with OI

A Guide for Families and Caregivers

Edited by
Ellen Painter Dollar

OSTEOGENESIS
IMPERFECTA

OI

FOUNDATION

Osteogenesis Imperfecta Foundation, Inc.
Gaithersburg, Maryland

Osteogenesis Imperfecta Foundation, 804 West Diamond Avenue, Suite 210, Gaithersburg, Maryland 20878

ISBN 0-9642189-1-7

Library of Congress Card Number 2001116218

Foreword

Gemma Geisman

As I look back on my family's life with osteogenesis imperfecta, I can honestly say that I now perceive it as an exceptional gift of many dimensions that taught me how to love unconditionally, how to understand the incomprehensible, and how to change the things I could not accept. With this rare gift, I was also granted the ability and the resources to share with others the things that I learned along the way.

I feel very privileged to have been part of the movement to bring information about living with OI to those who need it the most—the affected families. This extraordinary effort has involved countless volunteers and staff members working diligently over a long period of time to bring families a series of informative fact sheets, brochures, books, and videos that has culminated in the comprehensive double-book set you are about to read on *Growing Up with OI*.

It is difficult to contemplate how different my family's life with OI might have been had such a book existed when our much-anticipated second child came into the world with an estimated 35 to 50 fractures. The only information available then was a sketchy description of osteogenesis imperfecta found by our family doctor in an old medical school textbook. Armed with this scant information, he pronounced a diagnosis that no parent ever wants to hear. Our child would not live for more than a few days or weeks. The rare fragility of his bones had damaged him beyond repair, and there wasn't the slightest reason to hope that he would survive. Compounding the pain of the doctor's dire prognosis was the well-intentioned recommendation that, if indeed Mike did live beyond the predicted time, we would be well advised to put him out of our minds and hearts and place him in an institution for incurable children. The same refrain was repeated over and over again by nearly all of the other health professionals we consulted during Mike's postnatal hospitalization.

They did not explicitly say, "Forget about him," but the implication was there when they said, "There is nothing anyone can do for him. Enjoy your normal two-year-old daughter. Have other children. Go on with your lives."

Go on with our lives as if nothing had happened, as if our tiny, blond, blue-eyed baby boy had never been born? Maybe there was nothing *they* could do for Mike, but there definitely was something *we* could do. We could take him home, care for him, and love him for as long as he was ours.

Two weeks after his birth, when Mike was discharged from the hospital, sporting a body cast but otherwise looking very healthy and alert, we ignored the well-meant advice and took him home. Thus, with all the dire predictions still ringing in our ears, we began our all-consuming experience of living with OI. It didn't take long for us to discover the sheer enormity of the task of caring for a child with osteogenesis imperfecta in a world totally oblivious to it.

Repeatedly, we heard the words, "We're sorry, there is nothing we can do." Or "We're sorry, there is no literature available." And, "We're sorry, we know of no chapters, support groups, or other families coping with the disorder."

Most of the time, I try not to remember the sound of pencil-thin bones breaking, the pain-filled cries that followed, and the frustrations we experienced because we did not know how to prevent or ease the pain. Nor do I like to recall the stares, the invasive questions I could not answer, the loneliness of long hospitalizations, and the pain of social ostracization. Also on the list of things I'd just as soon forget are the feelings of inadequacy my husband, Dick, and I experienced when our other children asked, "What about us?" when our caring for Mike consumed every bit of our attention and energy.

Other times, I *choose* to look back, for it is only in recalling the insensitivity and apathy that I remember that they were my reasons for sharing our very personal story about living with OI in the pages of a national magazine. They were my reason for putting together, with the help of the other mothers who responded to my article, a one-page, typewritten, mimeographed newsletter about OI, which was the start of the OI Foundation's bimonthly publication, *Breakthrough*. And, finally, it was because of our early struggles and those of the other founding members that the OI Foundation came into existence in 1970 and began to coax open the previously closed doors of clinics and laboratories; brought together individuals with OI, their families, and friends to share information and offer mutual support; and began the long and arduous mission of telling the rest of the world what "living with OI" is all about.

The OI Foundation has come a long way since that first rudimentary newsletter. Today the words "osteogenesis imperfecta" are mentioned on prime time television shows; written about in national newspapers; and discussed on the Internet, at national conferences, and at scientific meetings around the world.

Unfortunately, we still don't know how to prevent or cure osteogenesis imperfecta, but we finally do know how to combat ignorance about OI. Though gathering information about OI may seem simple, it hasn't been. It has taken years of trial and error, of caring and sharing among affected families and within the medical community, to be able to conclusively say that we now have the knowledge and the ability to provide accurate information concerning the medical, educational, and emotional resources that are available today, so that every parent of every child diagnosed with OI can have reason to hope that their child will have a fighting chance to live a long and worthy life.

The long-awaited publication of *Growing Up with OI: A Guide for Families and Caregivers*, along with its companion book, *Growing Up with OI: A Guide for Children*, addresses the specialized needs of children with OI, their parents, siblings, and friends. It is my hope that it will be the first publication placed into the hands of mothers and fathers whose infant has just been diagnosed with osteogenesis imperfecta, for it was especially with them in mind that this book was written with passion, conviction, and hope by those who have already experienced the inevitable heartaches and the tremendous joys of living with osteogenesis imperfecta.

GEMMA GEISMAN IS A FOUNDING MEMBER
OF THE OSTEOGENESIS IMPERFECTA FOUNDATION

Preface

The Osteogenesis Imperfecta (OI) Foundation recognizes that helping children with OI to grow into capable, healthy adults involves more than just setting broken bones or getting physical therapy. *Growing Up with OI: A Guide for Families and Caregivers,* and its companion book for children, fill a pressing need for information on nurturing children with OI physically, mentally, and emotionally, so that they can become happy and successful adults.

The medical aspects of OI can be daunting, and families need clear information to help them make decisions about treatment. The first six chapters of *Growing Up with OI: A Guide for Families and Caregivers* covers the basics of managing and treating OI, including a review of OI symptoms and genetics, first aid, treatment options, relationships with health care providers, preparing children and families for hospitalization, and the financial concerns of families facing specialized medical care.

Chapters 7 through 10 address the importance of whole-body health and well-being that go beyond the bones. These chapters cover independence in daily personal care, exercise, nutrition, and education. The final five chapters recognize that emotional balance, personal growth, and loving relationships often contribute more to a person's health and happiness than any medical treatment ever could. These chapters provide helpful advice on balancing independence and risk, maintaining healthy families, making friends, and coping with difference.

Each chapter begins with a summary of key points to help readers choose which chapters are most relevant to their situation, particularly if time for reading is in short supply. Many chapters end with a list of resources—books, articles, web sites, and organizations that can provide more information and support. We have also included photos and vignettes throughout the book—real-life stories of how families have dealt with the issues covered in the chapters.

Keep in mind when reading the vignettes that these are the personal reflections of families concerning their unique situations. Some vignettes discuss medical, health, education, or other decisions that led to positive or negative results. These vignettes should not be construed as providing advice for other families. Readers should talk to their family members and the professionals they trust before making decisions for their own own child and family.

This book was developed primarily for parents and other caregivers of children with OI. However, it contains information that will also be of interest to teens and adults with OI, other relatives of people with OI, medical professionals, educators, social service providers—in short, anyone who has an interest in people with OI and those who care about them. The companion book, *Growing Up with OI: A Guide for Children*, covers the same topics in language appropriate for school-aged children.

Growing Up with OI is packed full of advice from parents, people with OI, and professionals. Reading it cover to cover, some caregivers might feel overwhelmed by the sheer volume of information. As one of the authors, Kay Kriegsman, writes in her chapter introduction, "As you consider what follows, RELAX!" No family could possibly put all of this advice into action, nor should they. As the chapter authors write over and over, each person with OI, and each family, is unique. No two people or families have the exact same challenges or the same strengths. If this book provides help for a question or problem that has been nagging at your family, then it has served its purpose. Keep the book on your shelf and pull it out every now and then—as new challenges arise, information that once seemed irrelevant may suddenly make sense. If a particular piece of advice doesn't seem right for your family, leave it be, or talk with your family and your health care team about your concerns.

A short note on language: Some chapters have repeated references to a generalized "child with OI." These chapters sometimes refer to these children as "he," and sometimes as "she." This seemed less cumbersome in certain chapters than repeated use of "he or she" and "his or her." The editor made every effort to use "he" and "she" in approximately equal numbers.

The OI Foundation believes that this book is the most comprehensive resource to date on raising a child with OI. We hope that, in ways large and small, it makes life easier for families living with OI.

x

Acknowledgments

The OI Foundation gratefully acknowledges the Million Dollar Round Table Foundation, which funded the *Growing Up with OI* double-book set. The Million Dollar Round Table Foundation's financial support allowed the OI Foundation to garner the experienced volunteers, information, and collective wisdom needed to bring this project to life. Additional support from the Orrin T. Shapiro Memorial Foundation helped to expand the books' distribution.

No project this large could be accomplished without the help of many, many people who shared their time and talents with the OI Foundation. The project began with a volunteer advisory committee, who together hammered out not only which topics this book should cover, but also how they should be covered. The committee members—teens and adults with OI, parents of children with OI, and professionals from several fields—all have first-hand experience with what questions are most pressing for families living with OI, as well as what answers are most helpful. Once the book outline was complete, these dedicated volunteers read each chapter draft carefully, pointing out everything from missing commas to missing information. Their constructive criticism and praise helped authors refine their drafts and craft each chapter into a practical and well-rounded resource.

In addition to OI Foundation staff members, the advisory committee included Kristen Antolini; Lynn Gerber, M.D.; Heidi Glauser; Trey Glauser; Ashley Glicken; Michelle Hofhine; Mark Johnston; Jamie Kendall; Marnie King; Kay Kriegsman, Ph.D.; David Morrison; C. Michael Reing, M.D.; Barbie Simmonds; Beth Simmonds; Sue Simmonds; Peter Smith, M.D.; Priscilla Wacaster, M.D.; and Michael Whyte, M.D.

The authors (some of whom also served on the advisory committee) are a diverse group of busy people who generously gave their time to write these high-quality chapters. Many families would have to travel far and wide, or spend hours in the library or searching the Internet, to find the valuable information that these experts have shared in such a readable, concise format here. By contributing to this book, each author has truly made a difference in the lives of many families living with OI.

Early on, the advisory committee members agreed that we needed "real life" vignettes to put a human face on all of the information in these pages. Many of the committee members shared their stories, and many others responded to a posting on the OI Foundation web site. As I opened the envelopes of vignettes and photos that soon filled my mailbox, I was grateful for and humbled by people's willingness to share their hope and heartbreak, their struggles and successes with the people who will read this book. The families who contributed their stories have given all of us a tremendous gift. They are listed by name on page xiv.

I am grateful to Executive Director Heller An Shapiro of the OI Foundation for the opportunity to edit this book. It has been one of the most satisfying and rewarding projects of my career. This project allowed me to call on knowledge and experience I gained as a child growing up with OI, a writer and editor for several nonprofit agencies, an OI Foundation staff member, and most recently, the mother of a daughter who also has OI. At the same time, I learned a great deal from this project—information my parents did not have when I was growing up, and that will certainly make a difference in my growing family's life.

The rest of the OI Foundation staff each provided vital support to this project. Mary Beth Huber brought to bear her experience providing information to families affected by OI; her insights on what information families need and how it should be presented were invaluable. Alison Mistretta carefully checked the resource lists for each chapter to make sure that all of the contact information was accurate. Jan Davis and Ann Duvall helped with the technical details of book publishing. Desiree Swain took charge of sending out chapter drafts to the advisory committee and authors for review. Katya Thomas scanned and placed all of the photos and illustrations.

Finally, I am thankful to my family, who contributed to this project in many ways. My parents not only provided inspiration, as I recalled the wise decisions they made concerning my treatment and independence as a child with OI, but also babysat for my daughter to allow me an hour or two at the computer. My husband, Daniel, never failed to encourage and support my work, even when he came home occasionally to find me overwhelmed and exhausted from trying to be mommy, playmate, nurse, cook, housekeeper, financial manager, and editor all at once. As for my daughter, Leah— editing a book while also nurturing her through typical toddler troubles such as runny noses, earaches, picky eating, and hysterical bouts of separation anxiety (not to mention physical therapy and an x-ray or two) has been challenging, to say the least. But I can't imagine having done it without her. Being her mom made me a more knowledgeable and sensitive editor. I was frequently inspired to keep working despite fatigue or stumbling blocks by remembering that, in the end, this book will help me and Daniel to be better parents to Leah.

ELLEN PAINTER DOLLAR
EDITOR

Photo and Vignette Contributors

Christie Allen
Bill and Beth Bigos
Chris and Sandra Bouknight
Cathy Brown
Vito and Giovanna Bua
Juan and Luz Candelara
Daniel Cornejo
Miriam Cornejo
Tom and Regina Cummings
Melissa Davert
Angelo and Joyce DeLaRosa
Lorraine Dellasanta
Clara Dohm
Peter Dohm
LeeAnne and Abu Elhadi
Luchina and Egidio Fabrizi
Paul and Dina Granger
Rachelle Grossman
Juanita Gruenloh
Julie Hocker
Michelle Hofhine
Elizabeth Humphrey
Rosalind James
Michael Johnston and Bonnie
  Landrum

Cecilia Kerstiens
Donald and Christine Kraemer
William Lehr
Harold Long
Rijean Mahur and Diane Poulin
Kelsi Morgan
Tonya Muncy
Geza and Amanda Nemes
Margarita Pacheco
Joseph and Jill Pfalz
Mike and Amy Phelps
Monique Pierson
Marilyn Rapplean
Rich and Theresa Reed
Ronit Sanders
Maria Semprini-DeMartino
Juanita Shaw
Kara Sheridan
Wendy Shiflett
Barbie Simmonds
Ed and Mary-Lou Sims
Antonella Verderosa
Priscilla and Jeff Wacaster
Neil Wacaster

Contents

1
What is OI?

Ellen Painter Dollar

Key Points in This Chapter

- Osteogenesis imperfecta (OI) is a genetic disorder of collagen—a protein that contributes strength and resiliency to bones and other connective tissues. OI causes fragile bones and other physical symptoms.

- OI is a widely variable disorder that affects people in different ways. Symptoms range from mild to severe.

- There are several reported types of OI. Understanding the types can be helpful for affected individuals and families. However, it is important to focus on a child's particular abilities and challenges, regardless of his or her type of OI. No two affected individuals are identical.

- People with OI can and do succeed in all areas of life, such as school, family, employment, and social relationships.

When parents learn that their child has osteogenesis imperfecta (OI), they inevitably have many questions, and continue to have new questions as their child grows. Some questions are clinical: What causes OI? Why are my child's bones so fragile? Is there a treatment? But many parents are as concerned, if not more so, about how OI will affect their child's day-to-day life: Will my child walk? Will he need surgery? Will she be able to go to school, make friends, get a job, have a family?

This chapter will provide some basic information about osteogenesis imperfecta. It will go beyond purely clinical "textbook" information to address some of the more practical questions that families have about what OI is and how it will affect them. As anyone who has lived with OI can tell you, individual experiences with the disorder rarely fall neatly into textbook definitions. OI is a very variable disorder. Though people with OI have many similar symptoms and features, each individual with OI will have a differ-

I have a 13-year-old daughter named Monique. I first found that she had OI when I was seven months pregnant. I was referred to a genetic counselor. It was there they explained to me what OI was and did many tests to confirm that it was OI my daughter was going to have. I must have cried every day until she was born. I was just 17 years old and it was hard enough that I was so young. When Monique was born, she was so small and she had broken ribs, clavicle, and forearm, and poor skull formation. I thought, as well as the doctors, that she would not make it. But Monique is alive and as feisty as ever. I thought for her first five years, "If I can make it through five years it will get easier." I always make sure Monique is treated as a normal child—giving her responsibilities and consequences, scolding her when she behaves badly, giving her chores (although what child likes to do chores?!). I try not to limit Monique. She has a motto: "Don't say you can't do it unless you have tried a hundred times and each time failed."

Margarita Pacheco, mother of Monique Pierson, 13 years old

ent experience with the disorder—different abilities, different challenges, different outcomes.

What is OI and What Causes It?

Osteogenesis imperfecta (OI) is a rare genetic disorder that causes fragile bones and other physical problems. "Osteogenesis imperfecta" are Latin words that literally mean "imperfect bone beginning" ("osteo"=bone, "genesis"=beginning, and "imperfecta"=imperfect). In other words, people with osteogenesis imperfecta have a problem with their bones that was present from the beginning—when they were conceived. OI is caused by deficient or defective **type 1 collagen**, which is the main protein "building block" of bone and several other connective tissues (such as ligaments, tendons, and skin). There are additional types of collagen, and defects in them cause other disorders. (See the section on page 8 on "Why Are OI Bones So Fragile?" for more on type 1 collagen.)

The genetic problems that cause OI in a baby are not caused by anything that the mother or father did or did not do during conception, pregnancy, or birth. Parents should know that their child's OI was *not* caused by the quality of prenatal care, poor nutrition, exposure to drugs or chemicals, a difficult delivery, or other events during pregnancy or birth. Rather, OI is caused by a genetic mutation that affects the body's ability to produce type 1 collagen.

OI Genetics

Genes are units of hereditary material (DNA) that tell the cells in our bodies how to function. Scientists believe that each of us has approximately 30,000 different genes. When a baby is conceived, he or she receives two copies of each gene—one from each parent. Most of the time, genes function the way they are supposed to. However, genes can sometimes be altered by a **mutation,** in which there is a change in the structure of the gene's DNA. When a mutation occurs, it can disrupt the normal function of a gene.

Nearly all cases of osteogenesis imperfecta involve a **dominant mutation** in one of the two genes that must both work to make type 1 collagen. When a gene with a dominant mutation is paired with a normal gene, the mutated gene "dominates" the normal gene. In OI, a dominant genetic mutation causes one of two things to occur:

1. The dominant mutated gene directs cells to make some defective collagen protein. Even though the normal gene directs cells to make healthy collagen, the presence of some defective collagen causes Types II, III, or IV OI (these are the moderate to severe types of OI; the OI types are discussed in detail later in this chapter). In other words, moderate to severe OI results from a problem with the *quality* of type 1 collagen.

OR

2. The dominant mutated gene fails to direct cells to make any collagen protein. Although some collagen is produced through instructions from the normal gene, there is an overall decrease in the total amount of healthy collagen produced, resulting in Type I OI (the mildest form of OI). In other words, milder OI results from a problem with the *quantity* of type 1 collagen.

When a mutation is dominant, a person only has to receive *one* defective gene to have a genetic disorder. This is the case for most people with OI; they have one faulty gene for type 1 collagen, and one normal gene for type 1 collagen.

Some parents who have a child with OI, when there is no one else in their family who has ever had OI, wonder if they are a "carrier" of the OI gene. The term "carrier" is usually related to **recessive inheritance**, as opposed to dominant inheritance. At one time, physicians believed that severe forms of OI were caused by recessive inheritance. *However, most researchers now agree that recessive inheritance rarely causes osteogenesis imperfecta.* With recessive inheritance, *both* copies of a particular gene must be defective for a child to have a genetic disorder (cystic fibrosis is an example of a recessively inherited disorder). This occurs when each parent carries a single defective copy of the gene. The parents do not have the disorder (because they have only *one* faulty gene), but they are "carriers" for the disorder. With each pregnancy, there is a 25 percent chance that the child will receive both defective genes (one from each parent) and will therefore have the genetic disorder. If a child only inherits one of the faulty genes, he or she is a carrier for the disorder, like his or her parents, but does not have the disorder. Recessive inheritance generally does *not* cause OI; recent research indicates that the vast majority of people with OI have a dominant genetic mutation.

But if that is so, why do some families with no previous history of OI have a baby with the disorder? There are essentially three genetic explanations when a child is born with osteogenesis imperfecta. However, genetic issues are complex, and the advice of a clinical geneticist is important for individuals and families.

1. The most common reason a child has OI is that he or she directly inherited a defective type 1 collagen gene from a parent who also has OI. About 75 percent of people with OI inherit the disorder in this way. A person with OI has two genes for type 1 collagen—one gene is defective, the other is normal. Each time that person conceives a child, he or she passes on *one* of the two genes to the child. Therefore, there is a *50 percent chance* that his or her child will inherit the defective gene. Because OI is a dominantly inherited disorder, as explained previously, a child who has one defective collagen gene and one healthy gene (from the other parent) will have OI. If, on the other hand, the parent with OI passes on his or her normal gene to a child, that child *will not* have OI and *cannot* pass the disorder on to his or her own children. A child who inherits OI from a parent will have the same genetic mutation, and therefore the same type of OI, as the parent. However, the disorder may not affect the child in exactly the same ways that it affected the parent, and symptoms may be somewhat milder or more severe. The reasons for this variation within families are poorly understood.

2. Approximately 25 percent of children with OI are born into families with no history of the disorder. That is, a child is born with a dominant genetic mutation that causes OI, yet neither parent has OI. This occurs when the child has a "new"

or "spontaneous" dominant mutation. The gene spontaneously mutated in either the sperm or egg before the child's conception. As far as we know, this type of spontaneous mutation is random and is *not* caused by the parents' health, age, diet, behavior, or environment.

In most cases, when parents with no family history of OI have a child with OI, the couple is not at any greater risk than the general population for having a second child with OI. In addition, unaffected siblings of a child with OI are at no greater risk of having children with OI than the general population. In other words, a spontaneous mutation is an isolated event that is unlikely to occur twice in the same family. Remember, however, that any person with OI, whether the disorder was inherited from a parent or the result of a spontaneous dominant mutation, has a 50 percent chance of passing the disorder on to his or her own children, as explained previously.

3. In rare cases, parents with no family history of OI have more than one child with the disorder. Researchers believe that this is only very rarely due to recessive inheritance. Instead, the rare recurrence of OI in a previously unaffected family is more likely due to a phenomenon called **mosaicism**. Occasionally, a spontaneous mutation, instead of occurring in an *individual* sperm or egg, is present in *a percentage of a parent's reproductive cells*. Thus, although the parent does not have OI, the mutation present in a percentage of his or her reproductive cells can result in more than one affected child. It is estimated that 2 to 4 percent of families into which an infant with severe (Type II) OI is born are at risk of having another affected child because of this situation.

Families affected by OI are encouraged to see a geneticist or genetic counselor at their local hospital or medical center. These specialists can examine the family's medical history, explain inheritance risks for future pregnancies, and provide information about genetic testing and prenatal diagnosis, which is possible in some cases of OI.

Expecting our first child brought many new emotions and challenges for us. What sex would the baby be? What would we name the baby? Could we provide well for him or her? For me, mothering would be a full-time, stay-at-home job.

After eight months of a wonderful healthy pregnancy, it appeared that the baby's presentation was breech. An ultrasound confirmed this. At that time, no other concerns were noted. A c-section was scheduled. We quickly proceeded to "nest" and get our home in order for the arrival of our precious new baby. We had one concern. We had decided on only one name—Jonathan, meaning "God's gift."

On July 6, 1995, arriving on his own initiative and by c-section, our dear Jonathan was born. What a beautiful baby boy! Jonathan was presented to us wrapped in a bundle of blankets with the most precious face peering over them. Oblivious to the scurrying of medical staff and continued cries from the baby, we proceeded on in overwhelming excitement and joy. Later that morning, our pediatrician told us she was concerned for Jonathan due to noted bodily deformities and apparent pain and stress. She was unsure of the cause. Jonathan was transferred to a local children's hospital for evaluation. There, a geneticist, having just received a brochure about OI the day before, confirmed a diagnosis of OI.

That brochure was a gateway to resources and support for our family. It included information about a conference scheduled at a university in our state. So, at three weeks old, with casts on both legs and his right arm, Jonathan went to his first OI conference, along with his mom, dad, grandmother, and aunt. We connected with educators and families affected by OI. The support we established continues to be a great network for us to this day. The OI Foundation was and continues to be a valuable resource for us. From the conference, we also learned of research studies at the National Institutes of Health (NIH). At six months old, Jonathan and our family made our first trip to NIH. Their guidance has been instrumental in our decisions, timing of medical procedures and surgeries, goal setting, and optimizing activities of daily living.

Looking back, we thank God for the initial bonding we had with our dear Jonathan. Although our path has at times been arduous and exceeds "normal" childcare, we feel truly blessed by the abundant love and support from family, friends, neighbors, and church family. We feel very honored to have Jonathan as our dear son!

Theresa Reed, mother of Jonathan, 5 years old

Why Are OI Bones So Fragile?

To understand why the bones of people with OI are fragile, it helps to understand the structure of bone, and how this structure is weakened by insufficient or poor quality collagen.

The structure of bone is very similar to the reinforced concrete that is used to make a building or bridge. When the building or bridge is first constructed, a frame of long steel rods is first put in place. Cement is then poured around the steel rods. The rods and cement form a tight union, producing a structure that is strong and resilient enough to withstand some rocking motion while maintaining strength. Without the steel rods, the cement would be brittle and would fracture with only minor movement. Without the cement, the steel rods would have inadequate support and would bend.

The same organization is true of bone. Type 1 collagen rods are similar to the steel rods. The "cement" that surrounds the collagen rods is formed by crystals of minerals (including calcium and phosphorus). These minerals give the bones strength, while the collagen rods provide resiliency.

Collagen rods are actually formed by a strict interactive arrangement of rigid collagen fibers (molecules). The arrangement is similar to the way that bricks and mortar interact in a brick wall. A strong wall requires that the individual bricks be uniform in size and shape, so they can be aligned in an overlapping manner. Likewise, collagen molecules (rods) are also organized in an overlapping manner, and attached to other molecules in bone, and to the calcium that comes from the blood.

The collagen rods in OI bone fail to give the skeleton full strength, because the quantity or shape of the rods is abnormal. There is a defect in either the *numbers* or *structure* of collagen molecules, due to a genetic mutation, as discussed previously.

In the moderate to severe types of OI (Types IV, III, and II), the collagen rods are either "kinked" or broken, so that the structure is inherently unstable. The more severe the collagen fiber defect, the more severe the OI. Mild OI (Type I) results instead from the underproduction of otherwise normal collagen fibers. A genetic mutation inactivates one of the two collagen genes that we all have. The presence of only half the number of normal collagen rods has a moderate effect on bone strength, but is not as severe as the malformation of bone that results from defective collagen fibers, as in severe OI.

There are additional reasons why a collagen mutation affects bone strength:

- The defective collagen rods form an abnormal "mold" into which crystals of the bone mineral "cement" are poured. The cement is therefore placed haphazardly in the bone.

- The badly formed collagen rods are more susceptible to the body's normal process that detects and destroys broken molecules. Thus, the amount of already imperfect bone is further reduced by "housecleaning" cells (called osteoclasts) that remove the defective collagen rods.

- Bone is a living tissue that is always being built up and broken down. In OI, the cells that form new bone (the osteoblasts) are affected by their content of, and the nearby presence of, defective collagen molecules. Osteoblasts have great difficulty making abnormal collagen fibers and transferring them outside the cell. They become very inefficient—slow to divide and make new bone cells. However, the body demands that they make more bone, particularly during rapid growth in children. Unfortunately, the only bone that the osteoblasts can make is defective, so the strength is never improved. This spiral of ineffective bone formation is never-ending. This phenomenon probably explains why people with OI sustain more fractures in childhood than they do after reaching puberty, when the demand for bone formation is less. Osteoblasts can then focus on making only enough bone to maintain bone mass—they no longer have to add new bone to sustain rapid growth. In effect, the osteoblasts can begin to "catch up."[1]

---

[1] This section on bone structure and fragility is adapted from the Osteogenesis Imperfecta Foundation's fact sheet titled *Understanding the Structure of Bone in OI*, which was written by David Rowe, M.D., of the University of Connecticut Health Center, who serves on the OI Foundation's Medical Advisory Council.

Beyond Bones: How OI Affects the Body

Many people refer to OI as "brittle bone disease," and indeed, fragile bones are the hallmark sign of osteogenesis imperfecta. Everyone who has OI has bones that break more easily than normal, although someone with mild OI will have fewer fractures and bone problems than someone with severe OI.

Because type 1 collagen is present in additional connective tissues throughout the body, OI affects more than just the bones. Some common signs of OI include bluish sclera (whites of the eyes); short stature; a triangular-shaped face; a barrel-shaped chest; brittle teeth; excessive perspiration; spinal curvature (scoliosis); and bone deformity (such as arm or leg bones that are curved, or "bowed," instead of straight). Symptoms that affect some people with OI include hearing loss and respiratory (breathing) problems, which are linked to rib cage deformity that decreases lung capacity.

Although these are some of the more common signs and symptoms of OI, they do not affect every person with OI, or in the same way. Some people with OI may have very few signs or symptoms. To help identify the different ways that OI can affect the body, researchers and medical professionals use a classification system of four OI types.

OI Classification: The Four Types

If you entered a room where people with OI were gathered, you would immediately see that OI affects people in very different ways. Some people are average height, while others are very short. Some use wheelchairs, braces, walkers, or crutches, and some walk independently. Some have had dozens of fractures, a few have had hundreds, and others only a handful. Despite this variation, however, by observing and interviewing the group, you might attempt to sort people into categories based on their signs, symptoms, and severity.

Researchers, clinicians, and other medical professionals generally separate people with OI into four categories, or types, numbered from I through IV. This classification system was developed by an Australian doctor named David Sillence in the 1970s. Recently, some researchers have proposed additional OI types; however, as of this writing, the four-type Sillence classification is still the most common way to identify people with OI.

The four types are defined primarily by clinical features—the type and severity of physical signs and symptoms that people with OI have. Because the definitions rely on subjective observations, determining what type of OI a person has is not always clear-cut. The four types and their associated clinical features are defined as follows. Keep in mind that many individuals with OI have only some—not all—of the clinical features.

TYPE I
- Most common and mildest type of OI.
- Bones predisposed to fracture. Most fractures occur before puberty.
- Normal or near-normal stature.
- Loose joints and low muscle tone.
- Sclera (whites of the eyes) usually have a blue, purple, or gray tint.
- Somewhat triangular face.
- Tendency toward spinal curvature (scoliosis).
- Bone deformity absent or minimal.
- Brittle teeth possible.
- Hearing loss possible, often beginning in early 20s or 30s.
- Collagen structure is normal, but the amount is less than normal.

TYPE II
- Most severe form.
- Frequently lethal at or shortly after birth, often due to respiratory problems. In recent years, some people with Type II have lived into young adulthood.
- Numerous fractures and severe bone deformity.
- Small stature with underdeveloped lungs.
- Collagen is improperly formed.

TYPE III
- Bones fracture easily. Fractures often present at birth, and x-rays may reveal healed fractures that occurred before birth.
- Short stature.
- Sclera have a blue, purple, or gray tint.

- Loose joints and poor muscle development in arms and legs.
- Barrel-shaped rib cage.
- Triangular face.
- Spinal curvature.
- Respiratory problems possible.
- Bone deformity, often severe.
- Brittle teeth possible.
- Hearing loss possible.
- Collagen is improperly formed.

TYPE IV
- Between Type I and Type III in severity.
- Bones fracture easily, most before puberty.
- Shorter than average stature.
- Sclera are white or near-white (i.e., normal in color).
- Mild to moderate bone deformity.
- Tendency toward spinal curvature.
- Barrel-shaped rib cage.
- Triangular face.
- Brittle teeth possible.
- Hearing loss possible.
- Collagen is improperly formed.

Because many people find it easier to think in terms of mild, moderate, or severe OI, it may be helpful to view these types along a continuum of severity, as shown in Figure 1.

Figure 1

Type I   IV   III   II

Mild   Moderate   Severe

Knowing what type of OI a child has can help the family and health care professionals understand the disorder and have some idea of what to expect in the future. However, two people with the same type of OI may have very different experiences with fractures, other health problems, and mobility. Even people with OI within the same family may have different signs, symptoms, and experiences. So although the four-type classification can be helpful, it is often more useful to base medical decisions and future expectations on a child's abilities, strengths, and weaknesses, rather than on his or her type of OI.

Looking to the Future: Focus on Function

A child's physician, physical therapist, and other professionals can work with the family to help the child function to the best of his or her ability. It is reasonable to expect children with OI to become independent in all major life functions (self-care, locomotion, recreation, social interaction, and education), with the help of adaptive

When Jonathan was first born, it was very overwhelming learning about OI. All I could do then was think about everything I would NOT be able to do with Jonathan. Now I think about what I CAN do with Jonathan. It takes a little time to know your baby and what he will or will not tolerate and, at least for us, this constantly seems to be changing. We could not hold or dress Jonathan for three weeks, we could not pick him up under his arms for four months. Now we do all these things. There is no way to tell what your baby physically will or will not be able to do. Just take things one day at a time and celebrate each and every little milestone. While this "not knowing" is frustrating, it also leaves a lot of room for hope. One day it hit me that there are SO MANY things Jonathan WILL be able to do—paint, play a musical instrument, read, write, enjoy computers, swim, golf, go to school, have a job! The list is endless!

Amy Phelps, mother of Jonathan, 1 year old

equipment as needed (see Chapter 7 for more on adaptive equipment). OI does not affect intellectual capacity, and people with OI can succeed in school, the workplace, family life, and social interactions.

Life expectancy for people with OI has not been clearly defined. Babies with the most severe type of OI (Type II) who survive after birth may die in infancy or childhood, though some people with Type II have survived into young adulthood. People with severe OI whose lungs are compromised by significant rib cage and spinal deformity may develop serious respiratory problems that can be fatal. However, other people with severe OI survive into old age. In general, life expectancy for people with mild and moderate OI seems to be average.

When I was 16 weeks pregnant, I went to Dartmouth Mary Hitchcock Medical Center for ultrasound and amniocentesis testing. Patrick was a much-wanted child and was to be my "dream come true." My friend and I watched the ultrasound technician with much excitement. The doctor went over and over the ultrasound pictures. Something was wrong with my unborn child. Five genetic specialists called it a "skeletal abnormality, a dwarfism of an unknown type." They eventually settled on a diagnosis of OI Type II. However, after I demanded a second opinion, other specialists performed additional ultrasounds and decided on a diagnosis of OI Type III. Two of the doctors said they could clearly see the right radial bone and ulna, and that the bone appeared to be too firm to support the diagnosis of OI Type II.

After his birth on February 4, 1987, Patrick was also diagnosed with hydrocephalus, or water on the brain, which has not affected his personality or intelligence. I loved my little boy Patrick long before I knew him. The love I felt was like no other. I am not a religious person, but it was not my choice to decide Patrick's fate. I knew that he would be born with this disorder, so I contacted as many foundations and organizations as I could. Educating myself helped me cope.

Lorraine Dellasanta, mother of Patrick, 13 years old

Many families benefit from pulling together a team of professionals, such as physicians, physical or occupational therapists, teachers, and others, who they can work with to maximize their child's health and abilities. A board-certified, knowledgeable, experienced, and compassionate pediatric orthopedist (a doctor who spe-

cializes in children's bones) is often the most appropriate medical professional to manage a child's OI. Children with OI also need to see a pediatrician regularly for immunizations and other routine care. Families may need to consult other medical professionals, such as a physical therapist or an ear/nose/throat doctor (for hearing loss), as the need arises.

OI is treated primarily by managing fractures and promoting as much mobility and independence as possible. Prolonged immobility can lead to muscle loss, weakness, and more fractures. Many orthopedists prefer to treat fractures with short-term immobilization in lightweight casts, splints, or braces to allow some movement as soon as possible after the fracture.

Many children with OI undergo a surgical procedure known as rodding, in which metal rods are inserted into the long bones to control fractures and improve deformities that interfere with function. In teens and adults, rodding and other surgery is often reserved for difficult fractures that are not healing well, or for alignment problems that interfere with function.

Physical therapy is appropriate for infants and children who have muscle weakness or motor skill delay when compared with same-age peers. Occupational therapy can help with fine motor skills and adaptive equipment to allow the child as much independence as possible in daily living. As a child with OI grows older, he or she will benefit from continued physical activity, such as adapted physical education and safe exercise. Swimming and water therapy are particularly well-suited for people with OI. Walking is excellent exercise for those who are able.

Various minerals and medications have been tested to determine if they strengthen bone in OI. Most of these substances have not been proven effective for OI. At the time of this writing, the bisphosphonate drugs (currently approved for use in preventing and treating osteoporosis in women and men) are being studied and show promise for people of all ages with OI.

Will there ever be a cure for OI? Researchers are exploring a number of gene and cell therapies to either 1) correct the genetic

My name is Kelsi Lynn Morgan. I am 11 years old and I found out in May 2000 that I have Type I osteogenesis imperfecta. I have broken nine bones since I was two years old. My dad is in the U.S. Army and we live in Germany. I broke my wrist at school in May

1999. In August, I broke the other wrist and three weeks later broke my collarbone. When this happened, the doctor at the health clinic in Vilseck, Germany, suggested that I be tested for a bone deficiency. The doctor in charge didn't approve this test. Three weeks after my collarbone healed, I broke the fifth metatarsal of my left foot. The doctors then realized that there was something wrong with my bones. It took the doctors two months to find a specialist here in Germany who could help me find out what was wrong.

Kelsi (right) with her brother, Reagan, and sister, Amanda.

I was afraid to tell anyone that I had OI because I didn't know how they would react to me. Some kids make fun of me and call me "clumsy" and "klutz." Other kids say that I am faking when I have a cast on. Most kids understand though. I can still play with my brother, sister, and friends. I love to rollerblade, ride my scooter, and bike. I just have to wear kneepads, elbow pads, wrist guards, and helmet. My favorite sport is soccer! My favorite player is Mia Hamm. I'd like to play like her but I might break a bone if I do. The doctor told my mom and dad that I could do some things that I used to, but I would risk breaking bones. But he said my bones will heal the right way when they break.

I think I would like to be a bone doctor when I grow up. My doctors think it is funny because I know the right names for the bones that I have broken. Being a doctor for kids like me would be fun!

Kelsi Morgan, 11 years old

defect that causes OI, or 2) help the body replace weak bone with healthy bone. If successful, some of these therapies would improve the quality of bone, but not actually cure the disorder, while others could lead to a cure. These therapies are still being studied and perfected in laboratory animals. The OI Foundation and other organizations support this research by funding fellowships and grants.

Though a cure may still lie in the future, the prognosis for children with OI is very good. They and their families will certainly face challenges, but most people with OI lead satisfying and successful lives. Let's return for a moment to our earlier image of a room full of people with OI. In that room, you would not only observe people with a wide variety of outward signs and symptoms, but you would also soon discover a wide variety of interests, lifestyles, and successes. You would meet doctors, writers, actors, accountants, lawyers, computer scientists, artists, architects, small business owners, homemakers, and people in dozens of other professions. You would meet husbands and wives, mothers and fathers, and good friends. They would tell you about their travels far and wide, their strategies for physical fitness, and their hobbies, from gardening to reading, carpentry to boating. Overall, though they may know more than others about overcoming physical and other challenges, they would be very much like any other group of people.

This chapter has briefly touched on some of the key issues for children with OI and their families, such as choosing health care professionals, treatment options, exercise, and education. The remaining chapters in this book will provide more specific information about these topics and others, as well as highlight ways that people with OI have dealt with the challenges they face.

Resources

Genetic Alliance, Inc.
4301 Connecticut Ave. NW
Suite 404
Washington, DC 20008-2304
Phone: (800) 336-GENE
Internet: www.geneticalliance.org

National Parent Network on Disabilities (NPND)
1130 17th St. NW
Suite 400
Washington, DC 20036
Phone: (202) 463-2299
Internet: www.npnd.org

National Organization for Rare Disorders (NORD)
100 Route 37
P.O. Box 8923
New Fairfield, CT 06812-8923
Phone: (800) 999-6673
Internet: www.rarediseases.org

Osteogenesis Imperfecta Foundation
804 West Diamond Ave.
Suite 210
Gaithersburg, MD 20878
Phone: (800) 981-2663 or (301) 947-0083
Internet: www.oif.org

> The Osteogenesis Imperfecta (OI) Foundation has many fact sheets, pamphlets, videos, and books available to provide additional information about the causes, symptoms, and management of OI. The following titles specifically address the topics discussed in this chapter.

> *Fast Facts on Osteogenesis Imperfecta*
> *OI Issues: Genetics*
> *Understanding the Structure of Bone in OI*
> *Osteogenesis Imperfecta: A Guide for Medical Professionals, Individuals, and Families Affected by OI*
> *Caring for Infants and Children with Osteogenesis Imperfecta*
> *You Are Not Alone: Caring for Infants and Children with Osteogenesis Imperfecta* (video)

> Wacaster, Priscilla (ed.). 1996. *Managing Osteogenesis Imperfecta: A Medical Manual.* Gaithersburg, Md.: Osteogenesis Imperfecta Foundation.

The best part about having OI is having things like a three-wheeled bike. I know I'm safe when I ride it. The worst part about having OI is that you never know when you're going to have a break. My dreams for the future are to be an artist, to be in the circus, or to be President.

Neil Wacaster, 9 years old

I was told when Elizabeth was born, "Special children are born to special parents." I have come to realize, sadly, that this is not true. I wish every child who faces life with a disability could have a great family situation. I believe that when we face a difficult challenge like OI, it is an opportunity to *become* special—special to that child, to your entire family, and to your community. My Elizabeth has helped me develop into someone special.

Juanita Shaw, mother of Elizabeth, 12 years old

Understanding OI and the Structure of Bone: Science Experiments

Priscilla Wacaster, M.D., uses several science experiments to explain typical bone structure and OI to both children and adults.

Log Cabins

One of the simplest ways to show people about the different kinds of OI is to use log cabin building sets. Incidentally, it is also a lot of fun! In a group setting, such as a classroom, volunteers can help build each square from groups of logs prepared in advance.

1. To demonstrate typical bone, use the longest logs to build a solid square. Multiply how high you want the wall to be by four to decide how many logs to use. For example, if you want the wall five logs high, five times four is 20, so use 20 long logs. This structure is pretty solid and can support quite a bit of weight.

2. To demonstrate the kind of bone usually found in Type I OI (where there is not enough collagen in the bone), use an equal number of long logs and short logs, plus however many of the little tiny ones you need to balance the square. For example, if you want the wall five logs high, five times four is 20, so use 10 long logs, 10 short logs, and eight to 10 tiny ones. This

structure will be somewhat solid, but will fall apart with a little bit of pressure. My nine-year-old son thoroughly enjoyed crushing the square!

3.   To demonstrate the kind of bone found in other kinds of OI (in which the quantity of collagen is normal but the structure is abnormal), use an equal number of long longs and short logs, pipe cleaners, and a few of the tiny logs to try to balance the square. For example, if you want the wall five logs high, five times four is 20, so use 10 long logs, 10 short logs, and eight to 10 tiny logs. Wrap a pipe cleaner around one end of each short log, leaving four or five inches sticking out. The builder will quickly learn that it is difficult to build a solid structure with this combination, and the structure will topple with light pressure.

Braids

Another visual aid for showing the different kinds of OI is to use braids of rope and aluminum foil. This is not completely scientific in showing the properties of collagen fibers, but it demonstrates quickly the differences among normal collagen, Type I OI collagen, and collagen in Types II, III, and IV OI. You will need rubber bands to bind the ends of the braids, 10 two-foot-long pieces of rope (or shoestring), and two pieces of aluminum foil, each six inches wide. To demonstrate typical bone, braid six strands of rope or shoestring together. This represents a typical collagen fiber. To demonstrate Type I OI bone, braid three strands of rope or shoestring. This represents having half the amount of collagen as in typical bone. To demonstrate the type of bone in other types of OI, roll each piece of aluminum foil into a strand, and attempt to braid the two foil strands with one piece of rope or shoestring. This represents an irregular collagen strand.

Them Dry Bones

This experiment takes more time and preparation. It does not demonstrate types of OI, but it does reveal important properties of bone.

You will need several chicken leg and thigh bones, white vinegar, household bleach, isopropyl alcohol (rubbing alcohol), and two glass containers (scientists call these flasks, but your mom probably calls them glasses or pickle jars). This experiment must be done with full adult supervision.

1. Prepare the chicken bones by removing all the meat, skin, and cartilage. Bones that have been cooked work wonderfully and make for easier meat removal.

2. Divide the bones into three piles. In one pile, place at least one bone that will be left alone (scientists call this a "control"). This one will not have anything done to it, so will be an example of typical bone. Divide the rest of the bones into two piles. It will work with just one bone in each pile, but for all this work, having more bones means more fun in the end!

3. In one flask, place one pile of bones. Pour bleach in the flask to cover the bones. The bones will float and make bubbles. It is very important that an adult do this step, and that the flask be protected from being tipped over by a pet or  small child. Place the flask in a safe place for several days. Pour out the old bleach and replace it with fresh bleach each day when the bubbling stops. Again, adult supervision is needed each time this is done. The process will take five to seven days, and is complete when there is no bubbling when you add new bleach. When you remove the bones from the bleach, they will crumble under very little pressure.

4. In the other flask, place the third pile of bones. Pour vinegar in the flask to cover the bones. It is important that an adult supervise this step, and that the flask be protected from being tipped over by a pet or small child. Place the flask in a safe place for three to five days. The process is complete when the bone bends easily like rubber.

5.   Protect the bones that came out of the vinegar by storing them in iso-propyl alcohol. This will keep them moist, but not change their rubber-like properties.

6.   The bones that were in the bleach, and the untreated bones do not need any special storage.

What does all this mean? Bone has two major components. One part is collagen, which makes the bone a little flexible. The other part is calcium, which makes the bone hard. The vinegar dissolves the calcium and leaves only collagen, so the bone is very bendable. The bleach dissolves the collagen and leaves the calcium, so the bone is very brittle, like chalk.

Pet Mouse

Scientists have found a type of mouse that has brittle bones like the bones in people with OI. This type of mouse is called the *oim* mouse. Anyone can purchase one or more of these mice for a household or classroom pet, or for scientific experiments. One must commit to the care of, feeding of, and cleaning up after the animal. The mice live about two years. Children should be prepared for emotional attachment and issues surrounding the death of their pet. Scientists that work with these mice speak well of their temperament in general.

Younger children can follow the mouse's growth and weight using a scale that measures in grams (or thousandths of grams), and make a graph showing percent gain weekly or monthly, or compare it to the growth of a littermate without the *oim* gene, or to a pet store mouse. Older children may want to do further experiments on the mouse, involving things such as diet, exercise, or activity level. Very committed older students can do their own genetic study by breeding the mice. (Unlike human OI, which is caused by a dominant mutation, the *oim* trait is recessive.)

The mice may be ordered from Jackson Laboratory in Maine (207-288-6000). Ask for customer service. The stock name is BTC3Fe-a/a-Cola 2 *oim/ +.* The stock number is 001815. They cost around $60 each.

2
First Aid

Priscilla Wacaster, M.D.

Key Points in This Chapter

- When an injury or a fracture occurs, caregivers should take the following steps: 1) stay calm, 2) do a quick assessment, 3) comfort, 4) do a thorough assessment, 5) make decisions, 6) act, and 7) forgive.

- With each injury, caregivers need to decide whether to give pain medication, who to call, how and where to transport the injured person, and whether to apply a splint.

- Having a fracture immobilization kit and basic first aid supplies organized and handy will help caregivers respond in an emergency.

- Parents of children with OI often have good instincts about an injury and should trust their feelings. It is also important, however, to be willing to rethink one's initial conclusion, and to be calm and courteous even in a disagreement with a medical professional.

- When traveling, take along a letter confirming the OI diagnosis, and a few basic medical supplies.

"Here is the line which divides the effective from the non-effective...he can depend upon himself, and be sure of his own action in emergencies."

Charlotte Mason, educator

A child in a crumpled heap on the floor crying. A calmly stated, "My leg hurts." A sickening series of thumps down a flight of stairs. The slow-motion sight of a fall on a concrete patio. How should a parent of a child with osteogenesis imperfecta (OI) respond to these different situations and the many others like them?

Step 1: Stay Calm

The caregiver must stay as calm as possible to help the one who is injured.

Step 2: Do a Quick Assessment

Is the person conscious, breathing, and trying to move around? Is the injured person unconscious or bleeding profusely? Is he or she in danger of having a neck or back injury or otherwise in need of an ambulance? Call 911 if there is any doubt. Begin CPR if needed. Apply pressure to any sites of bleeding. Loosen restrictive clothing.

Step 3: Comfort

Attempt to calm the injured person and the others nearby. Children may need to be held, as long as no neck or back injury is suspected. Sing a soothing song or cool the person with a damp cloth. When my son, who has OI, was very young, I had a song I would sing when he would have an injury. I knew that if he was squirming to get out of my lap before the first verse was over, he was fine. But if I made it through all three verses and he was still screaming, I knew we were on our way to get an x-ray. When the injured person has begun to calm down a bit, then proceed to the next step.

Step 4: Do a Thorough Assessment

Now, ask questions regarding how the accident happened or where it hurts. Look at how the injured person is holding arms and legs for clues about the site of injury. Even a very young, nonverbal child will often hold the injured part close to the body or refuse to move it. Gently touch the arms and legs down the length of each, one at a time. Begin with the least likely areas to be injured. When checking the limb where the suspected injury is, begin as far away from the injury as possible. Example: The injury appears to be to the right ankle. Check arms first, then left leg, then right leg beginning at the hip. If there is a bump on the bone or a place where every time it is touched, the child screams in pain, it is probably a fracture.

If there is an obvious fracture such as a bend in the limb where no bend was present before (medical types call this angulation), or a bone or rod is protruding through the skin, do not touch the area nor try to straighten the bend. Do not try to push the bone or rod back under the skin. Check the other limbs to make sure there is no other injury. Place a sterile gauze pad on any cuts or sites of bleeding or where the rod or bone is protruding through the skin.

Examination of young children can be difficult. Does he or she cry when moved or picked up? If so, consider rib fractures. Unless the rib end is hurting the lung, usually nothing is done for rib fractures, but it does make it difficult for a caregiver to move a child. If there is no obvious site of injury, after the child is calm, attempt to have the child bear weight on the arms or legs if that is her usual activity. For example, the first time my daughter broke her arm, she fell right at bedtime. After a short crying spell, she went on to sleep and slept all night. The next morning, she cried when I tried to wash her hands for breakfast and every time she attempted to crawl. Therefore I knew we needed to head to the urgent care center for an x-ray.

Step 5: Make Decisions

Should we give pain medicine?

If the injury requires surgery or cast application under anesthesia, the stomach must be empty for several hours. That is why most people advise that nothing be given by mouth to someone who is injured, as food or medication in the injured person's stomach may delay anesthesia. If the injured person has recently had food or

> When a fracture occurs, the first thing we all do is cry! We administer Motrin® (this seems to be the most effective) and immobilize the area, applying a wrap if needed.
>
> Theresa Reed, mother of Jonathan, 5 years old

drink, a bit of pain medicine by mouth at home is not going to affect the wait before cast application or surgery. But if it has been several hours since eating or drinking has taken place, weigh carefully the benefits of giving pain medication (such as more comfort during transport, less screaming, etc.) against the possibility of extending the time you will have to wait before a cast can be applied under anesthesia.

Some people get good pain relief from regular acetaminophen (e.g., Tylenol®), or ibuprofen (e.g., Motrin® or Advil®), especially for minor fractures. Others need hefty doses of strong prescription pain medicine. When treating the ongoing pain of a recent fracture, it can be difficult to balance the need for pain relief with the need for alertness. Some people find that minor fractures are well controlled with over the counter medicines, or that these medicines are sufficient during the day, but stronger medicine is needed for a good night's sleep.

Pain relief is a good issue to address with the orthopedist before an injury occurs. The discussion should include what should be given and the dosage. It may be important to choose a dosage based on the child's body weight (rather than age) if he or she is small. Always check the expiration date of anything given, note the time and dosage on paper to give to the nurse, and take the medicine along when the injured person is taken for care.

Whom should we call?

Know if your health plan requires notification prior to an emergency room (ER) visit. If the injured person is relatively comfortable, a quick call to the primary care physician (PCP) or to the orthopedist's office can save some frustration later. Some insurance companies have given some people with OI a letter allowing a certain number of admissions to the hospital or ER without PCP approval. If you are in a health maintenance organization (HMO) and want to set up this sort of arrangement, contact your PCP and the insurance company's member services department. If going directly to the doctor's office, always try to call first.

Should a splint be applied?

A splint may make transport more comfortable. Splint the bone in the position in which it is found. Do not attempt to straighten the bone. Any firm item such as a magazine, newspaper, stick, or block can be used for support. Wrapping the hard object to the limb with an elastic bandage (such as an Ace®) is fine, especially for the ends of limbs. Make sure the fingers or toes are okay after putting on an elastic

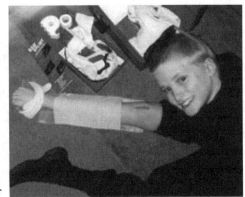

This splint was made with padded aluminum splinting material and an elastic bandage. Note the "fracture care" supply box nearby.

bandage. If they are cool to the touch or blue in color, the elastic bandage is too tight. Cotton gauze can also be used for wrapping. When putting an elastic bandage or cotton gauze on the top of the leg (femur) or arm (humerus), the wrapping movement over and around can cause considerable pain. Long socks or a neck tie can instead be tied around the hard object and the limb. Braces (orthotics) also make great splints if the bone is not bent out of the usual shape. A sling can be made with a towel or pillowcase and large safety pins. A splint or sling can also help the person rest if it will be several hours or overnight until being seen in the doctor's office, but it is not always necessary.

Do we transport the injured person and where?

Go directly to the ER if the bone is bent, or bone or rod is protruding through the skin. Most fractures in OI are not that severe, and time and money may be saved by going to the orthopedic doctor's office directly. It is a good idea to speak with the orthopedist to know how he or she would prefer to handle office vs. ER issues before they arise. An urgent care center or minor emergency clinic may be a better option than the ER for a minor fracture. These clinics have extended hours (evenings, weekends, holidays) and can usually do x-rays, order strong pain medicine, and apply a splint that will be sufficient for a few days until the orthopedist can be seen. As the caretaker gains experience, he or she will get a feel for how severe a fracture is, but if there is any reservation to waiting or the fracture seems unusual, listen to the gut feeling and go to the ER.

Many parents of children with OI treat uncomplicated fractures of fingers and toes on their own with a splint and pain medication. Some parents of severely affected children who fracture very frequently treat other fractures at home, to avoid the discomfort of a hospital visit and x-ray. It is important that parents talk to their child's doctors about whether home treatment might sometimes be preferable to a hospital visit, and get instruction on assessing fracture severity and applying splints. Even if a fracture is splinted at home, it is a good idea to follow up with a call to the orthopedist so he or she can record the fracture in the child's medical chart, and offer a "second opinion" on whether the fracture needs additional treatment.

Step 6: Act

Once the decisions have been made, act on them. This sounds simplistic, but the point is to think first then follow through. Other basic fracture care items often forgotten in the bustle are elevation of the injury and application of ice. In other words, put the leg or arm on a pillow if possible while calls are being made, and put on an ice pack. Incidentally, a bag of frozen vegetables works great!

Step 7: Forgive

This step is vital, not for saving the physical life, but for saving the emotional life. Forgiveness may need to be expressed to the one who caused the injury—the injured person, a friend or neighbor, a sibling, another caregiver, etc. Or forgiveness may need to be

In the emergency room, one thing that has always worked for us is to watch the medical staff carefully to see who is really listening to the patient and/or the parents. Once you identify that person, focus on him or her and make sure they realize how grateful you are that he or she is willing to listen. That person will almost always be the one to take your suggestions seriously, give you timely information, etc. Give that person the chance to go to bat for you. If you ever have someone who is rude or will not listen, ask them to leave and say you will speak to the doctor directly. In other words, if someone is clearly being rude or rough, do not let your child go for x-rays, etc., until you have spoken with the doctor yourself.

The worst times for us have always been in triage, x-rays, etc. Especially the x-rays. Technicians may not really understand how painful getting into place for those frontal and lateral shots can be. Of course, it has to be done. But it helps if the person working with your child understands how to be gentle and that the whole body can be turned easier and with less pain, rather than moving the injured limb against the isolated weight of the body.

Local hospital staff, and even some doctors, may not know as much as we think they do, or should, about OI. But most will learn with you, and are willing to listen if you let them know you are knowledgeable and ready to cooperate with them. You are your child's first line of care, despite what some personnel may imply. And always remember that deserved words of encouragement to hospital staff are amazingly few and far between for them, and you would be amazed at how far a "thank you" goes through tears of pain.

Elizabeth Humphrey, mother of Rhianna, 3 years old

expressed to yourself as the caregiver ("Why didn't I…" or "If only…"). My son once fractured his femur at an OI Foundation support group meeting. That night in the hospital room, I sat on one side of the bed and my husband sat on the other side of the bed. Neither one of us said much. Finally, I couldn't stand it any longer and blurted out, "I'm so sorry. I shouldn't have put him in those shoes. If he had on his play shoes, he wouldn't have fallen." My husband was surprised at my apology. All that time I had been sitting there blaming myself, he had been blaming himself. He was right beside our son when he fell, and my husband felt guilty that he wasn't able to prevent the fall. After expressing forgiveness to each other, we were better able to forgive ourselves. And the hospital room didn't feel quite so lonely anymore.

First Aid Scenarios: What Would You Do?

1. You are washing dishes when you hear crying. You turn around and see your young child in a heap on the floor. The first reaction is to ask, "What happened?" But the first priority is calming the child. One cannot examine a child who is hysterical. Sometimes a child who has had several recent fractures may overreact to a fall that doesn't result in injury. After the child becomes more calm, then ask what happened if the child can talk or if someone else witnessed the fall, and begin checking for injuries. Figuring out where the pain is can be difficult in a young child. Sometimes a young child will calm down or even fall asleep when held still, only to awaken screaming when the fracture site is moved. Depending upon the severity, one can decide where or if to go see the physician. Some aids to decision making with young children are:

    - Can the child crawl/stand/walk like he or she usually does?
    - Can the child move all limbs freely?
    - Does the child want to play or just be held?

2. An older child calmly says, "Mom, my leg hurts." You glance at the clock. It is 4:30 p.m. and a Friday. First, evaluate for evidence of fracture: Can the limb bear weight without pain? Is there a tender lump along the bone? Is there any redness or swelling or bug bite? Certainly fracture is the first concern, but there could be other valid reasons for the discomfort, such as sunburn, insect bites, poison ivy, scratches, blisters, orthotics too tight or too loose, etc. Most likely, a minor injury or fracture can wait until the next day to be seen by a physician. Some stable fractures could even wait several days with no weightbearing and appropriate pain medicines given at home. Trust your experience and intuition though, and seek immediate help if you are uncertain, or if the thought of waiting causes great anxiety in you or the child.

3. While visiting some relatives, you bathe your child in the only tub, which also happens to be by the top of a flight of stairs.

When the bath is over, you are straightening the bathroom when you hear a sickening series of thumps. Your child is on the floor at the bottom of the stairs. Assume there is a spinal injury unless there is a reliable witness who says the fall was just one or two steps. Do not move the injured person or let the injured person move unless absolutely necessary. Call 911. Begin CPR if needed. Transport by ambulance to an emergency room for full evaluation of bones, head, neck, back, and internal organs. Clearly inform all medical personnel about the person having OI.

4. The kids are playing out on the concrete patio. You see your child in what looks like slow motion take a short fall onto the concrete from a sitting position. Immediately evident is the blood flowing from a shallow scrape on the elbow. The child is distressed by the first sight of his or her own blood. Think first aid: Use a clean cloth (or sterile gauze if available) to apply gentle pressure on the bleeding site. Check the rest of the body for injury. After the bleeding has subsided, then check for fracture of the arm by gentle pressure on the bones and by having the injured person attempt to bear weight on the arm. Bruising will be tender to the touch, but the limb will be able to support weight without severe pain. Generally, a fracture will hurt with weightbearing. An x-ray may not be necessary, but if pain persists for several days, may be performed just to be sure. Also, for any cut, it is important that tetanus immunizations be up to date, which means a booster should have been given within the previous five years. (Note: One can go 10 years between boosters if no injury occurs.) There is a two-day window after the injury for the booster to be given without serious consequences. If no medical care is sought, clean the wound carefully and apply an antibiotic ointment before covering with a dressing. Check it daily for signs of redness, drainage that looks like pus, or increased swelling several hours or days after the injury. These are signs of infection and the person may need to be treated with an antibiotic.

When my daughter, who has OI, was 11 months old, I was sitting on the floor when she slipped off my knee and began crying "the cry"—you know, the one that says, "I just had a really bad pain that I don't understand!" After comforting her a few minutes, I began checking her. She was so upset that it took some time to

---

First Aid for Fractures at School[1]

School personnel should have a plan for dealing with fractures before they occur. The student's parent will usually teach educators how to deal with a fracture. Parents are experienced in dealing with fractures, and school personnel should follow their advice unless unusual circumstances require other action. A student with OI is often able to instruct adults in the best way to respond to his or her fracture.

Parents should tell school personnel ahead of time who to call in the event of a fracture. There are a few general tips to keep in mind when a child fractures a bone at school:

- Do not move the affected area unless it is absolutely necessary to move the child out of harm's way. The child will probably be able to tell you where the fractured bone is.
- Listen to the child's advice. He or she may instruct you not to move a fractured limb, or tell you how to gently place a pillow under the limb with minimal movement.
- Make the child comfortable while waiting for a parent or other designated person to arrive. If the child becomes chilled or nauseated, provide a blanket, a basin, or whatever else the child might need. However, do not provide food or drink; if the child needs surgery to set the fracture, this will interfere with safe administration of anesthesia.
- It may help to splint a fractured limb before moving the child, but school personnel should only apply a splint if the parent has instructed them to do so or if the child must be moved before a parent or other caregiver arrives. If a child wears braces, they may provide adequate support.
- It is best not to transport the child until a parent or other knowledgeable person arrives. If school personnel assist in moving the child, they should take care to keep the affected area as still as possible, and avoid jarring movements.
- Don't forget to comfort other children who may be upset by their classmate's injury, or feel responsible for the fracture. The situation will be much easier for everyone, particularly the injured child, if people remain calm and avoid panic and blame. If a fracture results from someone's carelessness, an apology may be appropriate, but will probably be more appreciated if offered later on, rather than during the difficult moments immediately following the injury.

[1] Adapted from Osteogenesis Imperfecta Foundation. 1998. *Plan for Success: Educating Children with Osteogenesis Imperfecta.* Gaithersburg, Md.: Author.

figure out where the consistent pain was. It was her right femur. I called the local general orthopedist's office and was told to take her to the ER. After waiting a few minutes in the waiting area, we were taken back to an exam room. I was pleased when the doctor ordered pain medicine before the x-ray. The nurse started an IV, gave the medicine, and sent us to the radiology department. After the x-ray, we waited a long time in the exam room, but at least my daughter had stopped screaming and was resting thanks to the morphine. Finally, the word came—the x-rays were negative and there was no reason to call in the orthopedist. We were to follow up in the office in a week. No matter how many times I insisted that it really was broken—I trusted the cry more than the x-ray!—the people in the ER said that they would take out the IV and send us home with no splint nor pain medicine. I was tired and angry and afraid of the consequences should the fracture go untreated. I did my best to be calm and polite to the ER personnel and requested a copy of the x-rays. I put my daughter in her car seat, drove home where my husband and son met us, and called the pediatric orthopedist who practiced about 60 miles from where we lived. We didn't even take the baby out of the car; we just drove to the hospital an hour away to meet the pediatric orthopedist. He thought the x-rays were negative, too, but he also recognized that an 11-month-old can't fake pain for six hours. He put her in a hip spica and follow-up x-rays confirmed the fracture. Sometimes, a new fracture is difficult to see on an x-ray. After a number of days, a callus (bump) forms, and the fracture becomes more visible.

I share this true story to make a few points. First, parents of children with OI should trust their knowledge of the child and of his or her reactions to injury. Children have different tolerances for pain at different ages and with different personalities. One child may be a screamer while another child calmly bears intense pain. Who can best determine from the child's reactions how much pain is there? The parent, of course. Second, when taking an injured child to the ER or an unfamiliar doctor, take proof of the child having OI, such as a copy of a letter from the PCP or geneticist, and have it attached to the child's chart. Respectfully request pain medicine prior to x-ray if the child is noticeably uncomfortable. I

What to Bring to the Emergency Room or Hospital

- Insurance information.

- Medical history summary.

- Any medications the child takes regularly, or has taken recently.

- Comfort item: favorite stuffed animal, blanket, etc.

- Recent x-rays, if applicable.

- Water bottle and snacks.*

- Phone numbers: pediatrician, orthopedist, relatives.

- OI Foundation material, such as *Emergency Department Management of Osteogenesis Imperfecta.*

- Proof of OI diagnosis.

- Ice pack for injured area.

- Pillow for support of fractured limb.

*Before giving the injured child anything to eat or drink, consider whether he or she might need anesthesia to set the fracture. If surgery is needed, it is best if the child hasn't had anything to eat or drink for several hours before.

was pleased in the above situation when the ER doctor ordered the medicine without my having to request it, but another time when we went to a children's hospital because of an obvious humerus fracture, I had to suggest it to the young physician in training. Third, and oh, this is hard, but try, try, try to be polite and calm even when the doctor says or does something that you dislike. Armed with written material from the OI Foundation, maybe your gentle rebuke will bring about change, but angry accusations will not help you or the child. Last, keep the phone number of providers you trust with you and don't be afraid to seek a second opinion. A corollary to this is to be willing to rethink your own position. Sometimes, an injury is truly just a bruise and not a fracture. If there is any doubt, a week or so of immobilization with a splint, then another x-ray to confirm that there is no healing bone present is probably not going to leave any permanent damage. And if there really is a fracture, the immobilization will make the child much more comfortable until an x-ray proves the fracture.

Emergency Supplies

One great idea gleaned from an OI Foundation meeting is to have an emergency fracture box. This box contains several necessary items in an easily moved box, such as a small toolbox or fishing tackle box. When an injury occurs, the box can be brought to the injured person rather than someone running around, back and forth, to get what is needed. One could also be kept in the car or at daycare/school. Basic supplies, with examples of each, are as follows:

- Hard items for making splints: old braces (orthotics), magazines, cardboard, long blocks, rolled up newspaper, umbrella, etc. Splints applied at the doctor's office or ER can also be saved and used again. Adult finger splints make great arm or leg splints for small children. Foam-padded aluminum splinting material, such as a SAM® splint, can be folded or molded to fit a limb.
- Something to tie the hard item to the limb: elastic bandage, neckties, long socks, towels, stockinette, cotton gauze, etc.
- Something to make a sling: pillowcase, towels, large safety pins, etc.
- General first aid supplies: sterile gauze, antiseptic ointment, small bandages (Band-Aids®), tape, hydrogen peroxide, alcohol pads, cotton-tipped applicators, etc.
- Other possibly helpful items: egg-crate mattress pieces, moleskin, sheepskin, washcloth, etc.

Other basic medical supplies to have at home include the following:
- Syrup of Ipecac, to be given only under the guidance of a poison control center or ER to induce vomiting.
- Acetaminophen and/or ibuprofen for pain or fever.
- Prescription pain medicine to treat severe pain in a person with OI. If possible, ask the pharmacist to put the true expiration date of the medicine on the bottle so it is clear when new supplies must be purchased. Some pharmacies have a policy of

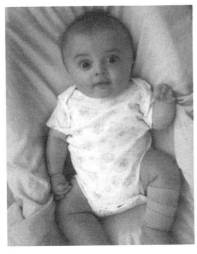

putting an expiration date on the bottle that is a few weeks or six months from the date the prescription was filled, rather than putting the true expiration date. If the child has grown or gained weight, the dosage may need to be adjusted by your PCP or orthopedist.

- Medicine for diarrhea.
- Hydrocortisone cream for insect bites, poison ivy, or minor allergic skin reactions.
- Pseudoephedrine or other nasal decongestant for colds and nasal allergies.
- Diphenhydramine (Benadryl®) or other antihistamine for allergic reactions. Incidentally, this may be given in the hospital to help children sleep. Ask your doctor if it may be given, if needed, the night before surgery or if a child is having difficulty sleeping in a cast.
- Some people may benefit from having more formal splinting material available if the family travels a lot or lives in a rural area several hours away from the ER or orthopedist. Your orthopedist should be able to help you obtain a box of plaster splinting material in a roll, or fiberglass wrapped in a cotton material (such as OrthoGlass®).
- A piece of plywood covered in eggcrate foam or pillowcases to use as a stretcher.
- A good, brief first aid guide for the emergency kit and a good, thorough family medical guide for the home.

A few closing reminders: Always check the expiration date before giving a medicine, every few months check the medicine cabinet for items that are expired or need to be replenished, and keep medicines well-protected from inquisitive children. Consider visiting your neighborhood fire and rescue station to explain OI and your child's use of mobility aids or a wheelchair. Some people even take a map of the house, highlighting the child's bedroom.

The firefighters truly appreciate such information and may give you a tour of the firetruck while you are there!

When traveling, take a letter from your PCP or geneticist stating the diagnosis of OI, the OI Foundation sheet on *Emergency Department Management of Osteogenesis Imperfecta*, and copies of x-rays if there has been a recent fracture. The OI Foundation support group list might also come in handy if there is an emergency away from home. Also pack in as safe a way as possible a few of each of the basic medical supplies listed above. Take prescription medicines in their original container only. Never mix different prescription medicines together in one bottle. If someone in the family is using liquid medicines, be sure to pack a measuring spoon. Oh, and enjoy the trip.

Resources

Osteogenesis Imperfecta Foundation. 1999. *Emergency Department Management of Osteogenesis Imperfecta.* Gaithersburg, Md.: Author.

Osteogenesis Imperfecta Foundation. 1999. *OI Issues: Fracture Management.* Gaithersburg, Md.: Author.

Reisser, Paul C. 1997. *The Focus on the Family Complete Book of Baby and Child Care.* Wheaton, Ill.:Tyndale House.

Wacaster, Priscilla (ed.). 1996. *Managing Osteogenesis Imperfecta: A Medical Manual.* Gaithersburg, Md.: Osteogenesis Imperfecta Foundation.

SAM® Splints

These foam-padded aluminum splints were designed for wilderness use. They are available from some outdoor supply catalogs and stores.
The Seaberg Company, Inc.
4909 S. Coast Hwy., #245
Newport, OR 97365
Phone: (800) 818-4726 or (541) 867-4726
E-mail: seaberg@samsplint.com
Internet: www.samsplint.com

Sample Form: Emergency Instructions for a Child with OI (to be given to other caregivers, teachers, etc.)

_____

(name of child)

My child has osteogenesis imperfecta, which causes his/her bones to be very fragile and break easily. Extreme care should be taken to prevent (name) from being bumped or lifted carelessly. My child has had numerous fractures, and is your best source for determining what to do in case of a fracture.

In case of a fracture, proceed as follows:

1   Do not move him/her if at all possible. S/he will be in pain and need time to calm down. There is no need to rush. Let him/her tell you where the fracture is, and please do not move that limb.

2   If it is necessary to move him/her for safety reasons, do so very carefully and slowly, being careful to support the injured limb and move it as little as possible.

3   Call (parent's name) at (parent's phone number). If you can't reach him/her, call (alternate) at (phone number).

4   My child's orthopedist (bone doctor) is (name). The doctor's phone number is (phone number).

5   Please do not call an ambulance or transport my child to the hospital unless the injury is severe and the people named here cannot be reached.

6   Don't forget to comfort other children or adults who may be upset or feel responsible for the fracture. These accidents are not to be blamed on anyone.

7   Sometimes, my child can get bumped, may cry a bit, and then settle down. Quite often, s/he has aches that prove not to be fractures, or are little "cracks" that we do not treat. Please let him/her be the judge and determine whether his/her level of comfort requires any action.

I hope this has helped. It means a lot to my son/daughter to be included in all activities.

Signed _____ Date _____

3
Relationships with Health Care Providers

Bonnie Landrum, M.D.

Key Points in This Chapter

- Children with OI benefit from having a team of health care providers (e.g., primary care physician, orthopedist, physical and occupational therapists, etc.) who work together with the family.

- Information sharing and good communication are hallmarks of successful relationships between families and medical professionals.

- Health care providers need parents of children with OI to provide them with the child's medical history and appropriate information about OI, if needed.

- Conscientious health care providers will keep families informed and involve parents (and when possible, the child) in decisions about how to treat and manage the child's health.

- Reasons to end a relationship with a health care provider include poor medical judgment, poor communication, or refusal to accept a second opinion.

- It is important that parents understand their health insurance policies, use formal grievance processes when they disagree with a coverage decision, and when they have a choice of plans, choose one that meets their child's anticipated needs.

When I was in medical school, I heard an often-repeated phrase, "Heaven spare you from being an interesting case." It was not until my daughter was born with osteogenesis imperfecta 20 years later that I truly understood it. Rare disorders present a dilemma to both families and providers. Families are searching for answers, treatments, and state-of-the-art, cutting-edge health care. Providers, on the other hand, have hundreds of other patients with more common ailments and cannot be experts on every rare disorder. There is an inherent conflict. As a doctor, I understand all too well our professional limitations. As a parent, I must demand the best care possible for my daughter. This chapter is designed to help parents navigate the health care system and optimize their child's medical care. Many parents find that to do this most effectively, they in essence become their child's case managers.

Children with OI often need multiple health care providers. Once this team is assembled, parents can enhance the members' effectiveness by following the general guidelines outlined in this chapter. They then need to assess each team member's effectiveness. Reasons to make changes will be discussed. The chapter concludes with a list of resources to aid families and their health care team.

Assembling the Team Players

All children need a primary care physician whose job is to care for the whole child. He or she needs to address general pediatric issues and how OI affects the child's overall health, growth, and development. Although most children's needs can be met by a family physician, children with a chronic disorder may be better served by a pediatric specialist as their primary care physician. Ultimately, the best primary care physician is one who inspires trust, engenders confidence, and with whom parents can have a partnership in their child's care.

In addition to a primary care physician, a child with OI needs a specialist best equipped to deal with the specifics of OI. This physician may be an orthopedic surgeon, a geneticist, or an endocrinologist interested in metabolic bone disease. His or her role is

When I was growing up, my pediatrician really wasn't involved in my OI-related care. So when my daughter was diagnosed with OI also, I did not expect her pediatrician to address her bone disorder. But I have been pleasantly surprised by his interest in her OI, and all he has done to help us find the resources we need to manage it. We met with him for a prenatal appointment to alert him that our baby might have OI. When she was diagnosed, he was the first health care professional we called. Though he  has never before treated a child with OI, he sees himself as our daughter's primary caregiver, and wants to be informed about all aspects of her health. He eagerly accepted the OI literature I offered him, and referred us to a geneticist and an orthopedist. When I told him I didn't think we needed to see a geneticist—my husband and I already knew a lot about OI genetics, and our daughter's diagnosis had already been confirmed through a skin biopsy—the pediatrician said, "You may know a lot, but I would like to know more. I would feel better if there is a geneticist familiar with your daughter who I can call if I need to." We went to the geneticist, and she has turned out to be a great source of information and support. Our pediatrician also referred us to our state's birth-to-three program, which allows us to get free physical therapy for our daughter through her third birthday. Our pediatrician has shown us the value of having a team of professionals working with our family. I have learned that the best doctors do not always need to be experts on OI, but they do need to be compassionate, interested in my daughter's overall well-being, good listeners, and willing to learn more about OI.

Ellen Dollar, mother of Leah, 1 year old

to monitor the child's OI and recommend therapeutic intervention, whether it is surgical or medical.

Many children with OI benefit from a physical therapy program. This may be directed by the primary care physician, an orthopedist, or a physiatrist—a physician who specializes in physical medicine and rehabilitation. The team should include both physical therapists and occupational therapists. The physical therapist's focus is to strengthen muscle groups and improve function. The occupational therapist's role is to help the child better accomplish the tasks of daily living. Together, this team will determine needs and prescribe appropriate assistive devices such as braces, walkers,

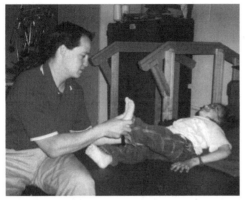

wheelchairs, etc. Aquatic therapy as an adjunct to this program can be of immense benefit in improving mobility and function in a buoyant, gravity-free environment. Success in the pool can lead to similar accomplishments on land.

Because of the possibility of hearing loss, children with OI should have their hearing tested regularly by the primary care physician. If an impairment is suspected, a licensed audiologist should do a complete hearing evaluation. Audiologists with experience working with children are preferable.

Children with dentinogenesis imperfecta (DI), a related condition to OI characterized by fragile, discolored teeth, need a pediatric dentist. Even children without DI need close dental follow-up with careful orthodontic evaluation to monitor growth of the upper jaw and maintain proper occlusion (i.e., bite).

What Doctors Need from Parents

To provide optimum care, a physician needs certain things from his or her patients and families. First and foremost, an accurate history is imperative. Parents should keep a detailed medical diary or log. Dates for developmental milestones, immunizations, fractures, surgeries, and other procedures are extremely helpful. Include any medications, allergies, reactions, or complications. Include a brief family history. If the log is quite lengthy, a one-page summary is a helpful refresher to remind the doctor of the child's course. Next, the physician needs specific information about OI. I gave a copy of *Managing Osteogenesis Imperfecta: A Medical Manual* (Wacaster 1996) to my daughter's pediatrician. Any new medical information parents acquire concerning OI should be passed along. Before an office visit, make a list of questions to be answered, and ask them in the order of importance. *Never leave the most important concern for last.* The physician may not appreciate its importance, and it may not receive adequate attention. Finally, follow through with the doctor's instructions. Busy physicians may not have time to monitor progress between visits.

What Parents Need from Their Doctor

There are several things parents must have from their doctor for a successful relationship. First of all, the relationship must be a partnership. Parents of children with chronic disorders rapidly become quite knowledgeable. Parents know their child better than anyone else and are expert in his or her day-to-day care and handling. Because of the enormous investment parents have in their child's well-being, they often become extremely up to date on medical

---

I called my doctor to set up an appointment to discuss getting surgery on my back [for scoliosis]. I really needed to get it done—my back hurt all the time and I also had a hump in my back by then. My doctor told me that scoliosis does not make your back hurt. When he told me that, I knew I did not want him operating on me. Several years went by, and my boyfriend and I discussed my getting surgery done. I called up my doctor and asked for a referral to another doctor. The new doctor compared my x-rays from several years ago. He came in to talk to me with a very comfortable attitude. He gave me the impression he was really concerned about what I had to say. He recommended surgery, and said he could put two rods along my spine with some hooks and screws. He explained everything to me, then asked if I had any questions. I asked him all I could think of. He sat with me for the longest time, talking about the surgery and the procedures before and after.

After the surgery, I was sent for physical therapy. I did not like watching all of the people there who could not walk. I knew I was going to walk. I explained this to my doctor, and he said if I feel I am going to walk and don't want to go to therapy any more, that is okay. I had trouble walking at first, but the doctor said not to worry, I would get better— I just needed to give myself time to heal.

Now it has been a year and three months since my surgery and I am doing a lot better. If it hadn't been for this doctor, I don't know where I would be today. He is the best doctor I have ever had.

Wendy Shiflett, adult with OI

advancements. Physicians must give parents credit for knowing their child and the child's disease. Age notwithstanding, the child should also be a partner in his or her care. Even very young children should be spoken to directly and included in medical discussions. A physician must be willing to participate in this partnership, and network with the other providers involved in the child's care. Ultimately the parent becomes the coordinator of care, often in conjunction with the primary care physician.

Due to the frequency of fractures, families need a plan for emergencies and other after-hours concerns requiring immediate attention. This plan *must* be worked out ahead of time. Know where to take the child if he or she needs immediate attention and how to reach the doctor.

An interview with a prospective physician is often enlightening and can help parents choose someone eager to work with them and their child. Lists of providers with special interest in OI are available from the OI Foundation.

Reasons to End a Relationship

Occasionally, despite proper "homework" and an initial interview, a relationship does not work, and families and their provider, for whatever reason, do not "click." Poor communication is the most common reason for a failing doctor-patient relationship. People often feel that their doctor is not listening, or is discounting their concerns, or is not adequately answering their questions. If the relationship is worth saving, speak directly to the doctor. Sometimes it is easier to express views in

---

Identify as soon as possible who will perform any rodding surgeries. Set up a tentative schedule. In the event of a fracture, you can quickly put your plan into action, minimizing "down time" in a spica cast. Our son was almost two years old when he fractured his legs in three places. The orthopedist who examined him said Jonathan would need a spica cast. The doctor said he would not perform rodding surgery at that time, as the bones needed to heal first. So our son spent four weeks in a spica cast, only to have to repeat spica casting several months later after rodding surgery. Since then, under the hands of an orthopedist experienced in OI treatment, we have found it much better to go ahead with planned rodding surgery if a fracture occurs near to the scheduled time.

Theresa Reed, mother of Jonathan, 5 years old

writing. If these approaches
are unsuccessful, find a
different physician. Reasons
to seek a new provider
include the following:

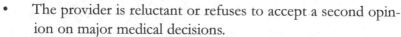

- The provider has lim-
ited knowledge con-
cerning OI or does
not seem interested
in learning more.
- The provider makes
errors in medical judgment.
- The provider is reluctant or refuses to accept a second opinion on major medical decisions.

Persistent conflict or antagonism between a provider and patient is not conducive to a productive relationship, and termination
may be the only option. If so, families need to communicate their
decision and the reasons to the provider, and request transfer of
medical records to the new provider.

When Away from Home

Children with OI will inevitably need care when away from home
or in an unfamiliar setting. Families can prepare for this event ahead
of time. Always carry documentation of the child's diagnosis. The
Shriners Hospital provided us with a laminated wallet-sized card
carrying our daughter's name, diagnosis, and emergency telephone
numbers. A medical alert bracelet can serve the same function,
informing potential caregivers of the diagnosis of OI, that x-rays
may be necessary, and of any emergency procedures that may be
required. Always carry the child's summary health history to aid
providers unfamiliar with the child.

A detailed emergency plan should also be in place in your
child's school as part of his or her Individualized Educational Program (IEP). This plan should also address day-to-day safety issues.
(See Chapters 2 and 10 for more on first aid and safety in school.)

Insurance

Many children with OI will access the health care system often. It is imperative that parents be familiar with their insurance coverage. (See Chapter 6 for more on obtaining adequate insurance coverage.) Read and understand the materials and be clear on coverage. If parents have a choice of plans, the child's needs should influence that choice. Review options thoroughly before deciding on a plan. For example, because children with OI may need to make frequent visits to specialists (such as an orthopedist), a plan that allows patients to see specialists without a referral for each visit is preferable. Coverage for supplementary services such as physical and occupational therapy is also important. Keep thorough records of medical care, including receipts. Review insurance payment records and medical bills carefully to detect mistakes and make note of insurance denials. Obtain prior authorization when needed to prevent denials. Get authorizations for care in writing, including the authorizing person's name and job title. Document the date and time and have witnesses if possible. Challenge denials of care if the interpretation is controversial. Most health plans and state health agencies have a formal grievance process. Learn about that process and use it!

Resources

Osteogenesis Imperfecta Foundation. 1999. *Osteogenesis Imperfecta: A Guide for Medical Professionals, Families and Individuals Affected by OI.* Gaithersburg, Md.:Author.

Wacaster, Priscilla (ed.) 1996. *Managing Osteogenesis Imperfecta: A Medical Manual.* Gaithersburg, Md.: Osteogenesis Imperfecta Foundation.

National Institutes of Health

This government agency is active in research and runs multiple clinical trials for patients with OI. Accepted patients receive comprehensive care free of charge.

National Institute of Child Health and Human Development
Heritable Disorders Branch
Building 10, Room 9S-241
10 Center Dr., MSC - 1830
Bethesda, MD 20892-1830
Phone: (301) 496-0741

Osteogenesis Imperfecta (OI) Foundation

The OI Foundation publishes information useful for people
with OI, their families, and their health care providers. It also
has a physician information list, and can link local health care
providers with OI experts for consultation.
804 West Diamond Ave.
Gaithersburg, MD 20878
Phone: (800) 981-2663 or (301) 947-0083
Internet: www.oif.org

Specialized Children's Hospitals

The following list includes a sample of hospitals that have programs
specifically treating OI and related disorders.

Alfred I. duPont Hospital for Children

1600 Rockland Rd., Box 269
Wilmington, Delaware 19899
Phone: (302) 651-4000
Internet: www.kidshealth.org

Cedars-Sinai Medical Center

Medical Genetics/Birth Defects Center
Marc Goodson Building
444 San Vicente Blvd.
Los Angeles, CA 90048
Phone: (310) 423-2224

Gillette Children's Specialty Healthcare

200 East University Ave.
St Paul, MN 55101

Phone: (800) 719-4040
Internet: www.gillettechildrens.org

Hospital for Special Surgery

535 East 70th St.
New York, NY 10021
Phone: (212) 606-1047

The OI Clinic at Kennedy Krieger Institute

707 North Broadway
Baltimore, MD 21205
Phone: (410) 502-8141 or 502-8100

Shriners Hospitals for Children

Shriners Hospitals, located throughout the United States and
Canada, provide comprehensive care to children with ortho-
pedic, neurologic, and other chronic conditions. Accepted
patients are eligible for care free of charge until age 18.
Shriners Hospitals for Children
General Offices
2900 Rocky Point Dr.
Tampa, FL 33607-1460
Phone: (813) 281-0300
Internet: shriners.com

National and International OI Conferences

The Osteogenesis Imperfecta (OI) Foundation holds a conference in the United States every two years, and there is an
International Conference on Osteogenesis Imperfecta held
every three years. Both conferences offer informative sessions
for people affected by OI and their health care providers, and
also provide informal and formal opportunities for people to
meet with medical experts to address specific concerns. Contact the OI Foundation (listed above) for information on upcoming conferences.

Sample Medical History Summary
(can be taken to the ER or a new physician)

Name: xxxxxxx

Date of birth: x/x/xx

Osteogenesis ImperfectaType I: Diagnosed at birth from cord biopsy

Birth history: Delivered by cesarean. Discharged at four days with mother.

Medical History Summary:
- Referred to early intervention provider at four months of age.
- Began physical therapy on a weekly basis at six months of age.
- Began walking with Kaye walker at 14 months of age.
- Bilateral AFOs.
- Began independent ambulation at 18 months of age.
- First dose of IV pamidronate September 2000 (3 years of age).

Fracture history:
8/98 R femur
9/98 Ribs
1/99 L tibia
3/99 Ribs
6/99 L radius
9/99 L tibia and fibula
2/00 L radius
5/00 R humerus
6/00 Refracture of R humerus (crack)

4
Making Treatment Decisions

C. Michael Reing, M.D.

Key Points in This Chapter

- Treatment decisions are frequently forced on a child and family by acute fractures, worsening deformity, and changes in other medical conditions. The "best" treatment for each person is individualized and based on knowledge of the treatment options currently available.

- Treatment options include rehabilitative therapies, bracing and casting, medications, and surgical intervention for fractures, deformities, and other medical problems associated with OI. Knowledge of what is currently available and what might become available in the future will help parents assess the various treatments, and ease the decision to begin treatment.

- Parents should freely question their health care team about not only the medical aspects of the treatment, but also their concerns about the effects on the child and the whole family.

- Each treatment, including participation in experimental treatments through clinical trials, has risks and benefits to be weighed. Not all treatments or investigative trials are for everyone. Because someone else is doing it doesn't make it right for every child with OI.

Decisions to begin treatment on children with osteogenesis imperfecta (OI) cannot be avoided. In reality, no decision becomes a decision! As treatments have improved because of technological advances and a better understanding of the underlying disease process, we have moved from passive intervention to a much more active role in treatment to maximize each person's potential. It was not many years ago that I remember an experienced pediatric orthopedist recommending to a mother that she carry her child with OI on a pillow, and not perform any type of therapy. Fortunately, we have moved beyond that, and the goal of any treatment should be to maximize each person's ability to function as painlessly and with as little intrusion into their "normal" life as possible. Keeping this goal in mind will help with the decision-making process.

This chapter will cover treatment options from "soup to nuts." It will explore surgical as well as nonsurgical treatments from a historical perspective, a current perspective, and what the future might bring.

Even as new information and techniques become available, the general guidelines for assessing treatments in this chapter should remain useful. Readers should consult their own physicians for current information about treatments and whether they are appropriate for a particular child.

Surgery and Fracture Care

I open with this discussion of surgical intervention because it is probably the one treatment modality that causes the most anxiety and anguish for children and their families, as well as the most disruption of family dynamics. The first choice of treatment is rarely surgical intervention, although there are instances when it is first. The mainstay of treatment for OI is still active rehabilitation with aggressive orthopedic and medical management—for example, therapy and exercise to improve strength, and use of adaptive equipment such as braces or walkers to promote mobility and independence. Surgery is often indicated as an adjunct to rehabilitation. Surgery is not just related to fracture care, but is also of benefit for deformities such as bowing (curving) of the long bones, scoliosis (side-to-side spinal curvature), and kyphosis ("round back").

Usually, doctors and families ask three questions about surgery: Why should surgery be performed? When should surgery be performed? What surgery should be performed? I would add three more questions: How effective is the surgery expected to be? What is the "degree of difficulty" of postoperative care? What are the potential complications? Parents should keep these questions in mind when deciding on a course of treatment with their child's health care team.

Often there is a great deal of emotion at the time of treatment decisions. It might be that the child is in pain, or it is incredibly bad timing for upcoming family plans, or frequently the child has had other fractures treated and other surgical intervention, and doesn't want anything more to be done. While the child's wishes need to be considered, it is not appropriate for young children to make the decision for or against treatment. As children mature, and especially when they become teenagers, they have a better understanding of the problems related to OI. Their feelings and opinions about whether and when surgery is done should be considered. It has been my experience that the more input older children and adolescents have regarding their own care, the more cooperative they are in participating as part of their health care team.

This chapter provides information and guidelines for both surgical and nonsurgical options, to help make families' decisions a little easier.

Surgery for Acute Fractures

Fractures in people with osteogenesis imperfecta heal at the same rate as in people without OI. This is because the defective or deficient type 1 collagen that causes OI is *not* the type of collagen that is laid down in healing or "woven" bone. The healing bone collagen is not defective in people with OI. Therefore, the normal criteria and time to heal fractures generally apply to people with OI. To effectively treat acute fractures, some form of immobilization of the fracture site is required. The decision to use external immobilization (e.g., a cast) or internal fixation (e.g., an intramedullary rod) relies heavily on which bone was, or bones were, broken, and to a lesser extent on the child's bone quality.

Why an acute fracture should be treated is clear—pain control, protection of the fracture site, and prevention of deformity. *When* is also obvious. Acute fractures need to be treated soon after they occur. However, fractures usually do not occur at a convenient time, nor frequently in a convenient location. A trip to the local emergency room and adequate splinting of the fracture will usually suffice until the child can see her usual physician, or another physician who is familiar with osteogenesis imperfecta.

What treatment to undertake is a more difficult question. Nonoperative treatment is still the most common—a splint, cast, brace, or a combination. As long as the cast or splint can be applied relatively painlessly, expected to maintain the proper position of the fracture, and removed in a reasonable period of time, then external immobilization is appropriate.

The choice of internal fixation, or rodding, is not as simple. Frequently, fractured bones already had underlying deformity. We know that if the bowing, or curve, was greater than 40 degrees, then the fracture was inevitable, and we need to improve the deformity if it is to be treated properly. Closed manipulation (setting the fracture under anesthesia by pulling on the bone, without making a surgical incision) and casting can sometimes improve the deformity. Sometimes we are able to take advantage of the situation and correct the deformity at the time of a fracture using internal fixation, e.g., an intramedullary rod. Another reason to consider internal fixation in acute fractures is if we know from experience that the fracture will otherwise be difficult to hold in good position, and therefore will require close observation and prolonged casting to get an adequate result. In this instance, internal fixation might allow earlier motion and rehabilitation, and a better end result. This concept is especially important for children who are going through a series of fractures and have been immobilized over a prolonged period. The longer the limb is immobilized, the weaker the muscles and bones get, and a cycle of fractures develops.

If a decision is made to perform surgical intervention and internal fixation on an acute fracture, then another decision needs to be made. What type of internal fixation should be used? In general, plates are not the treatment of choice for OI; rather, some type of intramedullary (down the center of the bone in the "marrow" cavity) fixation device is used. Here, parents should question their surgeon about what device he or she plans to use, realizing that the final decision has to consider the surgeon's experience and comfort level with what has worked for him or her in the past, and his or her familiarity with the equipment.

Historically, intramedullary rodding in people with OI was first reported in 1956, almost a half century ago. These early rods were nonelongating stainless steel rods that were passed through the medullary canal in a "shish kabob" fashion. They did not elongate as the child grew, so needed to be replaced. In 1975, experience with a Bailey-Dubow rod was reported. This was an elongating (or "telescoping") stainless steel rod. Elongating rods, when they work as designed, lengthen with growth, and the rate of repeat surgeries to replace rods drops. In general, the complication rate is higher for elongating vs. nonelongating rods. New materials and new metals are currently being used for both elongating and nonelongating rods, including titanium "flex" rods.

Even with new materials and techniques, the complication rate of surgery in patients with OI is high. Fortunately, the complications are usually minor, and the success rate is also high. Factors to consider in embarking on an operative course include which bone is broken, and the child's bone quality. Leg fractures more frequently require internal fixation because of the weightbearing stresses across the fracture site. There are also some people with OI (although increasingly rare with today's surgical technology) whose bones are not amenable to surgical intramedullary fixation. These people have "soap bubble"-appearing bones. The bones are so thin and soft that they will not hold the rod. In general, these types of bones can only be treated with casting.

There are other considerations before deciding on surgical intervention. The child's medical history needs to be carefully evaluated. The heart, lung, and other organ system problems that can occur need to be taken into account, and the risk of surgical intervention vs. the expected benefits needs to be considered. Great strides have been made over the past two decades in anesthesia, and the safety of surgery has been much improved. However, the anesthesia team's experience with people with OI needs to be considered, and it is best to have the surgery performed in a setting where the anesthesia team is experienced and comfortable with OI patients. People with OI have special temperature regulation problems during surgery, and have special hematologic (blood) needs. Fortunately, they rarely have increased blood loss during surgery.

Last but not least in the decision-making process is the patient's and the family's situation. I have made the decision with families more than once to splint or cast a new fracture so that the child did not miss the beginning of school, or a long-awaited family vacation. We reserved operative intervention for the future if the result of casting or splinting was not optimal.

The future holds promise of new and more effective treatment for people with OI. These include the ability to better stimulate bone growth, and bone cement that will actually "glue" fractures back together. It is good for parents to be aware of what is on the horizon, but treatment cannot be delayed for the promise of something better in the future.

Surgery for Treatment of Deformity

There are more clear-cut criteria about the surgical treatment of deformities in children with OI, but the decision is still not easy. The decision to undergo such surgery is elective, and hence the timing can be somewhat controlled. This sometimes puts an even greater burden on the parents who have to make the decision.

Deformities can be divided into two categories: deformity of long bones, and deformity of the spine. There is one constant measurement for both. A curve of more than 40 degrees in the spine can be expected to progress, and with a curve of more than 40 degrees in the long bones, we know it is only a matter of time before a fracture occurs. In other words, it is not a matter of *if* the bone will break, but *when* it will break. With this is mind, treatment of long bone deformity can be planned at a "convenient" time for the child and family, realizing that if a fracture occurs before the planned surgery, the surgery can be moved up. Unless there is some unusual

circumstance, cast immo-
bilization for a fracture followed by surgery a few
months later should be
avoided, because this sce-
nario adversely affects
bone density and leads to
muscle atrophy.

It is generally *not* recommended that rodding
surgery be done solely for cosmetic reasons. In other words, if a
bone is somewhat curved, but repeated fractures are not a problem and the curve is much less than 40 degrees, it is not advisable
to perform major surgery only to change the limb's appearance.

The long bones in the legs are the femurs (thigh bones) and
tibias (shin bones). They are usually amenable to osteotomy (cutting the bone at an angle), together with intramedullary rodding,
and the results are generally good. However, femur surgery usually
requires a hip spica cast that goes up to the abdomen or chest. This
is difficult for anyone, especially a teenager, to be in for a prolonged period. As soon as possible, the cast should be removed
and the rehabilitation started.

In most cases, intramedullary rods do not need to be removed
unless they are causing problems. The softness of OI bone frequently allows the rod to migrate, or even "cut out" of the bone.
The hard metal wears away the bone, and the bone gradually yields
to it, like a knife cutting through butter. If a migrated rod causes
pain or damages the joints or muscles, then it should be removed.
The rod does not always need to be replaced, if the bone appears
to be sufficiently strong and healed that it is unlikely to fracture
again. This is a judgment call for a particular child's surgeon.

Leg length discrepancy is common in people with OI. Sometimes, the longer leg can be shortened during rodding or another
surgical procedure. The Ilizarov technique has greatly improved the
success of limb-lengthening surgery in the general population. However, it requires the use of an external fixation device, with pins
through the skin and into the bone, through which traction is ap-

plied. People with OI, particularly those more severely affected, cannot tolerate this traction, and the pins can migrate through the bone.

Spinal deformity is also treatable with current technology. Though bracing may be effective for some children with mild OI, in general, bracing is not effective for correcting a spinal curve associated with OI. In rare instances, a back brace may be used to control a curve and buy time before surgery. A brace can also be effective for controlling pain associated with the progressive collapse of the vertebrae in children whose spines are severely affected. The reason a brace doesn't correct a curve in children with OI is that the forces that the brace generates to correct the spine are too strong for a fragile rib cage, and rib fractures or deformity often result. Surgical correction is therefore the only long-term option for severely affected children. The "why" of spinal surgery is important, because a progressive scoliosis deformity of the spine also rotates and deforms the thoracic cavity (rib cage). The cavity's volume becomes markedly diminished as the curve gets worse; this crowds the heart and lungs and can lead to other health problems. Spinal deformity should be closely monitored because it can progress quickly in children with OI.

In people without OI, spinal surgery can usually obtain 50 percent correction of a curve. Thus, a 40 degree curve can be corrected to 20 degrees. In people with OI, we cannot push or pull on the spine as much, and less correction is possible. Therefore, it is important to make a decision to start treating a progressive spinal deformity in OI as early as possible. Slightly more kyphosis (round back) can be accepted before beginning treatment, and bracing is of more benefit than it is for scoliosis, but a progressive kyphotic deformity also needs to be addressed surgically.

The one other progressive deformity that needs to be addressed in people with OI is basilar invagination, or BI, of the base of the skull. Here, the skull presses down on the spine and becomes deformed. This can involve the brainstem from lack of neck support, and brainstem pressures can result. This is a serious condition and needs to be monitored, but rarely needs to be surgically corrected unless there are signs of spinal cord compression. The surgery is technically difficult, but the results are usually good.

Rehabilitation

The single most important treatment for OI is aggressive rehabilitation. Once the diagnosis of OI is made or suspected, a child should embark on an organized rehabilitation program, including physical and occupational therapy, and exercise that matches the child's interests and abilities. (See Chapters 7 and 8 for more on therapy and exercise to achieve strength and independence.) This applies to infants as well as older children. Parents especially need to learn and participate in a program of mobilization and strengthening even before a fracture occurs. Once a fracture occurs, the broken bone will be immobilized, but a program should continue for the other muscles and parts of the body not affected by the fracture.

The decision to mobilize a fractured limb must be made by the health care team with the parents' input. In general, early mobilization and strengthening is desirable to prevent weakening of the muscles and bone. For this reason, doctors may choose to limit the child's time in a cast, moving as soon as possible to a splint or brace that can be removed so that the child can periodically exercise the limb in a bathtub or pool. In recent years, braces have become much lighter and more functional from an orthopedic and design standpoint. They are useful in mobilizing extremities soon after fractures, maintaining alignment of bones and joints, and allowing children to maintain a functional position for use and ambulation. Braces can help make walking and standing easier, and allow more independence.

With an organized program of physical therapy, specific muscle, tendon, and ligament groups can be isolated and strengthened. The decision to start therapy must be made early, and families need to be committed to continuing rehabilitation despite the setbacks that will occur.

Dental Treatment

The best dental treatment is prevention. Some people with OI also have dentinogenesis imperfecta (DI), which leads to increased wear of teeth, breakage, and dental decay. Attention to rigorous oral hygiene can prevent or lessen dental problems. Once problems occur, they can be treated with standard dental treatment methods, including caps and crowns. The dentist can help assess whether a fluoride supplement or treatment will be helpful.

Medical Treatment and Treatment with Medicines

Medical treatment of OI focuses on the organ systems other than bone that are sometimes involved, including cardiac (heart), pulmonary (lungs), and hearing. The heart problems encountered by some people with OI are fortunately rarely as severe as those associated with other connective tissue disorders. The two most common heart problems are aortic insufficiency and mitral valve prolapse syndrome. These syndromes usually respond to medical therapy, and are well tolerated over a period of many years. Consultation with a cardiologist experienced in OI will be helpful in making treatment decisions and evaluating options.

People with OI frequently have chest and spinal deformity, and the volume and movement of the chest cavity are diminished. This can lead to some increased risk for lung problems, and also increase the risk of surgery to correct skeletal deformities. Careful evaluation and treatment by a pediatrician or a pulmonologist (lung doctor) are essential if there is any suspicion of lung problems due to chest deformity. Respiratory illnesses such as bronchitis and pneumonia should be treated aggressively in children with significant chest deformity to prevent additional complications.

People with OI may also have hearing loss because the small bones in the ear are also affected by the OI collagen defect. There are two basic types of hearing loss—conductive and sensorineural—and both can occur in people with OI. Sensorineural hearing loss can be treated with a hearing aid (amplification). Mild to moderate conductive hearing loss can be improved with a hearing aid, while severe conductive loss requires surgery. Potential complications of hearing surgery include further hearing loss, a degree of permanent dizziness and ringing in the ears, or fractures of the small bones of the ear. Children with OI should have their hearing tested regularly starting at the age of three or four. A hearing test

Being a mother of twins with OI, I know how difficult it can be to make decisions regarding a child's medical care. Each time my husband and I are presented with medical options, we must weigh the potential benefits against the pain and discomfort our children may experience during their treatment.

One of the most difficult decisions we have grappled with is whether to allow our children to participate in growth hormone treatments. After much deliberation, we decided not to choose this option for our children. The primary reason for our decision is that the treatment is not medically necessary for our children to live healthy lives. Second, we know that whatever treatment is offered to our children, they will never look like the "average" person. We want them to grow up accepting their disability and truly liking themselves for who they are. The size of their bodies will not determine the amount of happiness they will experience in their lives.

Part of our decision comes from my own experience as a woman with OI Type III. I can remember as a child the time when I realized how different I was from my friends and family. I remember looking in a mirror and seeing my skinny and bent little arms and legs, as well as the rest of my deformities. I must admit, I avoided looking in mirrors most of the time. One day, I made a wonderful discovery. I happened to look down at one of my legs, and I realized when I didn't compare my leg to any other person's leg, my leg was actually just fine. As a matter of fact, my other leg and arms seemed just fine too. I discovered that when I didn't compare myself to anyone else, I really liked my body just the way it was.

Through my personal experience with OI, I learned that although having OI can be challenging, it also comes with a gift. The gift is the ability to learn to like myself for who I am. We want our children to discover their gift, and we want them to grow up to know that happiness does not come from being like "everyone else."

Melissa Davert, mother of Austin and Michaela, 2 years old

in a noisy doctor's office or school setting may not pick up subtle hearing losses. A soundproof room and an audiologist experienced in testing children are necessary for a valid hearing test. Often, this requires a visit to an ear, nose, and throat doctor (ENT), although a pediatrician may be able to refer a child directly to an audiologist.

Treatment with medicines is different than medical treatment. One of the most frequently asked questions from families is whether a particular diet or vitamin supplement can strengthen bones. Little research has been done on how traditional and nontraditional diets and supplements affect OI symptoms, but it is certain that no food

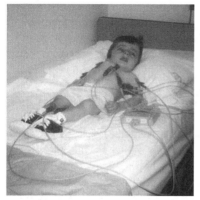

or supplement can correct the underlying collagen problems that cause OI. However, diet is important for adequate nutrition and weight control. Families should consult a physician or registered dietitian before putting a child on a special diet or supplements. (See Chapter 9 for more on nutrition.)

Pain medication helps control the pain of fractures and will help a child get moving faster. Chronic use of narcotics should be avoided. Anti-inflammatory medications, such as ibuprofen, can help relieve the soreness associated with a rigorous therapy program.

Two medications that are currently experimental for OI do hold promise for strengthening bones in people with OI. The first is growth hormone (GH). It is still under investigation for OI, but preliminary findings suggest it is effective in about one-half of the patients who take it. Why it is not effective in the other half is not known, and discussion is beyond the scope of this chapter.

The other drug group under investiagation for OI is the bisphosphonates. These medications have been used effectively to treat women with postmenopausal osteoporosis, and are being investigated for children with juvenile osteoporosis. Bisphosphonates work by inhibiting the body's resorption (breakdown) of bone. Bone is constantly being made and broken down in our bodies. By diminishing the amount broken down, these medications are designed to strengthen the bone by increasing bone quantity. Results of bisphosphonate studies in people with OI of all ages are increasingly encouraging.

Any medication, including bisphosphonates and growth hormone, has the potential for side effects. Parents and the health care team need to evaluate the potential side effects before treatment. Currently, growth hormone is only available through clinical trials. The bisphosphonate medications are also being studied in clinical trials as well as in laboratory animals. However, because initial research results are promising, some physicians and OI clinics have begun prescribing bisphosphonates to their young patients. Parents should be aware that, though they are becoming more widely prescribed, bisphosphonates are a relatively new treatment at the time of this writing. The long-term effects of these medications, particularly on children who begin taking them as very young infants, are still being studied. Currently, neither growth hormone nor bisphosphonates are FDA-approved for OI treatment.

Clinical Trials

This brings us to the final topic concerning treatment decisions: When should parents consider participating in a clinical trial (study) with their children? There is an unavoidable emotional component to this decision. Parents hope that the experimental treatment will help their child, and indeed, in some instances they will "try anything." However, most trials are "blinded," meaning that some children will *not* get the experimental medication, but instead will get a placebo (such as a sugar pill). To make the study objective, neither the family nor the doctors administering the medication can choose or know which children are getting the experimental medication and which are not. This will only be revealed at the end of the study. Also, there is some significant inconvenience (such as travel, paperwork, and repeated medical tests) involved in clinical trial participation. Parents need to realistically assess their family's ability to comply with these requirements. Fortunately, most clinical trials are well-constructed, making the child's safety paramount and minimizing the impact on the family. Parents should be informed of the potential risks and benefits, so they can provide informed consent. Parents should discuss with their health care team whether their child is eligible, the risks are acceptable, and participating is "doable" for their family. There is a certain altruism associated with participating in such research, and parents need to be commended for doing so. However, parents should also realize that just because other families have children involved in clinical trials, it might not be right for their child or family.

Conclusion

The decision to begin treatment in children with OI is never easy. Increased awareness of what is available now and in the future will help make that decision less difficult. Communicating freely and openly with the child and health care team is essential to arrive at the proper decision. A better understanding of the need for and goal of treatment for the child and his or her family also aids that decision. The final decision makers are the parents, with guidance from the health care team. A number of organizations, including the OI Foundation, strive to provide families with honest and objective information about treatment options (see resource list).

Resources

Binder, H., A. Conway, and L. Gerber. 1993. Rehabilitation Approaches to Children with Osteogenesis Imperfecta: A Ten-Year Experience. *Archives of Physical Medicine and Rehabilitation* 74:386–390.

Cintas, Holly, and Lynn Gerber. 1999. Physical Therapy for Children with OI. *Breakthrough: The Newsletter of the Osteogenesis Imperfecta Foundation* 24(4):9–10.

Cole, W.G. 1993. Early Surgical Management of Severe Forms of Osteogenesis Imperfecta. *American Journal of Medical Genetics* 45:270–274.

Engelbert, R.H.H., P.J.M Helders, W. Keesen, H.E.H. Pruji, and R.H.J.M. Gooskens. 1995. Intramedullary Rodding in Type III Osteogenesis Imperfecta. *Acta Orthopedica Scandanavia* 66(4):361–364.

Gamble, J.G., W.J. Strudwich, L.A. Rinsk, and E.E. Bleck. 1988. Complications of Intramedullary Rods in Osteogenesis Imperfecta: Bailey-Dubow Rods Versus Non-Elongating rods. *Journal of Pediatric Orthopedics* 8:645–649.

Glorieux, F.H., N.J. Bishop, H. Plotkin, G. Chabot, G. Lanoue, and R. Travers. 1998. Cyclic Administration of Pamidronate in Children with Severe Osteogenesis Imperfecta. *New England Journal of Medicine* 339(14):947–952. 1 October.

Harvey, Stephen. 1999. Surgery to Correct OI-Related Hearing Loss. *Breakthrough: The Newsletter of the Osteogenesis Imperfecta Foundation* 24(3):1,4–5.

Nicholas, R.E., and P. James. 1990. Telescoping Intramedullary Stabilization of the Lower Extremities for Severe Osteogenesis Imperfecta. *Journal of Pediatric Orthopedics* 10:219–223.

Osteogenesis Imperfecta Foundation. 1998. *Care of Infants and Children with Osteogenesis Imperfecta.* Gaithersburg, Md.: Author.

Osteogenesis Imperfecta Foundation. 1998. Montreal Shriners Hospital Study Advances Potential Drug Treatment for Children with OI. *Breakthrough: The Newsletter of the Osteogenesis Imperfecta Foundation* 23(5):1–2,4.

Osteogenesis Imperfecta Foundation. 1998. What Are Controlled Clinical Trials and Why Are They Important? *Breakthrough: The Newsletter of the Osteogenesis Imperfecta Foundation* 23(5):5.

Osteogenesis Imperfecta Foundation. 1999. *Fracture Management Fact Sheet.* Gaithersburg, Md.: Author.

Osteogenesis Imperfecta Foundation. 1999. *Nutrition Fact Sheet.* Gaithersburg, Md.: Author.

Osteogenesis Imperfecta Foundation. 1999. *Rodding Fact Sheet.* Gaithersburg, Md.: Author.

Porat, S., E. Helle, D. Seidman, and S. Meye. 1991. Functional Results of Operation in Osteogenesis Imperfecta: Elongating and Non-Elongating Rods. *Journal of Pediatric Orthopedics* 11:200–203.

Reing, C.M. 1995. Report on New Types of Intramedullary Rods and Treatment Effectiveness Data for Selection of Intramedullary Rodding in Osteogenesis Imperfecta. *Connective Tissue Research* 31(4):S77–79.

Smith, Peter. 1999. Rodding Surgery. *Breakthrough: The Newsletter of the Osteogenesis Imperfecta Foundation* 24(3):9–10.

Wacaster, Priscilla (ed.). 1996. *Managing Osteogenesis Imperfecta: A Medical Manual.* Gaithersburg, Md.: Osteogenesis Imperfecta Foundation.

5
Preparing Families for Treatment and Surgery

Peter A. Smith, M.D.
Caroline Anderson, Ph.D.
Melanie Bland, CCLS, CTRS

Key Points in This Chapter

- While nothing can eliminate the stress and pain of hospitalization and surgery, preparation and coping strategies can benefit all family members.

- Parents frequently experience guilt, anger, sorrow, depression, fatigue, or stress when their child requires treatment or hospitalization. These feelings are normal and understandable.

- Hospital staff, including nurses, psychologists, social workers, and child life specialists can help parents and children deal with the stresses of hospitalization.

- Children are better able to cope with medical procedures when they understand what is happening and have strategies that help them feel in control of the situation.

- Coping strategies that help children feel more in control include medical role playing, guided imagery, preadmission hospital tours, and bringing comforting objects from home to the hospital.

Children with osteogenesis imperfecta (OI) face the prospect of many trips to the doctor's office or hospital. These can be emergency visits after a serious fracture, or they can be scheduled trips for routine evaluations, elective surgery, or drug treatments. Although a certain amount of anxiety is unavoidable, there is no doubt that a patient and family who are prepared and knowledgeable can minimize problems and improve the outcome of care.

The most important consideration is to verify that the visit is to the right place at the right time, and will benefit the child. (See Chapter 4 for more on making treatment decisions.) Many fractures can be splinted or suitably immobilized at home, to await definitive evaluation and treatment during regular office hours by a physician familiar with the child. Many people with OI have had the experience of waiting for a long time in the emergency room to be seen by a doctor or nurse with little knowledge of OI. If the child has a significant fracture at night or in an area where an orthopedist is not available, then the emergency room is an unavoidable necessity so that the fracture can be properly assessed with x-rays and treated with splinting or casting. Emergency staff are very competent at evaluating fractures and providing appropriate splinting. They do not need to be experts in osteogenesis imperfecta, especially if the child or family can provide brief information about the child's diagnosis and fracture history. This information will expedite treatment and smooth over any embarrassment or anxiety on the part of parents or medical professionals. Parents can also help ease the child's emergency room experience by requesting pain medication while waiting for treatment, and asking if there is a quiet area or playroom where the family can wait until they are called in.

Similarly, clinic visits and hospital admissions for medication or surgery should be carefully considered and discussed with the responsible doctor beforehand. It is reasonable to expect a two-way discussion of the risks, benefits, and alternatives of any procedure and to be satisfied as to its necessity. This will lead to increased peace of mind for everyone concerned and ultimately lead to better outcomes. (See Chapter 3 for more on communication and partnerships with health care providers.)

When surgery is scheduled, parents should talk with the physician before the child is admitted, and with the physician and other staff while the child is hospitalized, about immediate postoperative needs—for example, adaptive equipment to aid mobility, exercises for the arms and legs that were not operated on to maintain strength and fitness, and plans for physical therapy as soon as it is safe.

Helping Parents Cope

It is normal for parents to be anxious about a hospitalization, surgery, or medical treatment for their child. Part of that anxiety relates to the fact that parents are the primary decision makers, especially for younger children, and medical decisions are frequently complex. Although parents clearly want what is best for their child, they must take responsibility for making the final decisions on whether or not an elective surgery should be done, whether they should seek a second opinion, or whether they are comfortable with a recommended course of treatment. The stress increases if spouses disagree or other relatives, especially grandparents, voice criticism of the plan, or if physicians have offered conflicting recommendations for treatment.

Added to the anxiety of making medical decisions are multiple other emotions related to the child's need for treatment. Guilt is often present when a parent takes a child with OI to the hospital because of a broken bone. Perhaps parents worry that the child should not have been allowed to play ball, should have been watched more closely, or should have been warned to be more careful. And no matter how careful they are, parents or other caregivers may accidentally cause a fracture. When unfortunate events occur, second-guessing and self-blame are common.

A corollary response that a parent may have is anger. If a child was told not to play ball, did it anyway, and broke a bone as a result, or if another child or adult contributed to an accident by being careless, the parent may be justifiably angry. The disruption of the family's schedule, the agony of another trip to the emergency room, and the feeling that the emergency could have been avoided are all stressful. Anger in this situation is perfectly normal and natural, although it is often difficult for parents to acknowledge this anger. Their feelings

My son once fractured his femur at an OI Foundation support group meeting. That night in the hospital room, I sat on one side of the bed and my husband sat on the other side of the bed. Neither one of us said much. Finally, I couldn't stand it any longer and blurted out, "I'm so sorry. I shouldn't have put him in those shoes. If he had on his play shoes, he wouldn't have fallen." My husband was surprised at my apology. All that time I had been sitting there blaming myself, he had been blaming himself. He was right beside our son when he fell, and my husband felt guilty that he wasn't able to prevent the fall. After expressing forgiveness to each other, we were better able to forgive ourselves. And the hospital room didn't feel quite so lonely anymore.

Priscilla Wacaster, mother of Neil, 9 years old, and Lillie, 3 years old

are conflicted and difficult to sort out—how can I be angry with a child who is suffering so much? Parents may blame themselves for feeling angry, adding to the problem.

Sadness, sorrow, and frustration are equally common responses as parents deal with their child's pain and disappointment, the restrictions that a surgery or splint require, and the realization that once again OI has disrupted the family's plans. Depression and fatigue may also set in as parents deal with having a child in the hospital while balancing the needs of siblings, jobs, financial realities, babysitters, and household chores.

Once a child has entered the hospital, parents have the additional stress of losing their parenting role, to some extent. A parent no longer has control of the child's schedule or environment. It may not be clear when doctors will visit, or procedures and medication will be administered. Even more stressful, the parent is unable to prevent many of the invasive and painful events that will occur.

Helping parents deal appropriately with their own stresses is the first step in enabling them to provide the most effective support for their child. Whether the surgery or medical treatment is elective and carefully planned or a sudden emergency, parents will benefit from receiving clearly stated information, plenty of opportunity to ask questions, and repetition again after they have had time to process the implications of the plan. While physicians are primarily responsible for discussing the medical or surgical plan with parents, it is also helpful for parents to talk to nurses, social workers, or psychologists, who can assess parents' emotional response to the treatment plan and answer any additional questions that arise. Once parents feel comfortable with the medical or surgical plan, they often have numerous other questions: Can I stay at my child's bedside? Where will I sleep? Is there a cafeteria? Can siblings visit? Finding the answers to all of their logistic concerns will be very reassuring to parents. Parents should not hesitate to approach hospital personnel until they get the information they need.

Most children's hospitals practice family-centered care, where parents can stay overnight with the child. In general, this is helpful and improves the child's medical care. Hospital staff, including nurses, psychologists, and child life specialists can help parents interact with their child at the hospital in ways that are most comfortable for both child and parent. Many parents want to continue to do as many caring activities as possible with their child, including bathing and dressing. If needed, hospital staff can teach parents how to manage despite IVs, casts, or pain (although it is also common for parents to show hospital staff how to handle their child). Communication between staff and parents is critical to ensure that parents feel confident in the care they are providing, and that both nurses and parents are happy with the decisions about whether hospital staff or family members are responsible for specific aspects of care. Although most parents prefer to do their child's care themselves, there are also times when they may need a break.

Throughout the course of a hospitalization, parents may benefit from opportunities to talk with a psychologist or social worker away from their child. This allows parents to vent about anxieties that they might not want to express in front of the child, and gives the health care professional an opportunity to support and acknowledge that a parent's feelings of anger or frustration are perfectly normal. Most hospitalized children will also display behaviors that are unusual for them; they regress, become angry with their parents, or act out in ways that embarrass their parents. Parents may become distressed about these behaviors; the social worker or psychologist can reassure them and suggest strategies to help manage the behavior.

Finally, parents often benefit from information about concrete resources or services that will make their lives easier during a stressful time. If the hospitalization is too far from home to allow easy travel back and forth, parents may need to know about a local Ronald McDonald House or other reasonable housing and transportation options. Help negotiating through all the issues with their insurance company or planning for their child's return to school can be reassuring and calming to a parent. Even encouraging parents to spend time at home with the siblings or take an afternoon away from the hospital for themselves can be valuable, enabling the parent to take a needed respite without feeling guilty.

Helping Children Cope

When a child arrives at a hospital for surgery or a procedure such as a cast change or splinting, they are entering a world with strange sights, sounds, and smells. Even for children who have been frequently hospitalized, these changes in atmosphere can create significant fear and anxiety. Fear of the unknown and surprises leads to increased anxiety and an inability to cope with planned surgeries and procedures. By preparing their child ahead of time, parents can eliminate unneeded stress and anxiety for trips to the hospital or treatment center.

When parents learn a child may need surgery or a medical procedure, they can start to implement age-appropriate coping strategies. A coping strategy gives children a sense of control over their body and what is happening to them. The control might be counting to three before an IV starts or playing "I SPY" during a blood draw. This perception of control will enable the child to handle the procedure positively.

If surgery is scheduled for a child, parents can ask the hospital for a preadmission tour. It is helpful to encourage the child to

When our son had his rod replaced when he was seven, we took pictures to help him later as he dealt with his memories. To our surprise, our daughter Lillie, who was two at the time, was the one who wanted (needed?) to look at the pictures and talk about the experience.

Priscilla Wacaster, mother of Neil, 9 years
old, and Lillie, 3 years old

become familiar with the setting, including the location of the playroom and patient rooms. Parents and staff should use child-friendly and simple language. An honest approach, telling the child what will happen and how it will feel, is best. This is a great opportunity to deal with any misconceptions children might have, while also building trust. It is during this conversation that a coping strategy may be discussed and chosen. Both parents and child can ask many questions; they can never have too much information about what they will be experiencing. Also, the more secure and knowledgeable the parents are about what the child will undergo, the safer the child will feel. Parents may also want to ask if the hospital has age-specific storybooks or coloring books to familiarize the child with the surgical process. Again, taking away the element of the unknown helps a child to understand or cope with the experience of surgery or treatment.

Other coping strategies may entail bringing support from home to the hospital. Often a favorite stuffed animal, blanket, or familiar object provides a sense of security, enabling children to feel more comfortable with their surroundings and what is happening. Parents should help the child understand when he will be with the family and when he will be apart. Separation often has a lot to do with how anxious and traumatic an experience is. Parents can also ask the hospital if preoperative teaching is available from a child life specialist. A child life specialist can explain the surgical process to the child in age-appropriate language, and

> When Nicole has surgery, they always allow us to wait for her in the recovery room before she is brought in. This makes Nicole feel calm and at ease when she arrives in the recovery room. We also make laminated signs for her bed and her medical chart stating that she has OI and to handle her with care.
>
> Michelle Hofhine, mother of Nicole, 6 years old

provide medical play to work through anxieties or fears if needed. By taking the time to thoroughly prepare children for a procedure, parents eliminate unneeded stress.

Postoperatively, parents should continue to foster positive coping skills by using distraction techniques such as guided imagery, deep breathing, or using toys to engage a child in play. Parents can use guided imagery to take a child's imagination to a safe and secure place by asking questions such as: Where is your favorite place to go when you are scared? Where in our home do you feel the safest? Can you describe it to me? What was your favorite family vacation? A child's imagination can serve as a powerful tool during difficult or painful procedures. Often, children can forget about the pain associated with an uncomfortable procedure when they are participating in an enjoyable activity or talking about a favorite thing. This type of purposeful play enables children to work through the treatment process in a more desirable or pleasant manner.

Parents should bring a camera to document the surgical process for the child. Take pictures before and after to illustrate the improvement and show why the surgery was beneficial. Parents might also provide a journal for remembering favorite roommates, nurses, or funny sayings. Encourage siblings to visit and understand what the child is having done, and perhaps what the child or cast will look like after surgery. Let them be part of the experience. Another idea is to create a calendar of when the follow-up visit will be or what day the cast comes off. Then the child can put a sticker over each day and have mastery over the situation.

With age-appropriate education, parents can expect that their child will be as ready as possible for situations they will experience in the hospital. Procedures can be accompanied by pain or discomfort, but preparing the child with knowledge and coping strategies is the key to having as positive a hospital experience as possible.

Resources

Albrecht, Donna G. 1995. *Raising a Child Who Has a Physical Disability*. New York: John Wiley and Sons.

Avis, Brenner. 1997. *Helping Children Cope with Stress*. San Francisco: Jossey-Bass.

Osteogenesis Imperfecta Foundation. 1999. *Emergency Department Management of Osteogenesis Imperfecta*. Gaithersburg, Md.: Author.

Thompson, Richard. 1985. *Psychosocial Research on Pediatric Hospitalization and Health Care: A Review of the Literature*. Springfield, Ill.: Thomas.

Books for Children

Brazelton, T. Berry. 1996. *Going to the Doctor*. Addison Wesley Longman.

Hallinan, P.K. 1996. *My Doctor My Friend*. Ideals Children's Books.

Berenstain, Stan. 1981. *The Berenstain Bears Go to the Doctor*. Random House Books for Young Readers.

To Give or Not to Give?

When a child is injured or hospitalized, it is natural for family and friends to want to give gifts or a special treat. When a child has a chronic condition such as OI, gift giving becomes more complex. Families have come up with different solutions for gift giving.

- Some families feel that giving a child with OI a "pick me up" gift after a fracture or surgery is appropriate. They often choose gifts that help pass the time during recovery, such as a book, video, CD, or game.

- If a child has siblings, parents need to consider how to include them in gift giving so they will not feel left out. Some families get a small gift for each child. If they wish, parents can use the gifts to recognize children's behavior or coping skills. For example, the child with OI gets a gift for being brave during an x-ray, while big brother gets a gift for holding his sister's hand and telling her a funny story on the way to the hospital.

- Purchase a family gift that everyone can enjoy, such as a new game, and present it to all of the children instead of just the child with OI. Or rent or purchase a movie that the whole family can watch.

- Plan a special family outing to a play, movie, or the beach once the child with OI has recovered enough to get out of the house. The whole family can celebrate the child's recovery together.

- Make a special "activity bag" for each child. The children can even choose what they want in their special bag. Put the bags away and save them for when someone in the family is injured, hospitalized, or ill. As time and money allow, add something new to each bag so that it continues to be a treat.

- Some siblings may benefit more from one-on-one time with a parent than from gifts. One mother remarked, "I don't think gift giving has to be one for one. When our daughter with OI had rodding surgery, we learned that making time for our other daughter to be with one of us, without her sister, worked better than giving gifts."

- As a general rule, it's best to avoid using candy or other food to comfort a child after a fracture or surgery, as this can lead to unhealthy eating habits. But in some cases, food can be an appropriate treat for the whole family, particularly if they are usually conscientious about healthy eating. For example, parents can prepare a favorite meal or special dessert to celebrate a child's coming home from the hospital. One adult with OI recalled, "On the way home from the ER after a fracture, my parents would sometimes let me choose where we should stop to pick up a take-out meal. This was a treat for everyone, as we rarely ate out, and we were usually hungry after several hours of waiting in the ER."

- If friends or family wish to give a gift, parents might suggest that a phone call, e-mail, card, or visit would be appreciated. Many children enjoy inexpensive gifts such as a favorite magazine or a video rental gift certificate, rather than yet another stuffed animal or balloon.

6
Brittle Bones, Fractured Finances

Financial Security for Families Living with OI

Mark A. Peck

Key Points in This Chapter

- Health insurance is vitally important to a family's financial security.

- Adults with OI may have difficulty getting health insurance because insurers may exclude people with "pre-existing conditions." However, there are several government programs and regulations in place to help adults with OI get insurance through their employer, or through state and federal insurance programs.

- Most states also have Children's Health Insurance Programs (CHIPs), which can provide coverage to children with OI if they are not covered or are underinsured by a parent's insurance plan.

- Life insurance is also important for a family's financial health. Though life insurance companies often accept people with pre-existing conditions, the rates may be higher.

- Parents of children with OI may wish to consider setting up a special needs trust for their child, rather than giving their child direct inheritance of their estate.

Author's note: *Any information provided here should be examined for relevance to the specific programs in your state, as well as the applicable probate code. This is not to be construed as legal advice in any way, and is the opinion of the author and not the Osteogenesis Imperfecta Foundation.*

Health Insurance

As a financial planner, I see many pitfalls that can devastate a family's financial health. None of these are as dangerous as the lack of health insurance, especially when a family member has a significant health problem. In a recent article in the South Florida *Sun Sentinel*, Nancy McVicar reported that a routine tonsillectomy at a hospital in that state costs more than $12,000 for less than 24 hours in the hospital! Certainly it's not hard to see how the lack of health insurance can destroy a family's financial well-being. Yet what about the family in which someone has OI? Getting health insurance can be difficult at best.

To better understand this problem, it is important to understand how insurance and insurance companies work. Insurance works on the principle of shared risk. By insuring large numbers of people, companies know that some will be unhealthy, while most will be healthy. Thus, the healthy people, by paying insurance premiums without incurring many medical bills, are paying the health care costs of the unhealthy. Insurance companies also add an extra amount to the premium for unexpected claims, and of course, their profits. If a company prices its coverage too high, other companies will bid away its customers by offering to sell the same or similar coverage at a lower premium. If the price is set too low, costs will exceed income from premiums. This in turn can cause financial problems, and possibly require the insurer to abandon that type of coverage or the entire health insurance market, as states impose minimum solvency requirements to make sure companies have sufficient funds to pay claims.

Private insurance companies compete with each other to write policies for individuals, families, and employer groups. Companies offer a variety of insurance packages that differ in price, deductible levels, limits on payments, conditions covered, and the regional composition of doctors and hospitals who may deliver services. The record shows that the private health insurance market can, with a minimum of government regulation and oversight, deliver insurance at a competitive price with a minimum of bureaucracy and waste.

Health Insurance for Adults with OI

In the case of an adult with OI, it can be difficult or impossible to obtain health insurance because insurance companies often exclude "pre-existing conditions." If they did not, they would be increasing the number of claims so much that the concept of shared risk would be destroyed and their estimates of health care costs thrown out the window. Few companies would have the financial means to stay afloat. Thus, insurance as we know it would end.

Nonetheless, there are a few possibilities for a person with OI. Over the years, state and federal governments have enacted a number of measures to help people obtain and keep health insurance. Congress and individual states have mandated conversion policies, continuation requirements, and portability provisions. The federal government enacted portability requirements as part of the Consolidated Omnibus Budget Reconciliation Act (COBRA), which allows an employee to continue health insurance coverage under their employer's plan for up to 18 months after leaving a job. The employee's covered spouse and children may continue their coverage for up to 36 months. COBRA only applies to employers with 20 or more employees. To continue insurance coverage under COBRA, the insured person is responsible for paying the *entire* monthly premium rather than just the "employee share" of the premium. In fact, the premium charged may be as much as 102 percent of the original premium. For example, if the employee's share of the premium while working was $100 a month, and the employer's share had been $300, the employee could pay as much as $408 per month to continue coverage under COBRA.

In 1996, Congress passed the Health Insurance Portability and Accountability Act (HIPAA), a law imposing broad access and portability measures. Under HIPAA, a person who has been covered under another plan (either group or individual) before joining a new *group* plan can use the prior period of coverage to offset the new plan's waiting periods for pre-existing conditions. Also under HIPAA, any waiting period imposed for pre-existing conditions cannot exceed 12 months.

In addition, some 66 million low-income and elderly Americans rely on Medicaid and Medicare, respectively, for their health care needs. It would be possible to fill this entire book with the details of Medicaid and Medicare, only to have the regulations be outdated by the time the book is printed. The Social Security Administration and Health Care Financing Administration's web sites are good starting references for current eligibility requirements and regulations (www.ssa.gov and www.hcfa.gov).

For more than 100,000 people who could not otherwise be insured, the answer is state-created Health Insurance Plans (HIPs). HIPs increase access to health insurance. These plans permit people to finance their health care needs by heavily subsidizing their claims. Some even help lower-income people pay for their share of the premiums. HIPs are not new. Many have been around for years, providing comprehensive medical coverage for individuals who could be considered uninsurable otherwise. Enrollment ranges from 198 people in Alaska's five-year-old program to about 26,314 in Minnesota's 22-year-old plan. One significant benefit of the HIP is that it allows the recipient to change jobs or look for a first job without concern over health insurance. As of 1998, the 28 states offering these programs were: Alabama, Alaska, Arkansas, California, Colorado, Connecticut, Florida, Illinois, Indiana, Iowa, Kansas, Louisiana, Minnesota, Mississippi, Missouri, Montana, Nebraska, New Mexico, North Dakota, Oklahoma, Oregon, South Carolina, Tennessee, Texas, Utah, Washington, Wisconsin, and Wyoming. To find out more about a particular state plan, or to determine if your state has been added to the HIP list, contact your state insurance commissioner's office.

Let me try and put this "alphabet soup" into English. First, people with OI who are employed or employable may be able to get insurance through their company's group plan. Insurance companies may waive their pre-existing condition limitations to make their services more appealing to employers. People who quit their job may

be able to continue coverage under COBRA legislation, which allows them to continue coverage for
18 months at their own expense,
as explained previously.

HIPAA allows a person who
has been employed with benefits for
at least 18 months without a significant break in service to change jobs
without exclusions of coverage for
any pre-existing conditions. In addition, if someone is employed yet
his or her current plan has such an
exclusion, that exclusion can only last for a maximum of 12 months.
Most relevant to a reasonably healthy person with OI is a requirement
that OI would only be a pre-existing condition *if* he or she has received *advice, diagnosis, treatment, or care for* OI during the six months prior
to enrolling in the new plan. For many adults with OI, this means that
OI is a pre-existing condition only if they have had fractures, x-rays,
surgery, etc., during that six-month period. Unfortunately, HIPAA only
applies to group plans and not individual policies.

Of course, other obvious ways to obtain coverage are through
a spouse's group plan, or a parent's plan, if the adult child is a
student and under a certain age (usually 26).

People with OI who are not employed and not covered by a
family member will almost always be eligible for Medicaid. If they
receive Social Security Disability Income, they should also be eligible for Medicare. These programs are tied to income and asset
restrictions. Generally, people who are unemployed will meet these
criteria. Also, most hospitals are required to provide free or subsi-
dized care for indigent patients. While this may not be an attractive
label, such assistance can make a huge difference.

Health Insurance for Children with OI

Children with OI are often covered under their parents' insurance
plans. The information above on COBRA, HIPAA, Medicaid, and

Medicare can be helpful to parents in obtaining and keeping insurance coverage for their entire family. For children with OI whose parents may or may not have health insurance plans, most states have Children's Health Insurance Programs (CHIPs) or similar plans to provide health insurance to children not otherwise insured. Most of these plans are needs-based, meaning that they are tied to income and assets. These plans can also serve as excellent supplements to cover deductibles and coinsurance on coverage parents already have. These programs are usually managed by either the state department of public health, or the state insurance commissioner's office.

Life Insurance

Another type of insurance that is often overlooked is life insurance. Life insurance is also based on the idea of shared risk. As a result, it may be difficult to obtain for those with OI. Unlike health insurance, life insurance does not always exclude coverage, but may simply "rate" the premium higher to compensate for the increased risk. Coverage will almost always be cheaper and more easily obtained at young ages. This is true because the company is not concerned with medical bills as with health insurance, but instead considers only the risk of death. The older the applicant, the higher the chances of death. In addition, as a person with OI ages, he or she may have other health complications such as asthma or even hazardous hobbies (such as, in my case, a student pilot license!). Infants can often be covered at standard rates as a rider on parents' policies for small amounts without any health questions. Coverage may be converted to the child's own name as a separate policy once the child reaches adulthood. Often, the coverage amount increases automatically at that time. This may be the only coverage the child will ever have and parents are well advised to see if they can obtain such a rider for their child with OI.

For the adult with OI who does not have dependents, the need for coverage may be limited to funeral and other final expenses. In most cases, this amount would be no greater than $10,000. This can often be obtained through an employer's group plan or well-advertised policies for "coverage that cannot be denied." Another source of similar coverage is membership in various nonprofit associations. This type of insurance is generally "decreasing term," meaning that the death benefit decreases with age and the policy has no cash value. Credit union membership often makes one eligible for this type of coverage, and the amounts may even be much higher.

For someone who has dependents, the needed amount may be much higher. Creativity may be needed to find the right coverage. By combining association membership, credit unions, employer group plans, and spousal plans, one can often obtain the amounts needed. One should never rule out applying for coverage where medical information is required. Although a policy may be rated (i.e., more expensive), the rating may well be worth the peace of mind. A trick of the trade I have used quite successfully is to apply for a policy around mid-December. Companies are often overwhelmed with applications at year-end due to agents trying to qualify for various incentives. Home office underwriters often overlook major medical requirements to get the business issued. It's not foolproof but it can work. If the policy is issued with a premium that is too high, the applicant can simply cancel the application and receive a refund of the deposit.

Two important caveats: People who have a lot more health problems than just OI can have the agent submit a "preliminary application." If this is rated or declined, it does not create a permanent file with the medical information bureau. Once such a file exists, the person will always be required to answer "yes" to the question, "Have you ever been rated or declined for coverage?" Also, applicants should never give false or misleading answers on an insurance application. Although they may get the coverage applied for, it will not pay the claim after their death if such fraud is discovered!

Special Needs Trusts

Also called "supplemental needs trusts," special needs trusts may be the most important aspect of financial planning for parents of a child with OI.

Most parents and grandparents want to provide for a child (even an adult child) with OI after their death. As a result, the child is made a beneficiary on insurance and may be given a larger share of the estate than other siblings. Some well-meaning but uninformed attorneys may even advise parents to do this. Well-meant as they were, the results can spell disaster for the child. As the owner of substantial assets, he or she is now disqualified from most needs-based government benefits.

The alternative is the special needs or supplemental needs trust. Using their will, the parents or grandparents actually "lovingly disinherit" the child. Instead, the child's share of the inheritance is bequeathed to the special needs trust. The trust in turn provides for any supplemental needs not provided for the child by government programs. Trust provisions are drafted so that any income or assets given to the child are kept below the amounts allowed for program

eligibility. Because in-kind (as opposed to cash) benefits do not disqualify the child from eligibility in most programs, the trustee pays for things directly rather than giving the child the cash.

Here's a true-life example. When I was in college, my tuition was paid for by a government program. I received Supplemental Security Income (SSI), which in turn made me eligible for Medicaid (these programs are always linked). At that

time, my parents were preparing a will. They told the attorney about me and he suggested that because I had OI, I should receive half of the estate while my three older sisters split the other half. Though I might have found this to be appropriate payback for just *having* three older sisters, it certainly would not have been fair! Fortunately my parents did not die at that time. If they had, not only would my sisters have forever hated me, but I would have also lost SSI, and thus automatically lost Medicaid, and my tuition grant. Yes, I would have had the cash to pay tuition, but because I had a major accident in my senior year, I racked up sizable medical bills, all of which were covered by Medicaid. Had I lost the Medicaid, the inheritance would have been spent on medical bills, not tuition or my own nest egg. If my parents had died with a special needs trust in place, the trust would have provided me the $65 per month income allowed under SSI, paid for trips home to visit my sisters, and, once I was on my own and working with benefits in place, the trust would have been paid out to me either in cash or as a monthly income. (**Author's note:** Under current regulations, the limits for SSI are $65 per month for income, and $2,000 of assets for an individual and $3,000 for a couple.)

The trust can be funded by a share of the estate, as in my example, or by purchasing a separate life insurance policy with the trust, not the child, as beneficiary. Parents should be absolutely certain that their attorney is experienced with the drafting of these trusts before beginning. The parents won't be there when the trust goes into effect, and it will be too late to fix mistakes.

Resources

Berger, Mark C., Dan A. Black, Amitabh Chandra, Carolyn Looff and Associates. 1999. *COBRA and Household Health Insurance Decisions.* Washington, D.C.: Pension and Welfare Benefits Administration, U.S. Department of Labor. **On the Internet at: www.dol.gov/ dol/pwba/public/programs/opr/H-RES/berger.htm.**

Hamburger, Paul M. 2001. *Mandated Health Benefits, The COBRA Guide.* Thompson Publishing Group.

McVicar, Nancy. 2000. Hospital Care Costs Shocking Patients. *South Florida Sun Sentinel.* 23 February.

Meier, Conrad F. 1999. *Extending Affordable Health Insurance to the Uninsurable.* Heartland Policy Study No. 91. Chicago: The Heartland Institute. **On the Internet at: www.heartland.org/studies/ meier-ps.htm#part2.**

National Partnership for Women and Families. 1998. *Guide to HIPAA.* Washington, D.C. : Author. **On the Internet at: www.nationalpartnership.org/healthcare/hipaa/guide5.htm.**

Pension and Welfare Benefits Administration. 2000. *Questions and Answers on the HIPAA Nondiscrimination Requirements.* Washington, D.C.: Pension and Welfare Benefits Administration, U.S. Department of Labor. **On the Internet at: www.dol.gov/dol/pwba/public/ pubs/faqs.htm.**

7

Personal Care for Lifelong Independence

Marilyn Marnie King, OTR/L

Key Points in This Chapter

- To learn personal care skills, such as dressing, bathing, using the toilet, and using household appliances, a child must first develop gross motor skills, such as reaching and sitting, which may be delayed or difficult for children with moderate to severe OI.

- Caregivers of children with OI can help them safely develop gross motor skills through protective handling, protective positioning, and protected movement, especially because frequent fractures can lead to frequent immobility and fear of movement.

- Equipment, ranging from simple pillows to specialized wheelchairs, can help children with OI develop gross motor and personal care skills even if they have muscle weakness or are recovering from a fracture.

- Water therapy can help children with OI develop skills in a gravity-free environment, before trying them on land.

- Energy conservation, joint protection, mobility, and household accessibility are key areas to address to help children with OI become as independent as possible.

- Traveling requires some advance preparation to make sure the child's personal care and medical needs can be taken care of away from home.

Author's note: *Parents and therapists can share the information in this chapter as they work together to find solutions to help a particular child achieve gross motor and personal care skills. The suggestions provided in this chapter are meant to be implemented over time as the child develops from a baby into a teenager. Chosen activities should address the child's particular needs, but should also appeal to the child's interests and sense of fun. Parents are advised to consult with their child's medical team—doctor, occupational therapist, and physical therapist—before pursuing any set of exercises on their own. To make it easier for readers to use the list of resources at the end of the chapter, I have numbered the resources and refer to them by number in appropriate places throughout the chapter.*

A Developmental Foundation Leads to Independent Personal Care

A child normally develops gross motor skills, such as sitting, crawling, and walking, with no apparent assistance or teaching required. These skills form the foundation for developing independent personal self-care. There is a typical ingrained order for achievement of gross motor or physical skills (Folio and Fewell 1983,1999). The order of development occurs from head to foot, and from the center of the body, or midline, to the ends of limbs. Compare this *gross motor* progression with the *self-care* milestones or progression in Table 1 (Parks 1988).

This typical gross motor skill progression builds trunk (torso) strength as a foundation for good stable posture, which enhances good hand function. This in turn will assist in developing independence in self-care. The foundation is like building a tower with blocks; the tower may be built higher if the base is solid. For developing children, there are increased cognitive (thinking) demands with more complex steps when doing purposeful self-care. For example, notice that self-feeding (done sitting) closely follows the achievement of independent sitting. The child's trunk strength and balance have become automatic and now the child is able to do two things at a time, sit *and* reach for food.

The normal progression may not be typical or possible for a child who has osteogenesis imperfecta (OI), depending on the severity of the disorder. The looseness of ligaments in OI requires

Table 1: Typical Developmental Milestones for Children Who Do Not Have OI

Gross Motor Milestones	Develop by (age in months)	Self-Care Milestones	Develop by (age in months)
Develops head control	3 months	Recognizes bottle/food	2–3 months
Rolls both directions fully	7		
Stays in sit when placed	5		
Circular sit-pivot	5–6	Holds own bottle	5–9
Sits independently indefinitely	5–8		
Gets to sit independently	6–10	Finger feeds	9–12
Moves (transitions) out of sit	6–10	Holds spoon	9–12
Pulls to a stand	6–10		
Commando crawls (on tummy)	8–10	Cooperates with dressing (holds out arm)	10–12
Creeps (on hands/knees)	9–11		
Cruises along furniture	9–13	Drinks from cup	12–18
Lowers from stand to sit	10–11	Indicates dirty pants	12–18
Kneels independently	11–13		
Takes steps alone	11–13	Removes sock or hat	15–18
Stands and pivots	12–14	Removes shoes (laces loosened)	18–24
Stoops/squats, returns to stand	18–23	Unzips large zipper	18–21
		Sits on potty chair with help	18–24
		Opens door by turning knob	21–23
		Puts shoes on with help	21–30
		Pulls pants down with help	24–26
		Undresses with help	26–32
		Pulls pants up	26–28
		Dresses with help	28–32
		Buttons	30–36
		Dresses with supervision, help with fastenings	32+

greater strength to assume positions. The lack of bone density permits muscle contractions to cause bending, bowing, or warping of the bones. Moving against gravity can cause fractures. What do we do to help the child with OI progress toward independence? Protective handling, good positioning, and protected movement are the first things to learn and apply in the child's daily life. These concepts will help the child build the foundation for independence in self-care. As a child grows from baby to toddler to preschooler, it is a good idea to include him or her in doing activities, even if the child can only do a part of the activity. This will develop the child's visual, cognitive, and problem-solving skills, which lead to independence. Problem solving will also help the severely involved child to direct his own care, permitting a less experienced caregiver to assist with his care in the future. Padding surfaces that the child will accidentally bump can prevent injuries and expose the child to increasing numbers of activities. Examples are padding bed rails with bed bumpers; padding the car seat, stroller, and tub; carrying an infant with OI on a pillow; and bathing the child reclined on a foam or inflatable floatation pad, as in Figure 1 (Resource 1,2).

Figure 1. Carrying on pillow   Bed bumpers and rail covers   Bath floatation pad

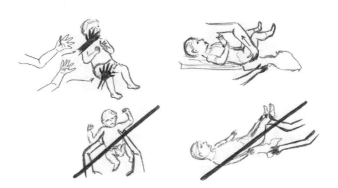

Figure 2. Hand positioning for lifting and diapering the infant

Protective Handling

Protective handling is done to prevent fractures, and avoid overstretching or adding to the joint hypermobility that is associated with OI. Lifting the child by using widely spread fingers under the back, neck, and buttocks will help avoid rib fractures (Figure 2). This should also be done to change diapers; lift the buttocks, not the legs. Or place the clean diaper over a piece of cardboard and slide it under the old diaper.

Example of a protective carrying position.

Carrying the child on a supported pillow will disperse support and pressure to the body. This will help everyone have greater confidence in moving the child. It is particularly useful for very young, fragile infants, and infants who startle easily when touched.

Protective Positioning

Protective positioning provides support during rest, and is essential for decreasing deformity and preventing overstretching of loose ligaments. The car seat, stroller, and bed must be analyzed to provide the best protective positioning for moderate to severe levels of OI. We all see children napping in every location, so examine the places that a child might fall asleep to provide support when she slumps.

It is important to help the child's spine and hips stay straight, the skull remain curved not flattened, and the neck to be symmetrical for head turning. The neck may be held positioned in the center with a neck roll, Velcro pads that attach to car seat straps (Resource 1,2), or pads that fit above the shoulders on the car seat. The seating equipment could have side pillows made of towel rolls or stuffed animals to assist in keeping the side of the trunk straight and the neck from drooping. Using a curved foam head pad or the gel pad created for premature infants will assist in keeping the skull from flattening at the back and permit some head turning (Re-

Figure 3. Best seated positioning in "big kid" sit, how to prevent slouching. Decrease "ring sit" whenever possible.

Figure 4. Gel pad under skull for contouring the skull. Wedges beside hips to avoid "frog legs" (hip abduction). A foam "trough" for back lying to decrease "frog legs" and support shoulders toward reaching midline.

Figure 5. Side lying for play creates different pressure on the skull for symmetry. This figure shows good positioning for play or sleep to decrease hip flexion and hip abduction, with gel pad under head.

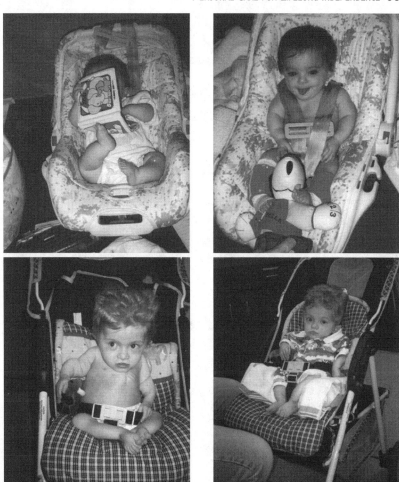

Cushions, stuffed animals, or towel rolls can be used to encourage children to use a "big kid" sit rather than a ring sit position in car seats and strollers.

source 12). A foam "trough" (Resource 1,2) will assist the infant lying on her back with support to the arms and legs, preventing the limbs from falling back and away from the center of the body (Figure 4). Placing a child on his side and encouraging a side reach to swipe at toys will vary the effect of gravity on the shape of the skull (Figure 5). When placing the child in a seated position, encourage a "big kid" sitting position, which means to support the hips, knees, and ankles at 90-degree angles (Figure 3). A seat cushion under the child's buttocks permits the feet to rest in a "big kid" sit in the car seat. This reduces the ring-sit effect (where the child sits with the soles of her feet together and knees pointed outward), which tends to increase the inward bowing of the lower legs and feet. When the child is in bed, use sandbags beside the hips or a thick body tube ("mermaid suit," described in Figure 13) that crosses the hips to keep the hips from bending up toward the face, and decreases the wide hip abduction (Figure 4). Children with OI tend to fold their arms and legs into their bodies, and then the bones curve or bow to follow that form.

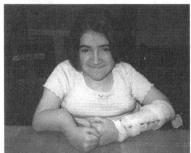
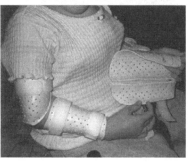
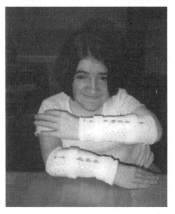

A nurse caring for a 10-month-old with moderate OI said that the child clapped when she saw her forearm splints. The child seemed to know that she could do more, sit, support herself, and reach for toys with them on! An older child who wore forearm splints from 10 to 14 years old had noticed a fracture cycle every two months and said her arms "needed to break." But when wearing the splints at night and during reaching activity, she found she could do more, and the two-month cycle became every six months.

It is especially important during the years of growth to attempt to maintain straight forearms. This can be done with "forearm circumferential splinting" to assist in moderate weight bearing to stimulate bone density when the child does partial crawling, scooter pushing, etc. (Figure 6). Straight arm bones will make a big difference in the child's ability to reach during such important activities as personal toileting. Older children with moderate to severe OI have used these splints for support during daily activity. As the child with OI reaches puberty, there is an increase in bone density and the need for the external support decreases. A research study being conducted at A.I. duPont Hospital for Children has a preliminary finding that children with OI have good hand function but poorer use of the limb if the arm is severely bowed, because the child's reach is decreased (Resource 10). Splinting of arms and legs can be utilized in water therapy to support limbs during new activities, such as bracing the legs to walk in chest-high water. Thus, external support will augment the strength of the inner skeleton and permit additional activity. For OI, a circumferential hinged splint design has been successful and can be made of the thinnest 1/16-inch perforated Aquaplast (Resource 9). As the child demonstrates confidence, less bracing may be attempted, first in the buoyant water and then on land.

When traveling with an infant, provide good head support because children nap in strollers and cars. It is important to keep the neck positioned in the center with a neck roll, Velcro pads that

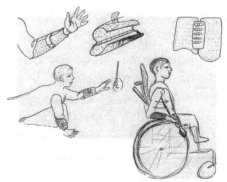

Figure 6. Forearm splinting to maintain limb straightness for mature ADL (activities of daily living), which also permits weightbearing or wheelchair pushing. The hinge is made of Velcro self-riveted to the splint material.

attach to car seat straps (Resource 1,2), or pads that fit above the shoulders on the car seat. Seat belts should have extra thick and wide straps to disperse the force of the car's motion. Velcro pads are available from automotive supply stores for widening the seat belts and were developed to cushion drivers' shoulders and necks. Vests with straps for transporting are also available (Resource 1,2, 5). These vests are useful for transporting a child with a fracture who must travel lying down. Due to the small size of the spinal bones, fractures occur easily in the spine. Equipment that permits frequent reclining will allow for more comfortable travel (and change in gravity forces) for older children.

Car seats are difficult to select for children with OI. Most car seats are designed for specific weights of children and may be used past the suggested age if the child still fits the car seat. Rear-facing in the car is recommended for infants and should be used as long as possible for the child with OI, as long as the child's feet do not reach beyond the car seat where they could be injured. Wide straps are available for some brands of car seats. See Figure 3 for the best positioning of side cushions. Recently, car seat manufacturers have developed a car bed for infants who need to be lying down. Some car seats are designed for children up to 30 pounds, and some new ones are for a larger, less capable 40-pound child. Fisher-Price has most of these recent products. (See Resource 15 for the car seat representative in your state.)

Protected Movement

Protected movement needs to be encouraged. This is a hard concept because caregivers tend to protect the child from fractures by limiting potentially harmful movement experiences. But not moving creates the problems of decreased strength, bowing from constant sitting, fear of movement and being moved, and dependence in all activity. Making slow changes in the child's position, placing items just beyond reach, encouraging the child to do short periods of activity, or only an easy part of an activity, and controlling the effects of gravity, give the child some confidence in moving. It is important to include the child in parts of activities, such as rolling out cookies but not stirring the stiff dough. This will expose children to various activities and builds a repertoire of experiences toward their future independence. Sometimes we tend to do what is the easiest; thus we "do for" and forget to permit the child to do for himself, even if it is just a part of the activity.

There is a general progression for developing skills in children with OI, usually provided through physical and occupational therapy. Therapy for children without OI usually moves faster. For children with OI, developmental concepts are analyzed more closely so that many small steps will lead to major achievements. The progression uses the same concepts of normal development that are listed in Table 1. As a level is done successfully and safely, then progression to the next level may be possible. This progression can also be used to recover from fractures. Various positions and movements against gravity will stimulate the development of greater bone density, permitting even more movement. Certain activities and positions will minimize fractures and deformities. Good positioning reduces spinal curves or scoliosis. "Big kid" sitting instead of ring sitting (see Figure 3) decreases the hip and tibia (lower leg)

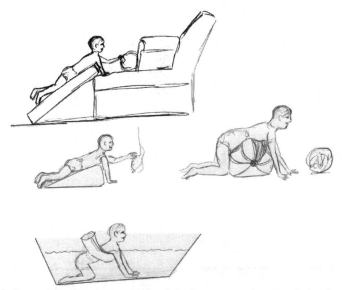

Figure 7. Prone playing for chest and spine. It is also a precrawl position that reduces some of the weight taken through the arms and legs. Lying prone over a partially inflated beach ball provides support for chest and arms, which reduces the effects of gravity.

bowing. Doing activities lying prone on tummy will stimulate bone density to decrease chest or sternum protrusions called "pectus carinatum" (Figure 7). This prone (tummy) position will also be needed when spinal discomfort or fractures occur. Emphasis needs to be on prone and sitting skills on land, with modified and supported skills in water, which eliminates the effects of gravity. Water is used to assist a child with moderate to severe OI develop greater mobility, first in water and then out of water.

Tolerance to being moved is a key goal for the more severely affected child. This can be accomplished by encouraging movement and by getting help from others when moving the child. To assist the child in increasing tolerance to movement, sandwich the child between two pillows with a wide base of support by bivalving the pillows (Figure 8) to turn the child over.

Sometimes it is safest to demonstrate or practice this movement with a doll so that it is done safely and the child knows what is going to happen. Begin new movement in supported positions, and then work on skills needed to transition to (move into) that position. It takes more strength and control for the child to do the transitions, such as rolling, going from lying to sitting, or from sitting to crawling, than to maintain a static still position. Note the child's tolerance for different positions, with the goal of slowly increasing the time spent in a position. This will develop strength, increase the child's confidence, and encourage automatic use of the position while doing something else, such as kneeling *and* reaching for a toy. Assisting with part of the transition may help the child develop the full skill. All positions should be combined with visual, auditory, or tactile activities that are fun, thus motivating a

Figure 8. "Pillow sandwich" or bivalve pillows to turn the child over.

Figure 9. Avoid hip flexion or "jack-knife" because it stresses the upper leg (femur).

child to tolerate positions that are new or disliked.

Some motions require a strong leverage that could cause fractures. Avoid having the child reach far forward from a sitting position, causing strong hip flexion ("jack-knife" or the "split"), which stresses the femur near the hip (Figure 9). Equally injurious is diagonal rotation (twisting at the trunk,) which affects the spinal vertebrae (Figure 10). Vertical bouncing should also be avoided due to the impact that could cause vertebral (spinal) compression fracture or foot bone fractures.

OI limits a child's ability to achieve developmental milestones independently, due to its effect on bone density, ligament stability, and muscle strength. Thus, the child with OI will require slow, graded introduction to being moved in progressively less supported positions. This allows the child to develop strength, confidence, and independence. Children with severe OI may not accomplish some of the developmental progressions. For self-care independence, the ability to reach and "shimmy-sitting" skills (the ability to scoot side-to-side or front-to-back in a sitting position) will go a long way to help the child with OI cope

Figure 10. Avoid diagonal trunk rotation because it stresses the spinal vertebrae.

as an independent adult in a modified setting. Some children will sit most of the time; some will never independently transfer but some will; some will be household walkers but not tolerate our active bumping society; and others will walk but with reduced endurance. Be-

Figure 11. Learning head control in supine (on back) on parent's chest. A safe hold on the child while standing, also permitting the child to practice head control. Note the caregiver's hand in a place *ready* to support.

Figure 12. Learning head control in prone (on tummy) on parent's chest. Lying on beach ball. Notice the caregiver's hand position *ready* to support.

cause we do not know what level of independence each child with OI will achieve, it is important to analyze the amount of stress any motion has on the body. Skills progress slowly from head to foot, and controlled weightbearing stimulates bone density. It is also important to position to prevent deformity that would limit the child's walking and personal care independence potential.

The following protected movement progressions are done within the child's comfort and tolerance. Only a few new activities should be introduced at one session. The progression may be used during recovery from fractures to regain previous skills.

For improving head/neck support and mobility, always provide good positioning with proper alignment (head straight in car seat, in house, and while feeding; using towel rolls or stuffed toys to keep head positioned when the child sleeps in the car seat). To strengthen the neck, decrease the child's head support for three to five seconds. Start with supporting the child bolt upright, sitting on the caregiver's lap. The caregiver then reclines slowly, moving the child gradually into a supine (lying face-up) position (Figure 11). Next try lowering the child's back onto the bed or into a chair slowly while the child holds her head in a chin-tuck. Caregivers can also help strengthen the neck by gently tilting the child to each side, forward and backward.

Prone positioning (lying on tummy) requires good head control. Older children with OI who have not been placed in this position often dislike it. Start as described above but with the child facing the caregiver's chest as the caregiver slowly reclines (Figure 12). One can also place the child lying partially prone on a foam wedge or sofa cushion at a 45-degree angle (Figure 7). Other ideas include lying on a partially inflated beach ball and rolling it slightly front to back, side to side.

Have the child progress to the prone position by placing him over a wedge or towel roll under the chest, with activities nearby to see and touch. Have the child prop on his forearms while a caregiver supports his head, and progress to three to five seconds without head support. Use visual distractions like swipe toys, pets, videos, or video games for older children.

In the **supine (lying on back) position,** the leg position should be monitored to avoid the wide hip abduction or "frog-leg" (Figure

Figure 13. "Mermaid suit" of stockinette to hold legs in neutral position.

4) position by using bolsters, wedges of towels or pillows, or a tube of stockinette over the hips called the "mermaid suit" (Figure 13). The "mermaid suit" can be made of the upper portion of old panty hose, or large stockinette or tubigrip. This long tube helps hold knees and hips together, leading to transitions from prone to crawl. The length of the "mermaid suit" is important; it should give support to the full length of the legs to avoid any leverage for fracture. When using the "mermaid suit," hanging soft toys on an activity gym will encourage arm reach and shoulder strength for later crawling.

Trunk (torso or main body) support and mobility will be enhanced by providing support, as described previously, for sitting straight in the car seat, in the house, while feeding, and while sleeping. Once head control emerges, providing less trunk support from the head down may be initiated to develop trunk strength.

Sidelying is also encouraged so that when tolerated, rolling can begin. Start with the child sidelying with support under her neck and side of face, and between her legs (to keep straight alignment of head and spine). (See Figure 5.) Then place a fun activity at arm's reach (swipe, pat, push, pull, or squeeze toys), and also at foot's reach for several minutes. Next time try the other side. Note any preferences but continue doing both sides for up to five minutes at a time.

Rolling can be encouraged in slow progressions. From a sidelying position, guide the child in half-rolling using the child's pelvis. Or use the pillow sandwich to help the child start the roll (Figure 8). Next, try to guide rolling to or from the sidelying posi-

Figure 14. Blanket to aid rolling, done slowly.

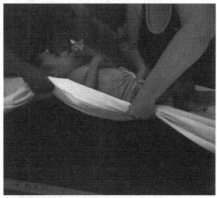

A blanket can also be used to help with transferring.

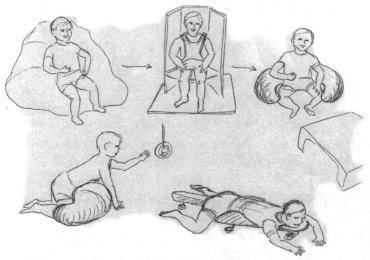

Figure 15. Progress from supported sitting in beanbag chair to corner chair to Boppy (crescent-shaped) pillow. Precrawl position over Boppy or scooter board ("crawlagator"). "Table" cut from cardboard box.

tion to prone (tummy) and/or to supine (back). Using a blanket under the child to begin the roll will distribute the force along the entire trunk (Figure 14). Having a towel roll or small pillow at the waist to stop the roll is another phase of half-rolling. Independent rolling will help with caregiving, permit easier dressing, and lead to other skills. Limbs should not be flexed up across the trunk when moving to the belly or the legs could get stuck. (See Figure 5.)

Supported sitting can begin with reclined support and offering things to reach. If the child requires a high back with neck support, place the child in a reclined supported sit in a beanbag chair; progress to a high chair with good side towel rolls and a complete trunk strap (Figure 15). If neck support is needed, try a foam-filled tube of stockinette around the neck and under the chin to limit the full movement of the head. As head control develops, provide more upright sitting supported with a corner chair (Resource 16) then progress to a "Boppy" crescent pillow to support and protect the back of the trunk for brief one to three minute intervals (Resource 1,2, 6). A crescent pillow can also be made from a large adult sweatshirt or sweat pants, stuffed firmly with towels for weight. A nursing pillow may also be used. Add activities on a tiny "table" cut from a cardboard box. Slowly increase sitting time if possible. Vary this position with the prone position on tummy over the Boppy, with a little of the body weight taken on the knees and extended arms. Advance to lying prone on tummy on a scooter

board or "crawlagator." Arm splints may be used for external support. (See Figure 6.) When the activity is tolerated, the bracing might be removed.

Unsupported sitting might occur if rolling and supported sitting are achieved. The goal is to have enough trunk strength to sit alone, which will make personal

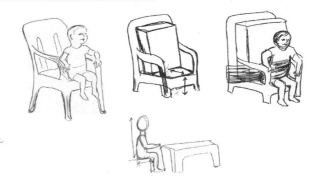

Figure 16. Resin chair cut to fit. Measuring for seat height. Box table height comes to elbows.

care possible. Shimmy-sit-scooting is the next goal to help with dressing, toilet transfers, etc. Using the Boppy and doing things at a table made of cardboard, or sitting on a bench with good foot contact to the floor will strengthen sitting. A child's resin chair (with the legs cut down so feet touch the floor) also has armrests for side support if needed (Figure 16). Initially, a wide hip strap can be used to keep the child safely seated. A back cushion made of upholstery foam covered with a towel or pillowcase may be needed.

Getting to a sit independently from a lying-down position may follow successful rolling and unsupported sitting. Encourage the child to try to roll to a sit using a sit-up motion and slight arm support on a cushion or your leg (Figure 17). Once the child gets to a sit independently, personal care independence will be most effective.

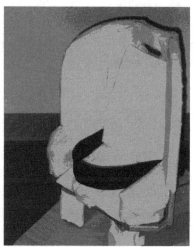

Corner chair (manufactured by Rifton) modified with padding, legs, and base for secure sitting.

Sit-pivot, sit-scoot, or "shimmy-sitting" while sitting on the floor is the next progression (Figure 18). Actual creeping and crawling may be too hard for some children's neck and arms. The sit-pivot or sit-scoot has a long-term value. It will assist in de-

Figure 17. Getting up to a sit independently using a Boppy pillow, cushion, or caregiver's leg.

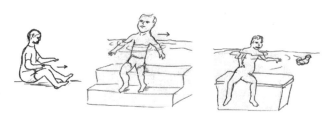

Figure 18. Sit-scoot ("shimmy sit") on floor and in water, with and without foot contact.

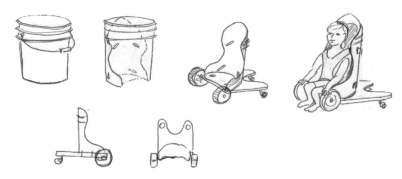

Figure 19. "Flower pot" scooter with a chest/hip vest, and child using hands and feet to move. Pattern is drawn on bucket with dotted lines. Views from the side and top show the design.

veloping bigger-kid and adult transfers from bed to chair and chair to toilet, and assist in general independence, especially during fracture recovery. If the child cannot shimmy-sit on the floor initially, this can be learned going sideways on the step of a pool, or on a bench stabilized in water up to the child's chest to decrease gravity and fear of falling on a hard surface.

Sitting and moving in "flower-pot" scooters (made from a five-gallon plastic spackling-compound bucket, two swivel casters at the rear, and a pair of six-inch wheels at the front) accomplishes several goals (Figure 19). It provides supported sitting, the child uses the arms to push, and the legs are in slight weightbearing position ("big kid" sit) with feet on the floor. This scooter can have head support and chest straps that are gradually loosened as the child develops more skills and confidence. This same bucket with the front cut down for the legs can be mounted on a foot-powered straddle toy if the child tolerates the activity (Figure 20). Often the height of commercial riding toys is too high for a child's leg length, causing the need for a homemade riding toy. While riding the toy,

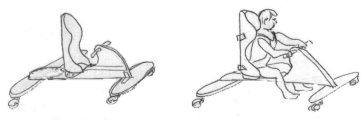

Figure 20. Mounting "flower pot" seat to other riding toys.

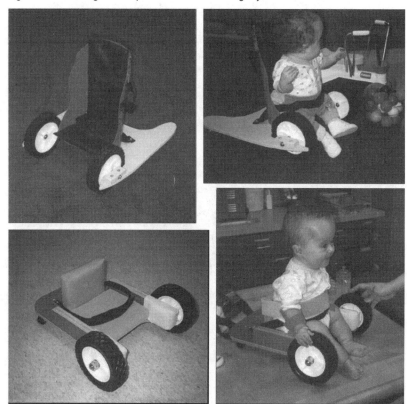

"Flower pot" scooters and low-back scooters provide supported sitting, and give children the opportunity to move under their own control.

the child also learns to reach for things and is more motivated to move under his own control.

Kneeling or pulling to a stand may require assistance from a partially filled beach ball, and support to the hips, such as described in the prone section above. The caregiver needs to provide increased support to a child who is bearing weight on her knees. Seat cushions stacked to the height of the child's armpits

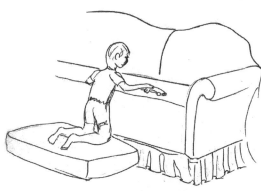

Figure 21. Using sofa cushions for kneeling.

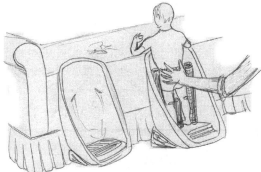

Figure 22. "Car seat prone stander"

Going from a sit to a stand in water.

when kneeling may be tried (Figure 21). If standing is approved by the doctor and tolerated by the child, a car seat may be used for a "prone stander" (Figure 22). This is an inexpensive way to begin supported standing. Usually with leg support or braces, the child kneels or stands facing backward in the seat, with a towel roll placed between the knees and feet. The car seat is leaned against the sofa for a soft play surface.

Water Therapy

Water therapy or aquatics utilizes the support and buoyancy of water that cushions, protects, and reduces the body's weight and speed of movement. Transitions from one position to another are less fearful for the child and require less use of pillows for specialized support. An aquatic environment may be the best

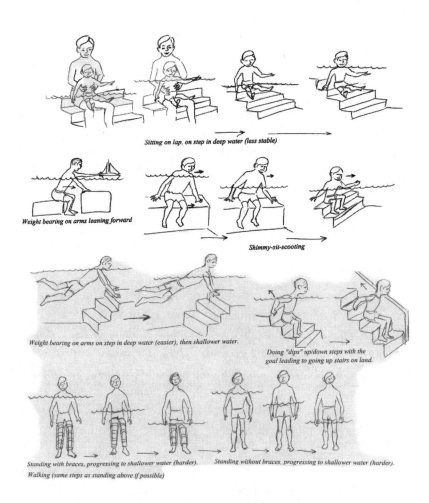

Sitting on lap, on step in deep water (less stable)

Weight bearing on arms leaning forward

Shimmy-sit-scooting

Weight bearing on arms on step in deep water (easier), then shallower water.

Doing "dips" up/down steps with the goal leading to going up stairs on land.

Standing with braces, progressing to shallower water (harder).

Standing without braces, progressing to shallower water (harder).

Walking (same steps as standing above if possible)

Figure 23. Progession levels of mobility in adapted equatics. Note the depth of the water. Not all children will be able to complete all levels, and may go back to the beginning when recovering from fractures.

place to learn the next step in some of the gross motor activities and positions listed above. Aquatics for lifelong activity will provide aerobic cardiovascular exercise. The water gives resistance to the entire limb, reducing leverage points to decrease fracture incidence. Doing the progressions previously discussed in this chapter in water can be used to regain skills after a fracture, before doing them on land. For example, the progress toward walking can be done in water in supported stages, using bivalve splints or braces in deep water. Then with ambulation success, the child can progress to shallower water, which has less buoyancy. Each step shown in Figure 23 should be slowly attempted; only one to three new levels should be tried at one pool session, according to the child's tolerance. Constant use of an innertube or ring under the arms can contribute to upper-arm bowing. A ski belt or swim suit with pockets for foam flotation (Resource 1,2) are recommended instead.

Cognitive Activities

Providing cause-and-effect activities that are cognitively (intellectually) stimulating helps increase inquisitive thinking. This will lead the child toward progressively more difficult problem-solving skills. Using a developmentally appropriate cognitive challenge might improve the child's physical strength and range of motion when using the activity to improve reach, strength of grasp, and balance. Examples are stacking things, working on puzzles, busy boxes, dressing dolls, playing with mobile poseable people in a dollhouse or garage, using cars in tracks, etc. These activities can be used when introducing the skill building in other positions described previously (prone on tummy, prone over Boppy, kneeling in front of sofa, standing in car seat, etc.) to distract the child from the new position or motion. All of this play will improve problem solving for self-care skills later.

Social and Communication Skills

Children with moderate to severe OI tend to be small, and may have a high-pitched voice, making them seem like much younger children. They should be encouraged early on to verbally state their age, and ask for things. Ultimately the child will be able to tell people how he needs to be moved or positioned. This will assist in communicating the actual age of the child, and help the child gain confidence and become responsible for accomplishing or directing his own care as he matures.

Self-Care Independence or Aids to Ease Care

Infant-Child Adaptations to Help Meet Self-Care Milestones

Developmentally, a child holds a bottle at about 10 months. To assist the child with OI to accomplish this, provide lighter or smaller bottles, "wings" for handles that fit on the nipple/lid, divided bottles, etc., available from toy stores (Figure 24). The "wings" especially will help if the child's arms are short.

Finger feeding comes next, once the child can sit. Silverware can be tried at 10 to 12 months, using sturdy plastic utensils as they are lightest. Children with OI should be encouraged to use a remote control for TV, a call-bell at night, and room

Figure 24. Wings for the bottle, divided bottle.

monitors to enhance independence as soon as possible. Removing socks and wiping face can be improved upon with proper position control, as described previously.

To encourage a child to move in bed, padding all hard surfaces is necessary. There are bed rail pads, in addition to crib bumpers (Figure 1). If the child sits independently, encourage play on a carpeted floor with all surfaces around the child padded to avoid fractures if the child falls. Padding for the edges of a coffee table or fireplace hearth is available from large home improvement stores or mail-order children's supply companies (Resource 1,2). These sources also have padded toys such as stacking rings, foam blocks, padded vibrating toys, padded busy boxes for front of stroller, etc.

Self-Care Independence for Older Children and Adults with OI

With equipment or compensatory techniques to overcome limits on gross motor development, older children and adults with OI may achieve independent self-care.

An important concept to utilize is **energy conservation**— economizing on motion and exertion where possible to maintain energy for the entire day. If transfers, walking, or standing take a great effort, try to conserve by reducing or pacing the activity. Utilize electric appliances, such as electric can openers, food processors, electric mixers, and blenders. A child can pace herself by doing shorter periods of an activity and then changing to something less stressful. To conserve a child's energy while performing daily tasks, set up work stations with all items in reach; for example, a computer station or homework area with all items on a lazy susan, or a hair care station with a hairdryer stand and long-handled brush.

Teens and adults with OI can shop through catalogs, newspapers, or the Internet instead of walking through stores. Other ideas include carrying things in a basket to make one trip through the house, and buying frozen convenience meals. If certain things are done frequently, try to set up the work area to return to daily, such as areas in the kitchen. Adults with OI can hire people to do really heavy things, including lawn mowing and cleaning the house.

Joint protection involves using the best body mechanics to avoid further injury. Caregivers of children with OI often support the child's whole body when lifting, turning, and positioning her. When children learn to do things independently, they should be taught to use the biggest muscle groups or body parts to do things. They can learn to protect themselves from injury with compensating motions. By sliding, rolling, or tilting heavy things, they will be able to do something such as tilting a carton of milk at the sink to pour into a glass that is

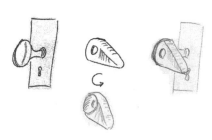

Figure 25. Door knob adapter to create a French lever.

down in the sink. Replace the need for a strong grasp with levers and tools. Examples are jar openers, faucets with lever action, and door knobs that are easier to turn, such as French lever-style knobs using a rubber snap-on adapter (Figure 25; Resource 6,7,8,9), or replacing knobs with hardware from a home supply source.

Mobility needs to be considered for independent self-care. If the child has good sitting tolerance and arm reach, but cannot walk, then a wheelchair is appropriate. If the child's arms are strong enough to push a manual chair, then the pushing of the wheel should be done in a direct line from hand through forearm, with armrests that can be flipped up and out of the way, as armrests can add to upper-arm bowing (Figure 26).

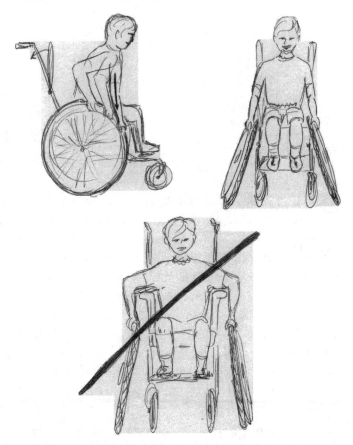

Figure 26. Pushing a wheelchair should be done in a direct line from hand through forearm, using flip-up armrests. Forearm splints may be used.

Figure 27. Power chair that has a seat elevator and power tilt.

A power chair that has a seat elevator and power tilt provides better reach by allowing the user to get closer to work surfaces or to the height of peers standing or seated (Figure 27). The seat's power tilt will help change the pull of gravity through the vertebrae. This permits the user to continue to function if spine movements are painful, and to rest with different degrees of gravitational pull. Permobil's "Chairman Robo" wheelchairs (Resource 4) currently offer these advantages. Due to the typical height of bathroom sinks, kitchen counters, and closet storage, a power seat elevator in a wheelchair is recommended for many people with OI.

For people using a wheelchair, tables need to be thin to get the knees under. Tables are easiest to roll under if the apron that holds a drawer is removed. Another method is taking a hollow smooth door or ¾-inch plywood and placing it between two sets of two-drawer file cabinets to serve as a desk or worktable.

Accessibility for household independence requires individual problem solving for each specific activity. To conserve energy and maximize mobility, living on one level is ideal (ranch house or apartment). If a wheelchair is needed, then a ramped outside entrance is necessary. Equipment

Foam "steps" allow this child to get in and out of bed independently.

that may be needed for people using a wheelchair includes an automatic door entry (Resource 13, 14), slide-in transfer benches for toileting and bathing, light switches at useable heights, lower counters and cooking surfaces, and a power wheelchair with elevating seat, etc. Routine activities can be set up by a parent or helper, such as the hair dryer plugged in and placed in a holder at the right height, on a dresser with comb and mirror in the child's room. Physical environments can be modified, such as widening doorways, creating open shelves for clothing, or lowering clothes rods. Work stations can be established, such as a desk with a lazy susan for desk items instead of a drawer, one pencil on a string, a computer, etc., ready for a child to roll up and study.

Families who live in multistory homes can keep necessary items downstairs and accessible to the child all day, convert a first-floor den into a child's room, or keep a potty chair downstairs for a young child if the bathroom is upstairs.

With these and other accommodations, semi-independence is a realistic goal for many individuals with OI. A healthy family "philosophy" makes as much as possible accessible to the child with OI, even if it means changing the way that others use household space or equipment. Some families end up doing too much for the child, rather than creatively figuring out how he can do for himself. Limiting independence can adversely affect strength and bone density, and leave the child less prepared for life as an adult.

The overall **working conditions** need to be considered. The heights of counters and tables may mean that barstools will provide a better sitting work height for teens or adults with short trunk and limbs. Long-handled items (such as brooms) might be stored more easily with hooks on the ends of the handles. Dishes and pots and pans may be stored vertically with slots built in cabinets or deep drawers; this decreases the need to lift a whole stack or reach overhead. Large appliances may be replaced with smaller ones, such as travel irons or mobile-home appliances. Stoves should have controls at the front, and sink faucets with a single lever can be installed on the side instead of the back of the sink. Small, shallow sinks can be ordered. A side-by-side refrigerator will allow more access because the door is lighter, opens beside a wheelchair easier, and has greater shallow door storage. Pull-out drawers or shelves will allow reaching to the back of the refrigerator. Closets need the rod within reach; rods can be lowered easily by hanging a broom handle from a chain or rope. Shelves and towel racks are best at eye level or lower. Table lamps can be changed to turn on with touch using a special bulb base, available from a hardware store. Telephones can be cordless, cellular, or voice-activated for ease of reach or weight. Means for carrying items must be developed. During walking, a light fanny pouch will carry small items, and a metal cart with shelves (such as a tea cart) may be pushed between the kitchen and dining area. A rolling hamper can move between the bedroom and laundry area, and cleaning supplies should be kept near the kitchen and bathroom. A person using a wheelchair can use a backpack or place a pouch beside the seat, and drag a laundry basket like a sled for transporting larger things.

To achieve personal care independence for children and adults with OI, families need to solve the above components of mobility, accessibility, joint protection, and energy conservation and then

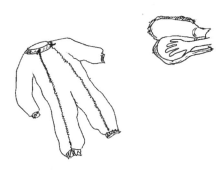

Figure 28. Jump suit with front closures, mittens with Velcro flaps.

solve each additional area by personal priority and need.

For easier **dressing,** look for clothing with front closures that are simple (t-shirts and loose elastic pull-up pants), coats that are "body bags" (Resource 1,2), or winter jump suits that have more zippers down the limbs (Figure 28). Avoid overstretching a child's fragile limbs and fingers; reach into a sleeve and enclose the child's entire hand in your hand while guiding it thorough the sleeve. Teach an older child to make a fist while reaching through sleeves. There are mittens that have Velcro fold-over sides to decrease the pressure required to dress a squirming child (Figure 28; Resource 1,2).

Clothing is very individual. For older children and adults with OI, sizes may be a challenge due to the length of limbs, and clothing may need to be altered. Some people might consider getting a pattern made for clothing that is easy to get into, and/or having the clothing custom made. Clothing should be age-appropriate to help the child look his age and foster his self-esteem. Avoiding finger injury on waist snaps or buttons on jeans may be accomplished by ignoring the snaps/buttons and using a belt instead. Slip-on shoes are an option for someone using a wheelchair. Dressing aids are available or can be made to assist reach to the feet, such as a sock donner, and dressing hook for pulling on shoes (Figure 29).

Toileting for independence may require a self-made potty chair for children with severe OI, as the right size is not available

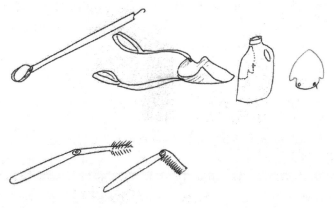

Figure 29. Dressing hook; sock donner may be cut from a detergent or bleach bottle; long-handled comb and brush

Figure 30. Resin chair potty seat; ring reducers (see Figure 16).

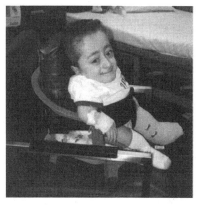

commercially. If sitting is tolerated, a potty chair with a back to provide supported sitting can easily be made using a child's resin chair, cutting down the legs so the feet touch the floor, cutting a hole in the seat (bucket beneath) and adding wide seatbelts and custom cushions if needed (Figure 30). For a child who is able to sit independently on a toilet, a toilet ring reducer comes in smooth or padded plastic, and reduces the size of the seat opening to 5 by 7 inches. A plastic folding (portable) ring reducer for children under 40 pounds is available at toy stores.

A urinal is easiest for boys. A toilet-paper extender will increase the reach of the hand if needed to wipe (Figure 31). This may be purchased (Resources 6,7,8,9) but it is large and heavy. It can be made at home with plastic-covered solid core copper wire from the hardware store, twisted into a coil around a broom handle and bent to form a handle, finished with electrician's tape or dipped in liquid plastic (Plasti-Dip® from hardware stores) so that all is washable.

From around five years old through adulthood, the shimmy-sit-scoot method may be used to **independently transfer from a wheelchair to tub or toilet** (Figure 32). This sit-scoot will also be useful during fracture recovery. A sliding transfer-bench tub/commode can be special-ordered from health care equipment companies (Example: ActiveAid's "Tubby II," Resource 3). If independent

Figure 31. Toilet paper extender of plastic-covered copper wire.

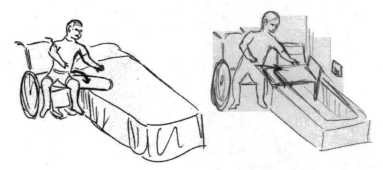

Figure 32. Shimmy-sit-scoot from wheelchair to tub or toilet seat.

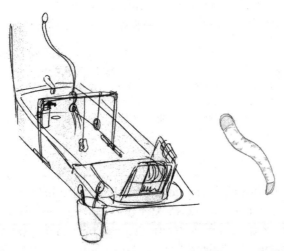

Figure 33. Bath pole/bar or bath seat with adaptations, such as long-handled items in can, washcloths over seat back, bar to hold soap-on-rope, hand-held shower, sponge, cup to hold shampoo, long thin wash cloth with handles, etc.

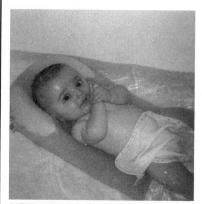

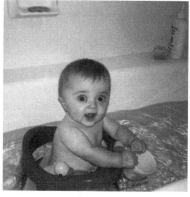

Bathing Jonathan was difficult at first. First we laid him on a gel pad, then we used a foam bathing pad. But with either of these I had to lean in and support his head with my hand/arm the whole time, or else only fill the tub with a little water and he would lie flat. I finally bought a bathing sling at a toy/baby supply store. It is a mesh cloth stretched across a sloping metal frame. I found that lying the foam pad on top of this sling put Jonathan in a perfect reclining position. I could fill the tub with enough water to bathe him and both my hands were free. We even starting lying him on his tummy after we washed him so he could play. This method worked great until he was old enough to want to sit up and roll. Now we use a plastic circular bath seat. We put a circular foam bath mat onto the seat to keep him from slipping. I have also found it helpful to have a piece of egg-crate foam on the floor next to the tub. I put his towel on the foam, and when his bath is over, I just lift him from the tub onto the towel and foam. I can wrap him up and move him on the foam to the counter to dry him off really well. This minimizes the distance I have to carry a wet, slippery baby.

"Boppy" pillows (C-shaped cushion pillows) are wonderful! We first used it to lay Jonathan in while he watched a video. Then we began using it for "tummy time"—it provided a good angle to support his upper body and allowed him to put a little pressure on his arms. It was also extremely useful as Jonathan was learning to sit up. It allowed him to practice without fear of falling over. Lately we have been using it to help him practice being in a crawling position.

Amy Phelps, mother of Jonathan, 1 year old

sliding is not possible, this technique will allow helpers of all sizes to assist the sliding, as the transfer does not require a full-body lift.

There may be a need to modify the bathroom size to accommodate the wheelchair and necessary equipment. The bathroom may require special "stations," with all of the needed devices stored at heights for independence. Bathing may include use of lightweight long-handled sponges or brushes, especially if arms are short. Washcloths can be placed on the arms of the bath seat, used by rubbing against them for washing the back, armpits etc. Devices may include items mounted to the wall, and a vertical pole or a bar in front of the bather to hold items too heavy to lift (Figure 33). Be creative! Keep supplies light and small because the weight of water and the length of long handles or reachers increase leverage forces.

Bathing and grooming require creative problem solving and perhaps assistance from an occupational therapist familiar with rehabilitation aids. The Little People of America provides ideas to assist with reach or height (Resource 11). Devices designed for people with arthritis who may have reduced reach and grip strength may also help (Resources 6,7,8,9). Long-handled combs, brushes, and dressing sticks both increase reach and allow arms to work together and closer to the body. The item may also be propped on a table and supported by the hands. (See Figure 29.) Towel drying the back may be possible by shimmying into a terry robe. Curling hair may be simpler with a short hairstyle or permanent, using curlers with Velcro hooks, or with a curling iron.

Kitchen activities will be easiest and most efficient if each frequent task is arranged in areas that serve as work stations. This might mean that drinking glasses are near the refrigerator or sink, the cutting board and knives are near the sink, the pans and potholders are near the stove, the microwave containers are near the microwave, and the napkins and silverware are near the eating area. Everything will need to be within reach. Cooking is easier with containers of reduced weight and size. Microwaves are useful because they use lightweight plastic cooking containers, reheat foods easily, and are quick. They can be placed on a table at the optimal height reached for a person with OI. When shopping for a microwave, consider the effort to open it and the direction of the door swing. If the door swings open to the side, this is best. If it opens by pulling down, it will be a wheelchair obstacle and reaching over the door will be hazardous. Modifications to the microwave door lock may be necessary and a "sliding ramp" might be made to slide containers out and down to the counter/table (Figure 34). "Tools"

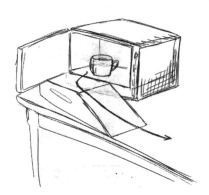

Figure 34. Microwave ramp.

taken from other purposes might be used to enhance reach (for example, a bread paddle, spatula, or pizza oven paddle could help get things out of the microwave or refrigerator, etc.).

Opening the refrigerator door may be too hard for some, but a hook or loop on the handle could be attached to a wheelchair to pull the door open (Figure 35). (This idea came from the helper-dog techniques!) Storage of kitchen items to assist reach may require creative planning. Using lazy susan turntables, reducing the weight and size of items, and lubricating drawers will help. There are devices that can be installed in closets to create rotating levels of shelving, or narrow shelves can be mounted on doors for ease of reach.

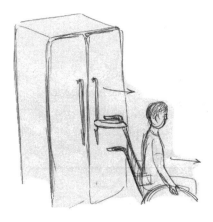

Figure 35. Opening refrigerator door with wheelchair.

Convenience foods in one-serving pouches are easy to manage. Opening containers may require ingenuity. A box, can, or frozen bag can be placed in a drawer for opening; while leaning against the drawer, the person uses a sharp tool to cut or pry the item open. Carrying hot items or liquids may be accomplished using small thermoses, in a basket, or in a walker/cart/wheelchair pouch.

Independent Living

Many people with OI are successful at independent living, with or without assistance. Using the "work station" concept discussed previously is helpful. If an individual can roll, sit-scoot, or help with her transfer and direct her own care, she can use helpers or friends and have a greater circle of possible places to go.

If more specialized care is needed for a person with severe OI, he or she might employ a personal care assistant, or live in a setting where independent living skills are provided or taught. Rehabilitation facilities may assist in finding such settings. Service dogs are an option. Professional housekeeping services can help with cleaning. Food can be convenient "heat and eat" meals. With energy conservation ideas, motivation, and innovation, many levels of independence are possible. Consider all options!

Traveling

Safe positioning is necessary when traveling with an infant and young child. As mentioned before, a child needs good support in strollers and cars, with seat belts having extra thick and wide straps to disperse the force of the car's motion. Velcro pads are available from automotive supply stores for widening the seat belts. Vests with straps for transporting are also available (Resource 1, 2, 5). These are useful to assist in transporting a child with a fracture who must travel lying down. Car seat information was mentioned earlier in this chapter and shown in Figure 3. Equipment that allows frequent reclining permits comfortable travel for older children. Due to the small size of the spinal bones, fractures might occur in the spine. Varying the tilt or recline of sitting position during the day is helpful following spinal compression or fractures. Self-care equipment for travel may include a folding toilet ring reducer or a small urinal.

Traveling with OI Identification and Splint Supplies

Parents should keep a folder of their medical references with them at all times while traveling, including their child's diagnosis of OI on medical letterhead. This avoids questions implying child abuse if the child needs medical help in an unfamiliar emergency room. Figure 37 shows wallet cards created for a parent of an infant and a teen

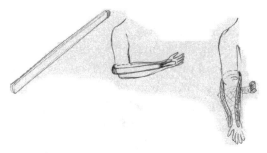

Figure 36. Sugar tong splint to transport a child with a fracture. It is bent along the limb or in a "U" and gently wrapped with gauze.

with OI, who both need assistance in monitoring the intensity of activity at hospitals, day care, school, camp, physical education, and with friends. Parents are also encouraged to carry gauze rolls and 1-by-12-inch foam-padded aluminum strips (adult finger splints) to form into tong-shaped splints that are gauze-wrapped to the limb for transporting a child with a possible fracture. The "U" shaped tong splint is gently wrapped with gauze to stabilize the limb (see Figure 36). (See Chapter 2 for more suggestions for first aid supplies.)

Communication for Assistance Before Traveling

When an adult or older teen is making independent travel plans, all needs should be listed and planned for ahead, because the spirit of "handicapped accessible" varies. Calling and asking for specific things such as a wide bathroom doorway, roll-in bath chair, etc., will help. For group tours when there will not be any help in the room at night, ask direct questions about walking distances; heights to step up into a bus, plane, or boat; if there is ramp access for wheelchairs; are there glass doors on the shower/tub, etc. These items may be taken for granted at home but must be requested when traveling alone.

Things to inquire about might include size, available equipment, and set-up of hotel bathrooms; requesting towels be placed low; reaching light switches, etc. Packing a reacher or reaching stick (with a fabric loop for the wrist on one end and a hook on the other) may be helpful for reaching small things if alone in a hotel room. Visual-

Figure 37. Sample wallet information cards.
For an infant:

MY CHILD , Susan X, HAS OSTEOGENESIS IMPERFECTA

This is a condition of brittle bones and joint laxity. I have been trained in joint protection and must be permitted to do the handling so that my child does not resist and have additional fractures. I must be able to modify or decline participation for her safety.

IMPORTANT PHONE NUMBERS
Doctor:
Physical/occupational therapist:
Other:

For an older child:

I HAVE OSTEOGENESIS IMPERFECTA
This is a condition of brittle bones and joint laxity. I have been trained in joint protection and must be permitted to modify activity or decline participation for my safety.

Activities to avoid: *Impact activity:* jogging, aerobics with jumping, trampoline, high springboard diving, bungee jumping, racketball, hitting a baseball or volleyball, horseback riding (beyond a walk), some amusement rides, etc. *Contact sports:* scrimmaging in basketball, football, karate martial arts, recreational competitive weightlifting, etc. *Overstretching:* gymnastics, some yoga positions, etc.
Activities permitted: Walk (preferably on soft surfaces), aerobic exercises (not jump or stepping), golf, canoe/row, bicycle with low resistance and knees slightly flexed, badminton, swim, dive off pool side, individual activities such as badminton on soft surfaces, archery, pool (billiards), T'ai Chi, Nordic track, cards and board games, drama, radio, electronics, light building, model building, arts and crafts, computers, etc. General strengthening activities are best in water where the resistance is over the entire length of the limb.

IMPORTANT PHONE NUMBERS
Parents:
Doctor:
Physical/occupational therapist:

---

ize the entire stay to anticipate other specific needs to help the trip go smoothly. Planning in advance will save many frustrations.

References

Binder, Helga, Linda Hawkes, G. Graybill, L. Gerber, and J.C. Weintrob. 1984. Osteogenesis Imperfecta: Rehabilitation Approach with Infants and Young Children. *Archives of Physical Medicine* 65:537–541.

Campbell, Suzann (ed.). 1994, 2000. Chapter on Osteogenesis Imperfecta. *Physical Therapy for Children*. Philadelphia: Saunders.

Folio, M. Rhonda, and Rebecca R. Fewell. 1983, 1999. *Peabody Developmental Motor Scales*. Austin, Texas: Pro-Ed.

Parks, Stephanie P. et al. (eds.) 1988. *HELP: Hawaii Early Learning Profile*. Palo Alto: VORT.

Resources

1. **The Right Start**
   P.O. Box 1259
   Camp Hill, PA 17011
   Phone: (800) Little-1 (548-8531)
   Internet: www.rightstart.com

2. **One Step Ahead**
   P.O. Box 517
   Lake Bluff, IL 60044
   Phone: (800) 274-8440
   Internet: www.onestepahead.com

3. **ActiveAid ®**
   Bathroom equipment, will assist with custom modifications, such as size of commode holes.
   P.O. Box 359

Redwood Falls, MN 56283
Phone: (800) 533-5330
E-mail: activeaid@activeaid.com
Internet: www.activeaid.com

4. **Permobil**
    Power wheelchairs with seat elevators and tilt.
    6961 Eastgate Blvd.
    Lebanon, TN 37090
    Phone: (888)-Permobil (737-6624)

5. **E-Z-On Products, Inc. of Florida**
    Transport vest for sitting and lying down.
    605 Commerce Way West
    Jupiter, FL 33458
    Phone: (800) 323-6598
    Internet: www.ezonpro.com

6. **Sammons-Preston Inc.**
    ADL (assistance for daily living) aids, splinting products.
    4 Sammons Court
    Boilingbrook, IL 60440-5071
    Phone: (800) 323-5547

7. **Maddak Inc.**
    ADL aids.
    6 Industrial Rd.
    Pequannock, NJ 07440
    Phone: (800) 443-4926 or (973) 628-7600

8. **North Coast Medical**
    ADL aids, splinting products.
    18305 Sutter Blvd.
    Morgan Hill, CA 95037-2845
    Phone: (800) 821-9319 or (408) 776-5000
    E-mail: custserv@ncmedical.com

9. **Smith-Nephew-Rolyan**

ADL aids, splinting products
P.O. Box 1005
Germantown, WI 53022
Phone: (800) 558-8633
Internet: www.smith-nephew.com

10. Islinger, R.B., M. King, and R.W. Kruse. *Hand and Upper
Extremity Function in Patients with Osteogenesis Imperfecta.* Ongoing research at A.I. duPont Hospital for Children.

11. **Little People of America**
Box 745
Lubbock, TX 79408
Phone: (888) LPA-2001
E-mail: LAPDataBase@juno.com
Internet: www.lpaonline.org

12. **Children's Medical Ventures**
Gel pad for skull support.
275 Longwater Dr.
Norwell, MA 02060
Phone: (800) 377-3449

13. **Power Access**
Automatic door opener.
106 Powder Mill Rd.
P.O. Box 235
Collinsville, CT 06022
Phone: (800) 344-0088
Internet: www.power-access.com

14. **Besam, Inc.**
Automatic door opener.
84 Twin Rivers Dr.
Hightstown, NJ 08520-5212
Phone: (800) 752-9290
Internet: www.besam.com/na/

15. **Car seat information**
    Internet: www.nhtsa.dot.gov or www.safekids.org/ home.html. Also check the Car Seat Safety Coordinator in your state, listed in the telephone book under County Extension, Safe Kids Coalition.

16. **Rifton Equipment**
    P.O. Box 901
    Route 213
    Rifton, NY 12471
    Phone: (800) 336-5948
    Internet: www.rifton.com

8
Exercise and Activity

A Balance Between Work and Play

Lynn Hurwitz Gerber, M.D. and Holly Lea Cintas, Ph.D.

Key Points in This Chapter

- Children with OI need a regular program to promote optimal function through muscle strengthening and stretching, aerobic exercise, and recreational pursuits.

- Families, school officials, and health professionals should work together to provide environmental modifications and adaptive equipment to promote participation in a wide variety of activities, including competitive sports when possible.

- Swimming for both recreational and therapeutic purposes is encouraged.

- Diet, weight control, and commitment to a healthy lifestyle are essential to longevity and the quality of children's lives.

Children today are, in general, less physically active than children were 50 years ago. Those with disabilities, unlike their predecessors, are being encouraged to be more physically active. While much discussion centers around the need for activity to enhance bone growth and mineral composition, cardiovascular fitness, and mental alertness, exercise also promotes peer relationships and helps children achieve something they value. Fitness, therefore, should be seen as a way to help children develop physically, emotionally, and socially, so they can be successful performers in all domains. Viewing fitness from the standpoint of performance, particularly that associated with pleasure or satisfaction, is an approach with potential for success.

Developing a program to achieve this depends on meeting the needs and desires of individual children, which vary widely according to their environment. A customized rather than a one-size-fits-all approach will have the most likelihood for success. Generalized exercise programs designed for children with specific types of OI rarely address a child's specific needs because they omit analysis of *that* child's level of function.

Children with OI are at risk of less-than-maximum performance because of several factors, including parental fear, which imposes restrictions on behaviors that are thought to be risky. While upright activity carries some risk, the benefits may far outweigh the risks. For example, unsupported standing may be considered so risky as to be unattainable, but proper choice of support devices and the timing of appropriate interventions may make this possible if viewed as a

long-term goal. The use of a supine standing device, the correction of long bone bowing to less than 40 degrees, muscle strengthening on land, and walking in water may help to accomplish this goal, particularly if the child's ideas and interests are incorporated to the greatest extent possible.

Each child matures at a different rate, which is neither continuous nor steady. Rolling, sitting, and adequate head and back control must precede standing. Body movement in water, which provides postural support for the back and neck, can be introduced to promote performance in, then out of water. Incremental points of progress, no matter how small the gains, add up to improvement.

Environment

Environments for performance enhancement are varied, and include home, school, and recreational facilities. Home is the mainstay of any exercise program. In general, progression at home begins with parents giving the infant or young child considerable assistance for positioning, movement, dressing, hygiene, and play (kicking in the bathtub, for example), while encouraging the child's cooperation to attempt and complete reasonable tasks as early as possible. This includes helping with dressing and undressing, washing and drying, and combing hair. Even though it takes more time initially, nurturing the child's interest in helping will benefit everyone eventually. As soon as the child can scoot in sitting, this activity should be encouraged for independent or semi-independent transfers, rather than lifting and placing the child, although this may be necessary after a recent fracture. Once the child can sit, some effort at home should be directed to standing every day. For nonwalking children, standing 30 minutes twice a day with a supine stander provides weightbearing for the legs while the child uses the tray to read, use the keyboard, or do homework. Ideally, this is combined with brief opportunities (five to 10 minutes) to practice standing from a high sitting surface, leading to secure standing, then walking. These are two of many options to promote standing

---

Physical therapy is very important to Alexis and her treatment of OI. She currently receives one-on-one therapy from an expert on OI on a weekly basis during the school year. The therapy has been extremely successful in building strength and improving performance. It has been instrumental in building Alexis' self-confidence, and has helped her immensely in her everyday activities. Therapy is a critical element in the treatment regime for OI. Alexis enjoys physical therapy and says it is fun.

Paul Granger, father of Alexis, 8 years old

and walking; others may be more appropriate for a specific child's needs. (See Chapter 7 for more on promoting independent personal care for children with OI. See also Cintas and Gerber 1996 for interventions linked to a child's performance level.)

Elementary school children should be independent for dressing and hygiene in most cases, but may need assistance or supervision with some exercises and standing or walking. To the extent possible, children should be encouraged to get around the house without using wheelchairs by walking, scooting, rolling, or riding a low trike or a big wheel. This is also important for children in middle and high school, although using a wheelchair at school may be essential for safety, or for covering long distances, even for children who walk. It is reasonable to expect school-age children to spend 15 minutes a day doing exercises specific to their needs to improve performance. This is most successful if parents take an active interest and perhaps even exercise with the child.

I am 42 years old and have been involved in wheelchair sports for more than 25 years. I feel that my involvement in a wide variety of adaptive sports and recreation opportunities has reduced the incidence of OI fractures. Currently, I compete in a circuit of wheelchair tennis tournaments. Tennis is a game that can be played by people with a wide range of disabilities. For people with OI, wheelchair tennis can provide a safe and fun environment in which to develop and improve physical fitness. The use of custom-made tennis wheelchairs will allow participants both improved mobility and the adjustability that is required for people who are short-statured. The technology in today's lightweight tennis racquets allows for tremendous power to be generated from even the most limited upper-body range of motion. Using a tennis racquet grip slightly smaller than average allows a wheelchair tennis player better access to the wheelchair pushrim, while maneuvering and continuously gripping the racquet. The U.S. Tennis Association and International Tennis Foundation have adopted the only rule variation for wheelchair tennis, which is an optional second bounce of the ball in which the first bounce must be within the play lines. Wheelchair tennis can be enjoyed while playing with other wheelchair users and nondisabled players.

Wheelchair tennis has allowed me to travel and compete throughout the United States and Europe. I may not win many tournaments, but the ability to make new friends and enjoy the company of old ones while visiting new places are my building blocks to a positive athletic lifestyle. This lifestyle did not seem possible when I was growing up, with many surgeries and nearly 100 fractures.

William Lehr, adult with OI

The school is responsible for providing a safe and accessible environment for the child's maximal educational benefit. In addition, we have a national commitment to fitness that requires the school to provide adaptive physical education, and possibly physical therapy. Lunchtime and recess provide opportunities for peer group physical and social interaction. Scheduling therapy or exercises during these times isolates the child and may lead to resentment, particularly in older children. A creative approach, and a sense of teamwork between parents and school personnel are critical to providing an environment that supports the child's evolving psychological and physical independence.

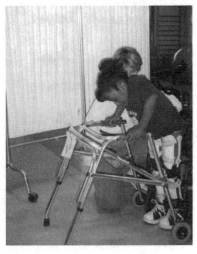

Children's needs differ greatly based on the severity of OI, age, grade, and the size of the school, but the general progression should be one of increasing independence and integration of children with their peers. Ensuring that the child has appropriate seating in school, and planning for opportunities for the child to be safely active out of the chair, are the physical therapist's responsibility. How this is achieved varies widely depending on the child and the school. Often the physical therapist develops the program and teaches it to a designated caregiver on site who can supervise it every day with the child. This approach is most successful if the focus is on what the child can do safely, and everyone understands the next goal to be attained. For example, if the child cannot transfer out of a wheelchair without being lifted, finding a way to do this in school is a high priority to increase independence in the bathroom. Spending time to address and solve this problem, perhaps through trial and error and selection of adaptive equipment, may be more critical than supervising exercises the child can do at home.

Activity

Factors that promote fitness and performance include reducing time spent in the same position. For infants and young children, this means frequent changes of position while awake, from the back to side to abdomen. Each position challenges muscles and joints to perform differently and provides the child an opportunity to practice activities specific to that position. Children with weakness are often happiest lying on their back, but will not develop sufficient back and neck strength for sitting and standing unless they spend

 some of their awake time positioned on the tummy. However, they must be supervised in this position, and positioning flat on the abdomen may not be safe for infants with severe OI if it compromises respiration. Sitting can be encouraged when the child can keep her head centered, and should be practiced with a straight back, perhaps using a small table or tray for arm support to keep the back and shoulders from curving forward. This, combined with an emphasis on reaching overhead from a sitting position for a toy or ball, promotes development of sufficient back and neck strength to progress to independent sitting, then standing, followed by walking.

For older children, sitting, even when at school, should be interrupted with standing, if only for brief periods, or lying down to extend the hips and knees as a respite from the flexed position. Children in preschool or elementary school may agree to use a supine stander for 30 minutes during the school day, but older children will typically refuse, as it is difficult to use this device in the average classroom. Thus, a creative approach to achieving 20 to 30 minutes of out-of-chair time during the school day can take many different forms. In general, standing, walking, or lying prone (on the abdomen), perhaps on the couch in the nurse's room, each day for a brief period is more valuable than walking for 45 minutes once a week. We discourage the use of diapers at school as a way of avoiding toileting. An aide can assist those in need, and time spent in interrupting the sitting posture, even briefly, is valuable.

Children who spend much of their day sitting should be encouraged to stretch even while sitting. They can unobtrusively bring their arms to their heads and bring their shoulders back to stretch muscles that are likely to pull the shoulders forward. Ankle pumping and straightening the knees can be done regularly even while sitting.

Poor posture in sitting may sap a child's energy; hence, back support and foot contact with footrests on chairs are essential for long periods of sitting. This is easily done with a regular chair by using a low stool or wedge for foot support, with the added advantage that this classroom desk or chair may be more like the chairs used by the other children, and moving from one chair to another at school is desirable from an activity standpoint. At home, children should be discouraged from sitting in the same position for more than 30 minutes.

Muscle contraction can be practiced intermittently during the day and does not depend on exercise sessions or physical therapy treatments exclusively. During school, this may be linked, at the most basic level, with the 20 to 30 minutes spent out of the chair. This brings up the issue of doing exercises during physical education (PE),

---

We are grateful to have doctors who are interested in doing more for Beth than fixing broken bones. Her orthopedist provides tremendous encouragement and guidelines for Beth to participate in sports and activities. She emphasizes activities that will meet Beth's needs for safety, muscle strength, and toning, and also has suggested looking for areas that allow Beth to participate in competitive events, either individually or as part of a team. For the last three years, Beth has taken tap dance classes and been a member of our swim team. Last year, she was awarded the Coach's Award for her efforts.

Barbie Simmonds, mother of Beth, 12 years old

We swim often! Jonathan stands up throughout the day and rides a tricycle. We use a reward system to keep us all motivated. At the end of the week we get a special treat, such as an outing to the movies or a special toy.

Theresa Reed, mother of Jonathan, 5 years old

Adam loves horses, but horseback riding is not on the top of the list for kids with OI. Just after he turned eight, however, Adam saw a miniature horse at a fair, and he spent half the day grooming her and yearning for the sweet animal. An unbelievably kind woman ended up giving him a miniature horse, Amy. Adam participated in horse shows, leading his  horse around the arena while I pushed his wheelchair, and eventually showing her on his own. Finding a home for Amy led us to live on a ranch, where a neighbor taught Adam and his niece and nephews (who are close to his age) to ride. I have pictures of Adam riding in a bright green cast.

We left our ranch life to go to Dallas for surgery on Adam's legs. We were staying with my sister and her family, who are avid kayakers. After Adam's spica cast came off, we drove to San Marcos to watch the Red River Racing Team's slalom kayak training sessions. As I wrestled Adam in his wheelchair through the woods so we could watch the team practice, I thought, "Gee, he could have floated down here a lot easier than this." With lots of help from coaches and family members, a new activity was born. Adam was outfitted with a safe flat-bottomed slalom kayak, helmet, and life jacket, and was made an official member of the Red River Racing Team, pre-junior division. It had never occurred to me that Adam could paddle down a river, but he didn't need strong legs to paddle a kayak! The years of manipulating his wheelchair helped Adam take to that slalom kayak like a pro. He knew just what he was doing the very first day, while I paddled in circles. He left me in his "river dust." We spent many happy weekends camped beside the Guadalupe River with the team kids and their families.

When Adam was nine, we moved to Hawaii. We looked for a way for Adam to again be involved with horses. What to do with a sad Hawaiian cowboy, yearning to ride on the range? The local paper featured a story about a woman with a string of gentle donkeys she used in her school, which was called Donkey Tales of Hawaii. Adam dug out his scuffed cowboy boots and his beat-up hat and he's been on his way ever since. A loveable donkey named Cyd is his new four-legged pal; Adam grooms him standing on a stool, and rides every week. He's training to use his legs to cue the donkey, balance himself, and post so that his legs do a lot of the work. He rides with his teacher in the Hawaiian back country. The wild things in the mountain wilderness are all new sights to marvel over. It's an adventure beyond conception for a kid with brittle bones.

Ronit Sanders, mother of Adam, 10 years old

or integrating with classmates during this activity period. There are many advantages to permitting and encouraging children with OI to play with their classmates during PE, including just having fun while joining in recreational pursuits that count as exercise. Increasingly, schools are finding ways to do this safely, but this varies from one school to another, and for some parents and school personnel, ensuring the child's safety does not permit this integrated approach. Adaptive PE is an alternative that permits a more individualized program whereby recreational activities are adapted for a particular child. Ideally, this is intended for a limited amount of time. Moving the child into regular PE often requires planning and discussion among the physical education teacher, adaptive physical education teacher, physical therapist, and sometimes the recreation therapist and physician. Parents are formally involved in this process in the Individual Educational Program (IEP) meetings. Finding the proper balance on this issue requires including the child in the decision, and possibly choosing to do some simple strengthening exercises at home to enhance the child's opportunities for inclusion and social growth at school. As parents are ultimately responsible for their child, an active and sustained interest in the child's daily activities, communicated in an enthusiastic and helpful manner, contributes to the child's safety and development. Children in middle school or high school can also participate in after-school sports in several ways, including cheerleading, announcing the games, and as a manager, among others. (See Chapter 10 for more on the school environment and physical education.)

Muscle Strengthening

Muscles that are most likely to need strengthening include those that lift the leg with a straight knee when the child is on his/her abdomen (hip extensors).

These muscles work with the back muscles to extend the body over the legs during standing, or to move the body when positioned on the abdomen. Lifting the leg with the knee straight while sidelying strengthens the muscles (hip abductors) that keep the pelvis level when one foot elevates to take a step. Sufficient strength in the abdominal muscles is necessary to change body positions, especially when getting up from lying flat. Gaining strength can be accomplished by lifting only the head when lying flat—a very minimal abdominal effort—supplemented by tilting the body backward while sitting with the legs flexed forward over the support surface. This can also be done by performing a partial sit-up beginning from a supported sitting position of 45 degrees. These methods represent minimal, but critical effort to gain abdominal strength over the entire arc from supine (lying down) to sitting. Arm strength is also important for changing body positions and walking with crutches or a walker. Easily done while sitting, pushing down on the armrests to lift the body one to one-and-a-half inches from the wheelchair seat is a means of strengthening the arms for walking or repositioning the body. The routine strengthening of thigh (quadriceps) muscles, calf (gastrocnemius) muscles, or elbow flexors (biceps) is usually not necessary. These muscle groups are often stronger than those mentioned above, and need strengthening only following fractures and periods of immobilization.

Equipment

Performance enhancement requires the use of proper adapted equipment. Walkers, crutches, low-riding three-wheelers, tandem bikes, hand-pedaled bikes, and bicycles with training wheels are all useful for mobility when used safely. If the child is viewed as an active performer, then appropriate equipment can be identified to enhance the child's performance in two domains: essential and recreational. Essential devices support optimal independence in everyday activities. To meet this goal, the task is to identify and prioritize activities, then concentrate on the planning and effort to achieve them. Frequently it is more successful to focus on one activity at a time and see it through to completion. Rehabilitation physicians, physical therapists,

I found it much more difficult to get involved in college than in high school. During my search for "my place" at college, I became more and more interested in one of my classes, fitness for the disabled. I set up an exercise routine tailored to my needs. I learned which machines I could use and how to adjust them for my height and stamina. With free weights and the standard resistance machines, I began to build muscle. I used a hand bike and rowing machine to increase my cardiovascular fitness. By Christmas break, I was proud to come home with my new-found muscles!

My trainer and the adaptive athletic director encouraged me to try swimming. Though I had been in the water a lot for healing and therapy, I had never swam even one length of the pool using a legal stroke. Sure, I was a great doggy paddler and could hold my breath for days, but anything else seemed near impossible during my first swim practice. But my coach displayed amazing patience and inspired in me the desire and belief that I could do it.

Each week I saw improvement. As I fine-tuned my technique I began to feel at home in the water. My weight training continued and I began to feel something that doesn't come easily to people with OI—I felt *fast!*

I began competing with people who have the same strength and level of disability that I do. I had never competed on a level playing field like this. I brought home bronze medals from my very first international meet. Adaptive swimming is not made easier because the participants are disabled; we swim under nearly the same rules as nondisabled swimmers. So if I faltered in my stroke on a turn, I was disqualified. But I worked on my mistakes. As my times increased, I swam faster in every meet and qualified for the 2000 U.S. Disabled Swimming Championships. It seemed unreal considering that less than a year ago I couldn't swim one stroke, and now I was considered one of the top swimmers in the country. At the national championships, I swam the fastest time of my life and am currently ranked fourth in the nation and 37th in the world for the 100-meter backstroke. In four years, I hope to make the Paralympic team.

Whatever your sport of choice, it will change your life. It reminds me that I need sleep for practice, healthy foods, and positive thoughts and surroundings. When I am stressed, I can feel my troubles sink to the bottom of the pool. My bone density has improved so much that I was disqualified from an experimental drug study because it was unclear whether the drug or the swimming had helped me more!

Kara Sheridan, 20 years old

occupational therapists, and recreational therapists can help analyze the obstacles to better function, and make suggestions for equipment options to improve it.

Recreational devices can be used to build confidence and to give children an opportunity to play by themselves and with their friends. Swim devices, such as vests and floatees, may require some trial and error to find the best choice for a particular child, but the effort supports independent exploration and playful activity. Participation in wheelchair sports may mean purchase of an additional, specialized wheelchair, but the opportunities for socialization and physical activity may be valuable life experiences if they are in concert with the child's interests. Just as is the case with therapeutic devices, a wide range of options exists. Other parents, rehabilitation professionals including recreational therapists, and school personnel are good sources of ideas. These devices also require careful assessment to link appropriately with a child's abilities and interests.

Aerobic Exercise

Activity that exercises large muscle groups and many body segments in a repetitive way is needed to increase heart rate and improve cardiac efficiency. This frequently needs to be done through noncontact and low-impact activity. Bicycling, swimming, wheelchair games, and mat activities under supervision are all possible. Children who have few problems with their arms can throw balls, do light weightlifting, and cycle using their arms. This will provide a good aerobic challenge. Those who have mild involvement of the legs can swim, cycle, and possibly walk for aerobic conditioning.

Children with OI can excel and derive great joy from being in the water. This can begin with the youngest infant backlying on a large towel in the bathtub, with water to or just above the ears. Talking to the baby usually elicits kicks, and the buoyancy provided by the water may provide the baby's first independent kicking experience. With practice, this will transfer to nonaquatic environments. In a similar fashion, using a swim vest or float so the child can move independently, without parent support, provides valuable experience with movement, and reinforces a sense of "I can do this myself."

This leads to the issue of adult-directed exercises vs. child-directed activities in the water. The pool or hot tub is a safe and supportive environment for children with OI to play in. If it becomes work (exercises), the fun may be lost along with the child's ability to make decisions reinforcing a sense of independence and competence. Therapeutic exercises after a fracture or surgery are often best done in water, and this may be the first medium in which a child can walk without a device. Thus, specific exercises or activities are appropriate under some circumstances, but if the goal is to establish a lifelong love of swimming, it begins with having fun for the youngest children, who may then progress to swimming lessons, and then, in some cases, participation on a swim team.

Diet

Proper nutrition and careful monitoring of caloric intake are important to support mobility. Children with large, protuberant abdomens are less likely to be active and are more likely to have significant pulmonary difficulty. The commitment to a healthy lifestyle includes adherence to diet and routine exercise designed to promote cardiovascular fitness through sustained activity. (See Chapter 9 for more on nutrition.)

Factors That Limit Fitness and Performance

- Long periods of time in the same body position.
- Limited opportunities for physical education or recreation in and out of school.
- Excessive TV, study, or computer time without activity breaks.
- Diet contributing to obesity.
- Exercise perceived as an unpleasant burden or another assignment for the child.

Factors That Promote Fitness and Performance

- Equipment choices that support optimal function and encourage as much independence as possible in all domains.
- Minimal long-term sitting or lying down without change in position during the day.

- Concept of an exercise bank: make deposits during the day.
- Focus on the next goal(s) for the child to accomplish rather than how many minutes of therapy he or she does.
- Developmental transition from physical therapy to adaptive physical education to peer group physical education.
- Dietary choices that discourage snack foods linked to long-term sitting.
- Recreation associated with satisfaction.
- Parental participation in an active lifestyle and good dietary choices.

Resources

Exceptional Parent Magazine: The May 2000 issue was devoted entirely to recreation, sports, and play for children with disabilities.

Exceptional Parent
555 Kinderkamack Rd.
Oradell, NJ 07649-1517
Phone: (201) 634-6550
Internet: www.eparent.com

Cintas, H.L., and L.H. Gerber. 1996. Motor Performance: Succeeding Despite Brittle Bones. In P. Wacaster (ed.), *Managing Osteogenesis Imperfecta: A Medical Manual.* Gaithersburg, Md.: Osteogenesis Imperfecta Foundation. Pp. 101–108.

Goldberg, Barry. 1995. *Sports and Exercise for Children with Chronic Health Conditions.* Champaign, Ill.: Human Kinetics, Inc. **To order, call (800) 535-1910.**

Disabled Sports USA
451 Hungerford Dr.
Suite 100
Rockville, MD 20850
Phone: (301) 217-0960
TDD: (301) 217-0963

E-mail: information@dsusa.org
Internet: www.dsusa.org

National Center on Physical Activity and Disability
1640 W. Roosevelt Rd.
Chicago, IL 60608-6904
E-mail: ncpad@uic.edu
Internet: ncpad.cc.uic.edu/home.html

Paralympics
Internet: www.ct2004.com/para.shtml

Rifton Equipment and Community Playthings
Adapted tricycles and other toys and equipment.
Phone: (800) 777-4244

Wheelchair Sports USA
3593 E. Fountain Blvd.
Suite L-1
Colorado Springs, CO 80910
Phone: (719) 574-1150
E-mail: administrator@wsusa.org
Internet: www.wsusa.org

9
Nutrition for People with OI

Sue Simmonds

Key Points in This Chapter

- Eating a varied diet low in fat and high in nutrients is important for good health and weight control for all people, including those with OI.

- The U.S. Department of Agriculture's Food Guide Pyramid provides guidelines for good eating. Whole grains, fresh fruits and vegetables, low-fat dairy products, and lean meats or other protein-rich foods are cornerstones of a healthy diet.

- Because adequate calcium is good for bones, this is an important nutrient for people with OI. However, OI is not caused by a calcium deficiency, so ingesting excessive amounts of calcium will not prevent OI symptoms, and may cause other problems.

- Because some people with OI have limited mobility and/or are smaller than average, general recommendations for daily calorie and nutrient intake may not apply to them. Consultation with a physician or registered dietitian will help people with OI develop an individualized eating plan.

Good nutrition is a way of life important to everyone. This is especially true for children and adults with osteogenesis imperfecta (OI). Although there are no foods or supplements that will cure OI or prevent its symptoms, compelling evidence shows that a balanced diet and weight control are crucial components of optimal health.

The wealth of information on diet and nutrition could fill an entire library, much less a chapter. The following is intended to provide general nutritional guidelines based on the six basic food groups, with a focus on nutrition and bone health. It is important to bear in mind that these are guidelines only. Factors such as age, weight, height, activity level, medications, personal tastes, and the severity of OI all help determine the appropriate dietary balance for any given person. Dental health may also affect the kinds of food people can eat, and how they are prepared. People with OI are encouraged to consult a physician or dietitian for an individualized nutritional assessment.

The Food Guide Pyramid

The U.S. Department of Agriculture (USDA) has developed a Food Guide Pyramid to help people make healthy daily food choices. The pyramid's value is evident in that, despite ever-increasing and sophisticated research, the Food Guide Pyramid has remained intact since its inception. The pyramid illustrates six food groups, offering guidelines for the appropriate daily number of servings from each group.

The three basic messages of the USDA's 2000 Dietary Guidelines for Americans are to aim for fitness, build a healthy base, and choose sensibly. More specifically, people are encouraged to aim for a healthy weight and be physically active each day. Let the USDA's Food Guide Pyramid help determine food choices, which should include a variety of grains (especially whole grains), fruits, and vegetables.

In general, choosing sensibly means choosing a diet that is low in saturated fat (such as the fat in butter and meat) and cholesterol, and moderate in total fat. Choose beverages and foods to moderate intake of sugars, choose and prepare foods with less salt, and, for adults who drink alcoholic beverages, do so in moderation.

Food Guide Pyramid

A Guide to Daily Food Choices

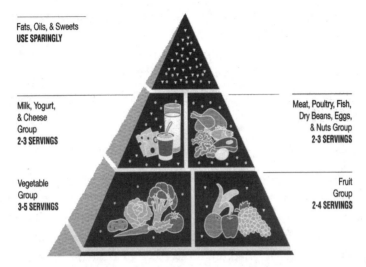

Fats, Oils, & Sweets
USE SPARINGLY

Milk, Yogurt,
& Cheese
Group
2-3 SERVINGS

Meat, Poultry, Fish,
Dry Beans, Eggs,
& Nuts Group
2-3 SERVINGS

Vegetable
Group
3-5 SERVINGS

Fruit
Group
2-4 SERVINGS

Bear in mind that the Food Guide Pyramid was developed for people of average body size and activity level. People with OI who have limited mobility and/or are smaller than others their age may only need the lower number of suggested servings in each group; again, check with a physician or dietitian to get individualized recommendations. Also, the USDA's definition of a "serving" is usually much less than the average person's definition. For example, the USDA defines a serving of pasta as one-half cup (the amount in an ice cream scoop), whereas many people commonly serve themselves two cups or more of pasta, equal to four or more USDA servings.

Grain-Based Foods

Eat 6 to 11 servings daily from the bread, cereal, rice, and pasta group. This group provides carbohydrates—a major source of energy—as well as fiber, vitamins, and minerals. A serving in this group is one slice of bread, one ounce of dry cereal, or one-half cup of rice or pasta.

Many people believe that carbohydrates are fattening foods to be avoided. Actually, these essential foods supply reasonable numbers of calories on their own. The calories and fat skyrocket, however, once cream sauces and butter are added. Large portions also add unneeded calories.

To increase fiber in your family's diet, choose breads, cereal, and other starches made with whole-grain wheat, oats, or bran. Check labels to see whether products contain whole grains; the most plentiful ingredients are listed first. Note that "wheat flour" (as opposed to "whole wheat flour"), "enriched flour," and "degerminated corn meal" are *not* whole grains.

Vegetables and Fruit

The USDA recommends three to five servings of vegetables, and two to four servings of fruit each day. These foods are naturally high in fiber and nutrients, and low in fat. A USDA serving is one cup of raw leafy vegetables, one-half cup of chopped vegetables (raw or cooked), one medium-sized piece of fruit, or three-quarters cup of fruit or vegetable juice.

In general, deeply or brightly colored vegetables and fruits pack the most nutrients. These include dark green leafy vegetables (spinach, kale, romaine lettuce), broccoli, carrots, sweet red peppers, winter squash (such as butternut), tomatoes, cantaloupe, strawberries, citrus fruits, kiwi, papaya, or mango.

Be aware that many "fruit drinks" have very little juice and lots of sugar. Choose 100 percent fruit juices. If weight is a problem, limit high-calorie juice of any kind, and opt for fresh fruit instead, which will help provide fiber and stave off hunger between meals.

Dairy Foods

The guidelines recommend two to three servings of milk, yogurt, and cheese daily, to provide protein and calcium (read more about calcium later in this chapter). A serving from this group is one cup of milk or yogurt, one-and-a-half ounces of natural cheese, or two ounces of processed cheese. Choose low-fat (1% or 2%) or nonfat (skim) milk for drinking and in recipes; they provide the same amount of calcium and other nutrients as whole milk. Children under two years, however, need whole milk for proper development. Choose reduced-fat products over their higher fat counterparts whenever possible.

Protein Foods

The guidelines recommend that people eat two to three servings from the meat, poultry, fish, dry bean, eggs, and nuts group. This group provides protein, B vitamins, iron, zinc, and other nutrients. A serving from this group is two to three ounces of cooked lean meat, poultry, or fish (an amount that is about the size of a deck of cards). One-half cup of cooked dry beans (pinto, black, navy, etc.) or one egg is equivalent to one ounce of lean meat, and two tablespoons of peanut butter or one-third cup of nuts also count as one ounce of meat.

Choose lean cuts of meat—extra-lean ground beef, ground turkey, loin or sirloin cuts of beef, and chicken or turkey breast. Trim visible fat from meat before cooking, and remove the skin from poultry. Because nuts and nut butters are high in fat as well as nutrients, consume them in moderation.

Fats, Oils, and Sweets

Use fats, oils, and sweets sparingly. For many people, the key is to work toward a moderate fat intake, rather than a no-fat diet. Fat is necessary for energy and development. Children less than two years old especially need fat for their development. To lower fat consumption, avoid buttering bread, cooking and frying in oil, adding fatty creams and sauces to foods, and snacking on high-fat chips or pastries.

Sweets and desserts can be part of a healthy, balanced diet. Low-fat cookie and cake recipes usually substitute a fruit purée (such as applesauce), or low- or

nonfat cream cheese, yogurt, or sour cream for some of the butter and shortening in traditional recipes. Pudding made with low-fat or nonfat milk is a good source of calcium. Remember, however, that low-fat does not equal low-calorie. Limit the portion size and frequency of low-fat treats.

The Importance of Calcium

OI is a genetic disorder of collagen, rather than a calcium deficiency. Taking calcium supplements will not prevent fractures. Children with moderately severe to severe OI often have excessive levels of calcium in their urine because the growing skeleton does not use all the calcium supplied by the diet. Accordingly, calcium supplements could potentially be harmful for these children. However, it is important for people with OI to include adequate calcium in their diets to develop and maintain bone mass, because bone loss can worsen bone fragility.

In 1997, the National Academy of Sciences developed the following Recommended Daily Intake (RDI) for calcium for people of *average* height and weight:

Young children (1–3):	500 mg per day
Older children (4–8):	800 mg per day
Preteens/adolescents (9–18):	1,300 mg per day
Men and women (19–50):	1,000 mg per day
Men and women (50+):	1,200 mg per day
Pregnant/lactating women (under 18):	1,300 mg per day
Pregnant/lactating women (19–50):	1,000 mg per day

A person of less than average height or weight may have lower calcium needs. It is recommended that people with OI, particularly if they are much smaller than average, talk to a physician and/or registered dietitian about their individual calcium needs. A measurement of calcium in a 24-hour urine collection may help determine if a person with OI is getting adequate calcium.

Calcium supplements are sometimes recommended for people who are not getting adequate calcium through their diets or who are taking certain kinds of medications, such as steroids or corticosteroids. Families should talk to their doctors about the effects of any prescribed medications on bone density, and whether a calcium supplement is necessary. Some medications, such as prednisone, can be quite harmful to the skeleton.

In addition to the amount of calcium in any given supplement, the solubility and absorption of calcium supplements must also be considered. For example, calcium citrate contains about half as much calcium by weight as calcium carbonate, but is far more soluble. There is also debate over whether calcium supplements are best absorbed if taken with food or between meals.

Dairy products are very rich sources of calcium. Fortunately, these products are increasingly available in nonfat and low-fat varieties, which contain the same amount of calcium as their higher-fat counterparts. One cup of nonfat yogurt, for example, contains approximately 450 mg of calcium, and a glass of skim milk contains approximately 300 mg. Cheese is also a good source of calcium. One-and-a-half ounces of cheddar cheese and two cups of cottage cheese, for example, each contain approximately 300 mg of calcium. People who cannot tolerate cow's milk may consider soy or rice milk enriched with calcium as alternatives.

Soy-based foods provide some calcium as well, and some researchers believe these foods contain other substances (phytoestrogens) that may boost bone health. Look for tofu, a solid form of soy, in refrigerated packaged blocks. (Be sure to choose tofu with calcium sulfate listed in the ingredients.) Tofu can be cut into chunks and stir-fried with vegetables and seasonings, shaped

---

We serve fruit with all meals and snacks. This has helped with digestive regularity.

Theresa Reed, mother of Jonathan, 5 years old

Children with dentinogenesis imperfecta may have a poor diet due to the inability to chew some foods if teeth are chipped or nerves are exposed. Our daughter had 15 caps placed on her teeth at age three. What a *huge* difference in appetite after that! We had no idea what she was missing. For constipation, we found that a mixture of apple juice and prune juice worked great since she hated prune juice alone. Also, we found regular calcium supplements very "chalky" tasting, and Nicole hated them. Now we use quick-dissolve fruit-flavored antacid tablets. No more fighting and she reminds us to give her calcium daily.

Michelle Hofhine, mother of Nicole, 6 years old

into meatless burgers, puréed into creamy pasta sauces and dips, or used as a custard-like base for pies or fruit smoothies.

There are also good sources of calcium beyond the dairy case, such as canned salmon and sardines (both with bones, which can be mashed). Many are surprised to learn that broccoli is a calcium-rich vegetable. One can also find calcium in dark-green leafy vegetables, such as kale, collards, and turnip greens. Dried beans and many nuts (such as almonds) may also provide supplementary sources of calcium.

Manufacturers are increasingly fortifying foods, such as orange juice, cereal, and breads with calcium. These products can easily be incorporated into an enjoyable and balanced diet.

The amount of calcium available to the body is not limited to intake; it can also be affected by what we drink. Caffeine and alcohol, for example, have been linked to decreased levels of calcium. Research suggests that the diuretic (water-losing) qualities of these products may promote calcium loss through the urine.

Other Important Nutrients

Vitamin D is necessary for calcium absorption. Exposure to sunlight usually allows the body to manufacture as much Vitamin D as it needs. Ten to 15 minutes of sun exposure a day is adequate. Vitamin D is also available in supplements and in some fortified foods. The RDA of Vitamin D is 400 international units (IU) per day. Taking supplements with more than this amount can be harmful.

Vitamin C has many functions in the body, including the production of healthy connective tissues, and the healing of wounds and fractures. Vitamin C is abundant in many fruits (such as citrus fruits, strawberries, and cantaloupe) and vegetables (including tomato, bell peppers, and sweet potato). There is some concern that

Vitamin C tablets can increase the risk of kidney stones in people who already have high levels of calcium in the urine. As explained previously, high urine calcium levels do occur in some people with moderate to severe OI. A well-balanced diet should supply all the Vitamin C that a person with OI requires.

People need water, and lots of it. Even slight dehydration can drain a person's energy. It takes an average of eight to 10 cups to replenish the water our bodies lose each day. To get a general idea of how much water an individual needs each day, divide his or her weight (in pounds) in half. The answer is the approximate number of fluid ounces he or she should drink daily. Many people quench their thirst with high-calorie, low-nutrient liquids such as sugary fruit drinks, sweetened iced tea, or soda. Drinking water instead not only meets the body's fluid needs more efficiently, but also cuts down on calorie intake.

Water plays an important role in every system in the body. It regulates body temperature; removes wastes; carries nutrients and oxygen to the cells; cushions the joints; helps prevent constipation; helps the liver and kidneys function more efficiently; and helps dissolve vitamins, minerals, and other nutrients to make them available to the body. Among its many benefits, water may help remedy constipation, a problem common among people with OI.

Weight Control

Extra weight can impede mobility, put additional stress on weak bones, and increase the risk of falls and other health problems. The best way for children and adults with OI to maintain a healthy weight is to get most of their calories from low-fat, high-nutrient foods, and to exercise to the greatest extent possible. (See Chapter 8 on exercise.) Consuming at least five fruits and vegetables each day is essential.

When mobility is limited, people with OI may gain weight, even if they are consuming a reasonable number of calories for body size, and eating a balanced diet. An individualized consultation with a dietitian or physician can help people with OI determine an appropriate calorie intake for their activity level, and/or develop a fitness program to burn more calories.

Avoiding Constipation

Constipation, a problem common among people with OI, can be caused by lack of exercise, certain medications, or a change in diet. To manage and prevent constipation, people with OI should 1) eat well-balanced, regularly scheduled meals to promote normal bowel function; 2) increase fiber intake; 3) drink plenty of water; and 4) be as active as their physician recommends and their condition allows. Fresh fruits, vegetables, legumes, and whole-grain foods (such as oatmeal or whole wheat bread)are good sources of dietary fiber.

Tips for Families to Promote Healthy Eating

* Choose a variety of foods for good nutrition. Because foods within most food groups differ in their content of nutrients and other beneficial substances, choosing a variety helps ensure that family members get all the fiber and nutrients they need. It can also help keep meals interesting from day to day. People who become bored by the same foods day after day may be tempted to splurge on high-fat treats.

* Try to incorporate foods with the full range of vitamins, minerals, and nutrients each week. Serving healthy foods every day will allow even a picky eater to still get adequate nutrients over the course of a few days or a week.

* Look for resources to help modify your family's diet. For people raised in the "meat and potatoes" tradition, it can be intimidating to cook new foods, such as meatless entrées or unfamiliar fruits and vegetables. Invest in a basic low-fat cookbook, or a good magazine that focuses on healthy eating. A number of food and nutrition web sites also offer low-fat, healthy recipes.

* Make a grocery list. Before you shop, select several healthy recipes to use in the coming week, and include the ingredients on your list. Having a list and a basic meal plan will help you avoid impulse purchases of processed junk food—and will probably save money too.

- Buy healthy convenience foods. Precut vegetables from the salad bar, prewashed salad greens in plastic bags, packaged roasted chicken breast, shredded reduced-fat cheese, and other convenience foods can cut down on preparation time and make healthy meals easy.

- Don't skip meals. Do allow healthy snacks between meals. People who are ravenous when mealtime comes around are more likely to overeat. Consider four or five smaller meals or snacks each day, rather than three large meals.

- Watch portion size. Most foods—even those that are high in fat such as peanut butter or ice cream—can be included in a healthy diet, as long as portions are reasonable. And even low-fat foods can contribute to weight gain if they are eaten in large portions. Try measuring portions occasionally to get an idea of what a cup of pasta or cereal looks like. When dining out, consider sharing entrées or taking home a doggy bag. Most restaurant portions are much too large for one person.

- To add whole grains to your family's diet, replace a portion of the white flour called for in bread, cake, or cookie recipes with whole-wheat flour. Make sandwiches on whole-wheat or oat bread, and try whole-wheat pasta, which tastes very similar to white pasta.

- Avoid using food as a reward or withholding food as a punishment. This sets up an unhealthy relationship between a child and food, which can contribute to weight control problems or eating disorders. Avoid using sweets and desserts to cheer up a child recovering from a fracture or surgery. This unhealthy eating pattern could last a lifetime.

- At mealtime, fill everyone's plate with moderate portions directly from the stove or oven, rather than putting the food on the table "family style." Assure children that they can have seconds if they're still hungry after eating their portion.

- Serve milk, water, and 100 percent fruit juices with meals and snacks. Reserve sodas for special occasions. Seltzer water mixed with orange juice is a good substitute for soda. Children may be more likely to consume healthy beverages if they see their parents doing the same.

- Keep healthy foods available for snacking. Single-serving containers of applesauce or pudding, carrot sticks with a low-fat dip, air-popped or low-fat microwave popcorn, and banana or apple slices with a little peanut butter are good alternatives to chips and cookies. Stock the fridge with a pitcher or individual bottles of water.

Resources

American Dietetic Association. 1997. *Calcium in Your Life.* Chicago: Author.

Duyff, Roberta Larson. 1998. *The American Dietetic Association's Complete Food and Nutrition Guide.* Chicago: American Dietetic Association.

Roberts, Susan B., Melvin B. Heyman, and Lisa Tracy. 1999. *Feeding Your Child for Lifelong Health: Birth through Age Six.* New York: Bantam Doubleday.

Tamborlane, William V. (ed.). 1997. *The Yale Guide to Children's Nutrition.* New Haven, Conn.: Yale University.

American Dietetic Association
216 W. Jackson Blvd.
Chicago, IL 60606-6995
Phone: (312) 899-0040
Internet: www.eatright.org
The ADA's web site includes hundreds of daily nutrition tips, nutrition

fact sheets, and information on finding a registered dietitian in your area.

Center for Nutrition Policy and Promotion
1120 20th St. NW
Suite 200, North Lobby
Washington, DC 20036
Phone: (202) 418-2312
Internet: www.usda.gov/cnpp/
This USDA-sponsored web site includes information on dietary guidelines, the Food Pyramid, a healthy eating index, news, and resources for teachers.

Cooking Light Magazine
P.O. Box 830549
Birmingham, AL 35283-0549
Phone: (800) 336-0125
E-mail: CookingLight@spc.com
Internet: www.cookinglight.com
Each issue of this monthly magazine offers dozens of light, lower-fat recipes for everything from main dishes to desserts, focusing on variety, good nutrition, fresh ingredients, and moderation. It also includes tips for exercise and an active, healthy lifestyle.

Five-A-Day Program
Internet: www.5aday.gov
This web site promotes the National Cancer Institute's Five-A-Day program to encourage people to eat more fruits and vegetables. It includes recipes and a health quiz.

Food and Nutrition Information Center
Internet: www.nal.usda.gov/fnic/
The U.S. Department of Agriculture, which publishes the Food Guide Pyramid, offers this resource to explain the pyramid and other nutrition guidelines. It includes links to the National Academy of Sciences, which publishes the Recommended Daily Allowance (RDA) of calories, vitamins, and minerals.

Healthfinder
Internet: www.healthfinder.gov
Healthfinder is a comprehensive federal government web site with links to hundreds of health-related web sites, including nutrition sites.

National Osteoporosis Foundation
1232 22nd St. NW
Washington, DC 20037-1292
Phone: (202) 223-2226
Internet: www.nof.org
The National Osteoporosis Foundation's web site includes detailed information on calcium and its relationship to bone health.

Nutrition Café
Internet: exhibits.pacsci.org/nutrition/
This children's site offers lots of nutrition information and games from the Pacific Science Center. Kids can be Nutrition Sleuths, visit the Have-A-Bite Café, and learn if they're eating right.

Nutrition Explorations
Internet: www.nutritionexplorations.org
This award-winning interactive web site was developed by the National Dairy Council for children of various ages, as well as parents, food professionals, and teachers.

Nutrition for Kids
Internet: tqjunior.thinkquest.org/3641/
This web site was developed by kids for kids. Learn about the function of nutrients, the Food Pyramid, foods kids should eat, and more.

10
Educating the Child with Osteogenesis Imperfecta

Maureen McCabe and Nina Rosalie

Key Points in This Chapter

- Many students with OI are eligible for special education services under the Individuals with Disabilities Education Act (IDEA). Under this law, schools receiving federal funds must provide specialized instruction and accommodation to allow children with disabilities to be educated in the "least restrictive environment." This means that, as much as possible, children with disabilities are educated with their nondisabled peers in regular classrooms.

- OI does not affect a child's intellectual ability. Many students with OI do well in school, although they may need help addressing physical and other challenges.

- A child receiving special education must have a written Individual Educational Program (IEP) that lists all services and accommodations the child needs to fully participate in school.

- It is important that students with OI participate in all school activities as much as possible, including classroom instruction, health education, physical education, field trips, and recess.

- Professionals such as school social workers or psychologists, physical and occupational therapists, or speech/language pathologists can help a child overcome problems related to OI that interfere with the student's full participation in school.

"The year of the millenium will guide us to a destiny where there are no disabled people, only people with varying degrees of ability. Hopefully, we will no longer use medical terms like amputee and paraplegic; we have the perfect terms now...man, woman, boy, girl, child. We should think of them as people...striving to be the same as the rest of the world."

Henry Viscardi, Jr.
Founder, National Center for Disability Services
and the Henry Viscardi School
June 1, 2000

The world of education for the parents of a child with osteogenesis imperfecta (OI) approaching school age can be compared to a bowl of alphabet soup. The soup bowl is full of letters in random order, which when brought together on the spoon can become words. Just as the parents become acquainted with the medical initials related to their child's care, such as OI, ER, PT, and MD, they now must broaden their "initial" knowledge. Parents learn that special educators, like medical professionals, also speak in acronyms. They talk about the student's "IEP" at the "CSE" and recommend services such as "OT" and "APE." In time, parents understand the educational jargon and learn to "talk the talk." It may be overwhelming at first, but it will also enhance parents' ability to communicate with the professionals involved in their child's educational life.

The ABCs of Special Education

It is important for parents to become acquainted with their child's rights under education law, and to advocate for the child to maximize the educational experience. The goal, of course, is for the child to become a consummate self-advocate and to achieve the life skills essential for higher education, career opportunities, and active community participation. Parents should become involved in the process that determines the best educational placement for their child.

Section 1401 of the Individuals with Disabilities Education Act 1997 (IDEA) defines categories of children with disabilities entitled to special education under the law. The law applies to "children with orthopedic impairments...who, by reason thereof, need special education and related services"; children with OI fall under this category. The federal law defines children's educational rights in broad terms; however, all states accepting federal funds must provide specialized instruction to children with disabilities from birth to age 21. The specific education regulations and related services eligibility vary from state to state.

The Individuals with Disabilities Education Act mandates that all children with disabilities have the right to a free, appropriate, public education (FAPE) in the least restrictive environment (LRE). This federal law, along with Section 504 of the Rehabilitation Act of 1973, prohibits discrimination on the basis of disability by any program that receives federal funding, including public schools. This means that children with disabilities have the right to receive an education with their nondisabled peers in a regular education setting. However, if the disability is such that supplemental aids and services provided within the regular education program do not appropriately enable the student to benefit from instruction, other options must be considered.

School districts are legally mandated to provide students in special education with "a full continuum of alternative placements ranging from regular classrooms to resource classes, special self-contained classes, special day or residential schools and hospitals" (Crockett and Kauffman 1999). To decide on the best placement for each individual, a multidisciplinary team evaluates all students receiving special education to determine each student's abilities and needs.

IDEA states that children who are eligible for special education are entitled to a written plan including the educational goals and related services required to meet the unique academic, social, emotional, and physical needs of the child in school. For students aged three to 21 years, the plan is called an Individual Educational Program (IEP).

Infants and toddlers who have delays in one of the developmental domains (cognition, communication, physical development, or psychosocial development) have an Individual Family Service Plan (IFSP), which is designed to meet the unique needs of this younger population. Early intervention programs for these children provide therapeutic services in the child's natural environment (e.g., the home). Early intervention programs vary from state to state; the local health department can provide information for a particular community. Families and professionals seeking further information about early intervention can contact the National Early Childhood Technical Assistance Center (listed in the Resources section at the end of this chapter).

Students not requiring special education under IDEA, as determined by a specially appointed school committee, but who may need modifications or adaptations in the regular classroom, are provided with a written plan called the "504 Plan" under Section 504 of the Rehabilitation Act.

The Committee on Special Education

Under the education law, the parents and members of a Committee on Special Education (CSE) make the decisions regarding a child's educational program. It is to the parents' advantage to be fully informed of their child's rights. The CSE comprises a multidisciplinary team, the parents, the child if appropriate, and, at the parents' discretion, any individual who has knowledge or special expertise regarding the child. The CSE uses the multidisciplinary team's evaluations and recommendations to discuss and determine a student's need for special services. The evaluation may include a physical examination, an individual psychological assessment, a social history, an observation of the student in the current educational setting, and other appropriate assessments or evaluations that describe the physical, mental, social, and emotional functioning. The Individual Education Program (IEP) is written by the CSE for the child's school to follow. The school is mandated to adhere to its stipulations. The IEP ensures that children receive all special services and accommodations necessary for them to benefit from the educational program.

Because OI is a rare disorder, many educators may not be familiar with its physical presentation. Therefore, when attending CSE meetings, parents may want to bring along a professional who is knowledgeable about OI and who can answer questions about the child's physical abilities. It may be helpful to direct team members to the OI Foundation for additional information. Also, a school representative may wish to visit the medical center where the child is treated to address any further concerns. For example, a school physical therapist who worked for the New York City Board of

---

Right from the start we decided we wanted Emily to attend regular school, and that included preschool. We wanted to give Emily the opportunity to show us that she was capable of being in a mainstream class. We had initial difficulty convincing the board of education that this was the right thing, but when they saw that we were adamant and prepared to litigate, they relented. I have mixed feelings about the experience. On the academic side it was great—Emily had a solid foundation for kindergarten. Socially, it was difficult. We were somewhat isolated. Preschoolers' play is very physical and Emily needed constant supervision. Playdates were very difficult. A few people at the preschool invited Emily over (she had to go with me and later, her little sister too), and Emily grew as a result. If I had to do it again, I might go to a preschool for children with disabilities. I think it's more supportive during this transition to school, but now Emily gets to tell her friends that she went to the same preschool as some of them, and I think it's good for her self-esteem.

When Emily went off to kindergarten, we opted out of school transportation. I drove her to school and picked her up. Academically, Emily continued to excel. Physically, she bounced back after her annual surgeries. Socially, I think it was a difficult time. The parents were not that anxious to have their children be friends with Emily. They were all polite but it took a while to find the few very good friends that Emily has made at elementary school. I've found that it helps to have a principal who allows me to be a part of the decision on what teacher Emily will have, and to have some say in which children Emily will have around her as a support. It took me a few years to speak up.

When she was younger and she couldn't participate in something like a field day event, or playground time at recess, she would be very upset. She has developed better coping skills. I think part of that comes from participation in the Junior Wheelchair USA sports program. She gets a lot of self-esteem from having a place where she fits in so completely. She swims and participates in track and field. She has also participated in children's theater programs. She's the only wheelchair kid but she gets right in there singing and dancing.

We don't complain about much at the school. We really pick our battles, so I think we have more credibility. We try to let the teachers and Emily work things out on their own. I put a lot of time and effort into the first two to three years, setting the tone at the school, so now we don't have to do it as much. They "get it" by now.

Rachelle Grossman, mother of Emily Seelenfreund, age 10

Education attended a student's physical therapy sessions at the Hospital for Special Surgery in New York. There, the therapist received instruction on proper therapeutic handling techniques and exercises, which reassured both the school physical therapist and the parents, who may have had reservations about their child's physical handling in school.

Based on the student's individual needs, the CSE will decide on the most appropriate program and placement in the least restrictive environment. The CSE must also consider the program's proximity to the child's home and the opportunity for involvement with nondisabled peers. Districts are encouraged to help identify resources and other agencies to provide support for the child in his home community.

A student with OI, like all students, can receive an education in a variety of settings, including public, private, parochial, special day  schools, and home schooling, depending on the student's needs and the family's preference. Parents should carefully consider each of the options. Special education under IDEA is specially designed instruction at no cost to the parent, to meet the unique learning needs of a child with a disability. Student needs are based on an individual evaluation, which will also be used to determine the related services that will best support the child in her educational setting. For instance, the student may be participating in a regular academic program with support services such as physical therapy to improve her mobility in school. Other parents may opt for a private school setting where the classes are smaller and the curriculum may be customized. If a child is extremely fragile, parents may consider a special day school or even home schooling, although home schooling is not reserved solely for severely affected children. Parents may consider home schooling for a variety of reasons— educational, religious, political, or medical. Most state departments of education can provide information about resources, rules, and regulations that affect home schooling. A number of national organizations, which are listed at the end of this chapter, provide information and materials to parents considering this option. The Internet, conferences, book fairs, and regional support groups also provide resources on home schooling.

When deciding for or against home schooling, parents should consider access to socialization opportunities with peers, access to recreational opportunities, the amount of time the child will spend with adults/parents vs. peers, and the abilities of the parent who will take on the role of teacher. Other concerns include the availability of safe transportation to and from school, the types of services the school system provides, how frequently the child is injured or hospitalized, the availability of school-sponsored home-based instruction when a child is recovering, the size of the public or private school being considered, and whether the school can provide the desired educational experience. Some schools are poorly equipped to provide "gifted and talented" services to a child who is also receiving "special education" because of a physical disability. On the other hand, some schools have strong academic programs, provide excellent therapeutic services and adaptive physical education, and can help families obtain adaptive equipment for the school setting. Cost is another issue. Home schooling is not free. In school districts that do special education well, public schooling can provide access to supplemental services, such as school-based therapy or a social worker to help obtain other types of assistance. By choosing home schooling or private schooling, families may have to piece together these services on their own, and possibly pay for them. Home schooling is an option that may or may not be appropriate for a particular family at any given time in their child's educational career.

The Educational Program

Classroom teachers are responsible for developing students' minds as well as nurturing their social, emotional, and physical well-being, and are the primary coordinators of a student's school day. It is critically important for the teacher to be informed about the child's specific physical abilities. Instructions on handling techniques and

My daughter, Alexis, has been diagnosed with very mild OI. Her problems include growth deficiency, loose joints, and some fracturing. She has experienced fractures to both feet, collarbone, and compression fractures in her back. For Alexis, dealing with OI in its mild form poses both physical and psychological challenges. Alexis does not display overt signs of a disability. However, her gait and ability to run and jump like her friends are not normal. Alexis tends to be cautious when participating in school and extracurricular activities.

Parental involvement and support is critical. Being cautious is smart; however, being overly cautious to the point where normal activities are compromised must be avoided. Despite the physical problems of mild OI, Alexis leads a very active life. She participates in

cheerleading, dance school (tap and ballet), Girl Scouts, and student council. All of these activities have helped to build self-confidence, and have assisted Alexis to overcome the potential psychological challenges of a mild disability. To promote school and extracurricular participation, Alexis' mother has volunteered to be an active parent leader/ member in the PTA, Girl Scouts, and football cheerleading. Alexis' mother is also very active in the classroom by assisting with various class activities and field trips. Active parent involvement also allows the activity to be monitored without being overly protective. Alexis is far from being the best cheerleader or dancer from a physical standpoint. However, she enjoys the activities and has made many friends. Activities that recognize achievement based on effort, participation, and cooperation rather than physical performance alone are important.

We set up a meeting at the beginning of the school year with the principal and teacher to review and advise school personnel on Alexis' mild OI and her current physical condition, with follow-up meetings throughout the year. School personnel are advised that "striking the balance" is very important when dealing with mild OI. It is important for Alexis not to be treated different or special. We do advise, however, that her activities should be monitored to avoid situations (such as contact sports, roughhousing, etc.) that could increase the risk of fracture.

Alexis advises that her OI is not a big deal. She hates to break bones, but knows she will get better. As a parent, it is evident that OI does not limit Alexis' enjoyment of life. Helping Alexis to feel normal while minimizing fracture risk—or "striking the balance"—is important.

Paul Granger, father of Alexis, 8 years old

fracture precautions are essential to ensure a safe school environment. Parents may want to keep the teacher apprised of all medical situations that might possibly affect classroom activities and/or absences. They should discuss with the teacher the specifics of how the child's physical information should be shared with other children and school personnel.

It is helpful for parents and children to meet with teachers before the school year to familiarize them with the child's needs, thus allowing for appropriate classroom setup. To help educate classmates, the parents and child can conduct an information session about OI at the beginning of the school year. As the child grows more comfortable, he can take more responsibility for this session each year, and can help decide how to describe OI and portray his abilities and restrictions. (See Chapters 14 and 15 for more about explaining OI to peers.)

The extent of the child's participation in regular education, and required program modifications *must* be specified on the IEP. All assistive technology devices must be included on the IEP (see the Assistive Technology section later in this chapter for more on special equipment). Classroom modifications and assistive technology may include the following:

- Classroom furniture may need to be rearranged to foster the student's mobility and accommodate her wheelchair and/or walking equipment.

- Items in the classroom should be within comfortable reach to prevent undo stress on muscles and bones.

- An air-conditioned environment may be needed because of the potential for overheating and sweating.

- Seating close to the instructor may be necessary when a hearing loss exists.

- Seating away from drafts might be recommended if the child experiences excessive sweating.

- Check the child's classroom desk to make sure that it is the appropriate height. An adjustable desk may be needed.

- A second set of textbooks can be ordered for home to avoid additional weight in the school bag.

- The availability of bookstands and automatic page-turners may be helpful to promote continued independence in the classroom, especially if the child is experiencing upper-body weakness due to a fracture or immobility because of surgery.

- Dictation into a tape recorder may be appropriate if handwriting tasks are too fatiguing.

- The use of a computer or word processor such as AlphaSmart or Dreamwriter may decrease fatigue.

- The use of special software can reduce the amount of typing necessary, thereby limiting fatigue.

A paraeducator, also referred to as a paraprofessional, teaching assistant, or teaching aide, may directly assist the child with the day-to-day school activities in the classroom, hallways, cafeteria, and school grounds. An aide working with a student with OI should be instructed in dressing techniques, feeding concerns, transfers, and wheelchair needs when appropriate. Deciding whether a child needs a personal aide in school requires an honest assessment of many factors, including the physical configuration of the school and playground; the student's ability to get to and from all areas of the school; the student's sense of personal safety in crowded corridors, playgrounds, or cafeterias; the impact that an adult aide may have on the student's interaction with peers; and parental concerns. A child's need for a personal aide at school will change as the student matures and her abilities change due to fractures, surgery, or changes in mobility and strength.

Even if a child does not require much assistance during the school day, it is vital that the teachers, teaching assistants, and personal aides be educated about OI and the child's abilities, not just his limitations. Parents should inform the classroom staff about emergency procedures regarding a fracture or injury (see Chapter 2 for more on first aid procedures). Fear of the unknown can result in overcompensation and overprotection, which will limit the child's independence and increase his own anxiety.

Class Instruction

Most students with OI are able to participate in a typical school program. Their learning styles are as varied as any student's in the general population. Unless a child has learning problems unrelated to OI, the curriculum does not usually need modification for academic content. Even when a student with OI is mainstreamed into a regular education program and following a general curriculum, frequent absences may require some instructional and management adaptations.

Because teachers may encounter only one student with OI in their careers, it is very difficult to draw conclusions about academic trends and learning styles associated with osteogenesis imperfecta. The professional staff of the Henry Viscardi School in Albertson, N.Y., shared their experiences for this chapter. Over a 30-year period, they have educated more than 30 students with OI from pre-K through 12th grade.

Each year, I write up an informational sheet about Beth's OI. I have amended this form each year since kindergarten with new medical information and our concerns at different ages. In the first few years of elementary school, I would arrange to meet the week before school started to discuss it with the teacher. In the later years, I would send in the form the first day of school with a note saying, "Here is some information you need to be aware of. Please call me with any questions or concerns at your convenience." The teachers responded very well to this approach. It gave them the information they needed immediately, and the flexibility to work a meeting or call into their busy schedule. I also ask that a copy of the information sheet be kept with the instruction packet for substitutes. As Beth has gotten older, she has become an excellent advocate for herself, answering most questions as well as I could.

Barbie Simmonds, mother of Beth, 12 years old
Sample form on page 208

Teachers and parents of children with milder OI report that the children usually do not require special modifications for classroom instruction. Parents' and teachers' concerns for these children revolve around the students' participation in physical education, sports, and recess.

Preschool is frequently the first point of entry into the formal education system. Parents may reluctantly send their children into this new environment filled with many factors they cannot control. The child may be ready, but parents are frequently concerned about the physical risks that may cause fractures. It may help for parents to spend a day in the classroom with their child to get the sense of a typical school day. Parents can suggest to the teacher how the child can actively participate in classroom activities. Parents should be specific about the type of seating, toys, and classroom materials their child can safely use; it cannot be assumed that the teacher will know.

Preschool and kindergarten are typically years when learning concepts are presented through a multisensory approach. Children perform activities using touch, taste, sight, sound, body position, and movement. Children with OI may have delays in gross motor skill development, which affect their ability to fully participate in movement activities. The teacher must create a physical environment that does not compromise the child's cognitive ability, and ensures that the child receives a complete multisensory "diet" in a safe manner.

Because children with OI tend to be passive and happily receive toys that are presented to them, they need to be encouraged to actively reach for things and move about. Toys operated by hand or foot switches, remote controls, or pull strings can help to establish an action-reaction relationship without the need for physical strength. Construction toys such as Duplos and Clipos encourage hand strengthening and fine motor coordination as well as imagination. Other manipulative materials such as clay, play dough, sand, and finger paints can provide additional sensory experiences to the hands and feet. By encouraging children to explore, parents help them build a strong foundation for the skills and knowledge learned in school.

The early elementary school years are a time to focus on strengthening the foundation for academic learning and increasing the physical stamina of a student with OI. Students with OI are often described as bright, high-energy students despite their physical limitations. They are quick to pick up new concepts and are often described by teachers as talkative and, at times, verbally precocious. This energy must be redirected when the child is expected to sit for long periods to avoid fidgety behavior. A child's imagination and creativity must be continually challenged to promote academic learning. Physical limitations should not lower educational expectations. There are creative ways to complete assignments even when muscles are fatigued. For example, students can dictate into a tape recorder or use a word processor to complete written tasks if necessary.

Delays in spatial awareness and organizational skills have been noted in children with moderate to severe OI (as well as children with other physical disabilities). This may affect how a child perceives instruction. Classroom activities to encourage organizational skills and spatial awareness include the use of cut-out window boxes, highlighting, and markers. These modifica-tions can be indicated on the IEP under program and testing modifications. Parents can encourage home activities such as meal preparation or laundry sorting to build the organizational skills necessary for classroom instruction.

Several older students and adults with OI have shared memories of feeling excluded from activities during their early years in their neighborhood school. To help create a better school experience, it is important for teachers to know that children with OI need to be active participants in all classroom activities, including sitting on the floor for "circle time" in the younger grades, or performing classroom jobs such as milk monitor or messenger in the older grades.

A child's teachers may need to work closely with his therapists to sculpt a program specifically suited to his needs. This will give the student an opportunity to fully experience and benefit from all aspects of school life.

Transition Services

By the time children with OI enter high school, they seem to have "caught up" developmentally. They experience high school much like any other teenager and transition successfully to college or the world of work. Students with OI who have typical real-life experiences do better with school work than children who have not been able to navigate and experience the everyday world.

As part of the Individual Education Program, all secondary education students with disabilities ages 14 to 21, and younger if appropriate, who are eligible to receive special education services must be provided with transition services. Transition services, as defined by the IDEA and Article 89, are a coordinated set of activities designed to prepare the student for adult life. Areas of transition may include community participation, postsecondary education, vocational training, employment, adult education, and independent living.

The purpose of an Individual Transition Plan (ITP) is to enable youths with disabilities to live, work, and continue to learn, with supports if necessary, as adults. Whenever transition services are discussed at CSE meetings, the school district must ensure participation of students and families, as well as agencies that may provide transition services.

It is recommended that parents of children with OI contact their state education department to get a copy of the requirements regarding transition services. The time to talk about transition is when children are in school. Transition needs to be thought about in terms of work situations, transportation, living arrangements, problem solving, agency resources, and recreation programs. It involves all of the activities that help make a person successful in the world outside of school. Families, students, and school personnel must be involved in transition planning and it must be started as soon as students can benefit from such a plan.

Health Education

Students with OI should participate in a regular health education program. Every issue in the health curriculum should be discussed. For example, students with OI are not immune from substance abuse because they may use a wheelchair, nor are they more inclined to use drugs. It is critical that no assumptions be made in either a positive or negative direction simply because the student has OI. Students with OI may have questions dealing specifically with their own situations. In the area of sexuality they may want to know if they will go through puberty like everyone else. They may also have concerns about having children or how alcohol affects any medication they may be taking. They may have concerns about fire escape plans in their home and/or in the school.

Physical Education

An IEP must address how a student with OI will participate in physical education. Exempting a student with OI completely from physical education (for example, sending her to the library during PE class) limits her opportunities for both physical fitness and the socialization that comes with group PE. A student with OI, depending on her situation, may participate in

- regular physical education,
- regular physical education with adaptations and/or special equipment, or
- adaptive physical education.

The PE program may change over the years, or within a single school year, as the student's abilities are affected by fractures and surgery.

Regular Physical Education. Some mildly affected children may be able to participate in all activities, using standard PE equipment.

Regular Physical Education with Adaptations and/or Special Equipment. Students with OI can participate in many physical education activities as long as their specific physical precautions are recognized. Many states require that the student's physician specify sports to be avoided. The Academy of Orthopedic Surgeons has designed participation guidelines for common physical disability groups including OI. Contraindicated sports where the risks outweigh the benefits for all persons with OI include: ice and sledge hockey and tackle football. Sports requiring hard running, tumbling, excessive twisting and volleyball may be appropriate for those with less physical involvement and must be evaluated on an individual basis. Sports recommended for most individuals with OI may include: swimming, tennis, field events, ball handling games and wheelchair sports (Adams 1994:205).

Chapter 7 of this book provides a sample card that a student can carry with him, listing which physical activities are allowed, and which are too dangerous.

The PE teacher should emphasize safety with the student and his classmates. The teacher can also help the student with OI to recognize his own physical limitations and voice his concerns if a particular activity seems risky.

Adjustments can be made to sports equipment, utilizing softer and more lightweight materials to allow the student to participate. The physical education teacher can replace the standard floor hockey stick with a child-size hockey stick. Smaller nylon beanbags substitute for heavy plastic pucks. Beach balls, balloons, and Gertie balls replace volleyballs. Nerf balls or lightweight playground balls replace basketballs. Oversized beach balls replace soccer balls. Lightweight children's lacrosse sticks with small wiffle balls replace standard lacrosse equipment. Equipment such as hockey sticks can be mounted to the wheelchair with a bungee cord if upper body strength or fragility is a concern. Students with OI may also be able to wheel or walk around a track while others run, or go to bat while another student runs on her behalf. Some children with OI develop good upper body strength from pushing a wheelchair or using crutches, and may be able to do push-ups or lift light weights.

Adaptive Physical Education (APE). All children love to play and children with OI are no different. Adapted physical education, which is federally mandated in accordance with education law, provides specially designed instruction, when appropriate, to meet the individual student's needs.

Some states have specialist credential programs required for adapted physical education teachers. Other states require the new Adapted Physical Education National Standards Exam. Parents may want to ask what the requirements are in their state and their own school district regarding the following:

- What are the qualifications of the physical education teachers who will be working directly with their child?
- What is the physical education curriculum?
- How do they see the child fitting into their curriculum?

A disability awareness program that includes information about osteogenesis imperfecta should be provided to the school personnel as well as the students. The focus should be on physical abilities so that the child can be included rather than excluded from activities. This will allow the child to play safely.

Physical therapy and occupational therapy are not substitutes for adapted physical education. However, input from therapists can be valuable when determining the following:

- How can the child move safely?
- How should the child transfer?
- Does the child need braces to crawl and walk for activities?
- Is it safe for the child to walk during class activities, or should she participate in a wheelchair?

Recess

For many younger children, recess is an important part of the day. Recess allows children to interact with each other informally, play games, get physical exercise on the playground, and take a break

---

When Nicole started kindergarten, the school had issues about her fracturing at school, as if we would sue them if she had a break there. We had to stress the importance of letting her be included in *all* activities. If she broke, we would fix it, but being with her friends was so important.

Nicole, both in kindergarten and first grade, went into the other classes to tell them why she was in a wheelchair, etc. It worked great! I've also heard from other teachers and parents that it helped them know how to handle her.

Michelle Hofhine, mother of Nicole, 6 years old

from intellectual work. As with physical education, it is important that students with OI participate in recess activities as much as possible. There is special playground equipment for children with disabilities, including swing sets that accommodate wheelchairs and sand tables that are at the proper height for a child in a wheelchair. Children with OI may also be able to use traditional equipment, such as slides or jungle gyms, with or without adult assistance. Even when a child with OI is able to play without assistance, adults may need to remind all students that safe and considerate play is important for preventing injury. Carelessly thrown balls or rough play can put the child with OI at risk of a fracture.

Gifted and Talented Programs

Students with OI are individuals; like other students, some will excel in school and others may struggle. Given the nature of OI, it is tempting to build protective barriers against interaction with outside experiences. It is also possible to overlook "giftedness" when the pressing issues of a disability diminish the role of academic achievement. Students with OI may also have hearing loss, which impairs responses to traditional testing situations. Therefore, the identification of giftedness in such students can be problematic. When identifying a child as gifted, it is helpful to keep the following definitions in mind:

> Students may have outstanding abilities in one area and/or in several areas including general intellectual ability, specific academic ability, visual or performing arts, creative thinking, leadership, and psychomotor abilities (American Mensa 1991:4).

The most prevalent characteristics of giftedness are: Students learn rapidly, have extensive vocabulary, have excellent memory, reason well, are curious, are mature for their age at times, have an excellent sense of humor, have a keen sense of observation, have compassion for others, have a vivid imagination, have a long attention span, have ability with numbers, are concerned with justice and fairness, have facility with puzzles and Legos, have a high energy level, are perfectionist, are perseverant in their areas of interest, question authority, are avid readers (Silverman 1992).

Academic achievement is often coupled with social isolation because the high-achieving student may not share peer interests. The student with OI may also be socially isolated based on frequent absences, protective barriers raised by school personnel, and parent concerns. "In addition, gifted children with disabilities often use their intelligence to try to circumvent the disability. This may cause both exceptionalities to appear less extreme: the disability may appear less severe because the child is using the intellect to cope, while the efforts expended in that area may hinder other expressions of giftedness" (Willard-Holt 1999:1).

It may be necessary for the gifted youngster with OI to have special home tutoring, accelerated classes, advanced placement classes, and enrichment activities to reach beyond the classroom setting. Colleges and universities offer programs that parents can look into. A student whose academic needs are not met may become aggressive, defensive, go off task, and/or lose interest in school achievement. Unfortunately, it is possible to ignore academic giftedness due to gaps in the sequence of educational delivery. These gaps may occur because of absences but may be misinterpreted as a lack of academic prowess. Gaps may also be related to developmental delays, but they do not mean that a child is not gifted. It is wise for the student with OI to retain an academic portfolio of accomplishments as testimony to academic achievement.

Although the IQ test stands as a measure of giftedness, it is also not the only measure. A student may be gifted in an area that is not measured by the IQ test or its equivalent. It is imperative that the IEP address the academic needs of a student with OI who is gifted. American Mensa offers information and web site links for parents who would like further information about meeting the challenges of having a gifted child.

Teachers should be aware that

commitment to identifying and nurturing the gifts of students with disabilities implies specific changes in the way educators approach identification, instruction, and classroom dynamics.

Include students with disabilities in initial screen phase. Be willing to accept nonconventional indicators of intellectual talent. Look beyond test scores. When applying cutoffs, bear in mind the depression of scores that may occur due to the disability. Compare with others who have similar disabilities. Weigh more heavily characteristics that enable the child to effectively compensate for the disability. Allow the child to participate in gifted programs on a trial basis (Willard-Holt 1999:5).

It is not unreasonable for parents to have high expectations for their child and to demand that schools have the same expectations. Challenging curriculum, creative projects, and the expectation of excellence are cornerstones of education for the gifted child.

School Planning for Community Activities and Field Trips

The term "accessible" means different things to different people. Museum directors may describe the museum entrance as "accessible except for one tiny step," or theater managers may identify their theater as "accessible except for the bathroom, which is down a flight of stairs." If it is possible, a visit should be made to the building or destination to determine the accessibility with regard to individual students' disabilities.

It is helpful for the parents and child to develop a list of questions to be asked before a field trip. Some of the obvious questions are:
- How wide is the entrance door?
- Are there steps to the door?
- Where is the bathroom?
- Is there an elevator and is it working?
- Are there assistive listening devices or closed captioning available for children with hearing loss?

Other, less obvious questions are:
- What is the floor like? Is it tiled? Is it carpeted?
- Regarding a hotel room: Is there a phone located on the nightstand?
- When going to a restaurant: Are there booths, high tables, or moveable tables?
- Will seating be provided close to the front of the bus to ensure a minimally bumpy ride?

A discussion with the school social worker and classroom teacher may facilitate the student's participation in field trips and overnight trips.

Unfortunately, there are times when the environment is not or cannot be modified. Again, in discussion with the child, family, and school there may be ways to get around the barrier. Perhaps using a different entrance, transferring (although this should be done cautiously), having a parent on the trip, etc., may help the student participate.

With the passage of the Americans with Disabilities Act (ADA), more establishments are willing to accommodate individuals with special needs. For example, on a recent overnight trip to New York City, a student needed a hospital bed. Working with the social worker and parent, the hotel was willing to move furniture, accept the delivery of the bed, and even have two workers on call if other accommodations needed to be made (such as temporary removal of the hotel room door). It is very likely that schools, workplaces, theaters, resorts, etc., will make accommodations, but they must be made aware of the child's needs and advised about how the accommodations can be made. Often, institutions are willing to try, they just do not always know how. It will take perseverance and a lot of legwork by the parents and teacher to make things possible. As the child with OI gets older and has watched his parents and teachers advocate on his behalf, he will be better able to advocate on his own behalf.

Related Services

The term "related services" refers to developmental, corrective, and other services that help a student with a disability to benefit from her educational program. These services may include speech/ language pathology, audiology, psychology, physical therapy, occupational therapy, counseling, social work, medical services, and assistive technology.

Related services are specified on the IEP and must be recommended by the Committee on Special Education. The specifics for each service must cover the frequency and duration of the therapy services, the maximum size of the group, and measurable annual goals. Parents should know exactly how related services will support their child in her educational program.

Social and Emotional Development

In the student's IEP, the section about social/emotional development discusses the degree or quality of the student's relationships with peers and adults, feelings about self, and social adjustments to school and community environments. In general, parents and teachers report that students with OI tend to have typical social and emotional relationships.

Psychology

In the broadest terms, school psychologists work to ensure that children are provided with opportunities that facilitate positive growth, development, and general well-being. School psychologists are knowledgeable about typical and atypical child and adult development and apply this expertise in school settings. They ensure that all children with disabilities are followed and reviewed regularly.

Because school psychologists are educated and trained in the early identification of sensory, learning, and emotional problems

---

Before we had children, we decided to home school when the time came to maximize learning opportunities. Now with two children with OI—a third grader and a preschooler—we are even more convinced that we made the right choice for us. Talk about the "least restrictive environment!" We adapt our curriculum to the children's interests and mobility levels, including lots of field trips. It is a lot of work, but there are many rewards.

Jeff and Priscilla Wacaster, parents of Neil,
9 years old, and Lillie, 3 years old

in children, they consult with other staff to implement instructional and behavioral interventions. School psychologists are also informational resources to children with disabilities and their families, as well as to medical personnel, teachers, and school administrators. They offer individual and group counseling to youngsters who are experiencing emotional distress, usually associated with school-related problems. School psychologists may also refer the youngster and his family for psychological evaluation and/or treatment in the community, depending on the nature and extent of the youngster's psychological needs.

Parents and educational staff should remember that, although frequently children with OI have normal intelligence, some youngsters may not be performing near their academic potential in school. This underachievement may arouse legitimate concern. School psychologists are instrumental in ascertaining the nature of the problem, and recommending educational intervention and remediation.

Social Work

The school social worker provides counseling, case management, and advocacy services to students and their families. Social workers serve as the link among the family, the school, and the community. They assist families experiencing financial hardships and assess students identified for possible abuse and neglect. The school social worker connects students to appropriate community resources, such as recreational programs, community case management, and financial resources.

School social workers seek to increase the social and emotional well-being of students by teaching age-appropriate social skills, encouraging the development of social relationships, providing crisis intervention services, and providing IEP-mandated counseling. Social workers help plan for students' long-term future and help them develop their own transition goals. In the early grades, school social workers help students adjust to separation from their parents during the school day.

For students with OI, the school social worker often assists in transitioning the child back to school after a fracture. Home instruction is required for students who are unable to come to school for medical reasons. However, returning to school as soon as possible after a fracture can reduce the amount of school time lost. Students need medical clearance from their physician to return to school, and special arrangements should be made for transportation that accommodates special casts or reclining wheelchairs. The social worker can work with the family and school staff to prevent and overcome barriers that may isolate the student from peer socialization and educational experiences.

School Nursing

The school nurse can assist students with OI in developing maximum independence with the safety precautions necessary to successfully carry out daily living activities. The school nurse, after educating him- or herself by talking to the parents and child with OI, can also instruct the staff on handling precautions, transfers, medical emergency procedures, and if necessary, toileting procedures. The nurse should be aware of any braces or orthotics, and know how to assist in adjustment or removal if necessary.

The school nurse is available to maintain and maximize comfort should a student experience a fracture in school. Parents should provide written information to the nurse (as well as the child's teachers) outlining procedures for handling a suspected fracture. In general, a student with OI is able to instruct the staff on which position will provide him with maximum comfort when he is experiencing pain. If directed to do so by the parents, the nurse can immobilize the injured part to prevent further pain and, if necessary, arrange for transportation to the emergency room. Many parents of children with OI prefer that they themselves (or a trusted family member or friend) transport the child to a familiar doctor or emergency room, even if it means that the child has to wait in a safe, comfortable area for a designated person to arrive. If a school has no nurse on site, an emergency plan for fractures needs to designate the appropriate personnel responsible for carrying out the plan. (See Chapter 2 for a list of procedures for fractures at school, and a sample form for emergency instructions.)

When there is an absence due to injury, fracture, or surgical procedure such as rodding or casting, the school may require a note from the child's physician, explaining the injury and restrictions of activity. A note from a parent may also be required for the child to return to school.

Speech/Language Therapy

Specific speech or language deficits do not appear to be associated with OI. The incidence of speech/language problems is similar to that of the general population. Hearing loss does, however, affect some people with OI. Hearing should be tested early to establish baseline data.

The speech/language pathologist designs and implements a program for children with communication problems such as speech and/or language impairments. Although students with OI may demonstrate thin high-pitched voices, this does not impede their ability to communicate. The speech pathologist can conduct a hearing screening to establish a baseline and may recommend otological or audiological intervention. If a hearing impairment is detected, the parents are advised to see a physician, audiologist, or ENT (ear, nose, and throat specialist) for a full evaluation.

Parents should make sure the speech/language pathologist is aware that

> there is a progressive hearing loss (conductive, sensorineural and mixed hearing patterns) associated with OI. This loss usually starts in the second and third decade of life and increases with age, though some may be affected as early as three years of age. The high frequencies are involved preferentially initially (Vernick 1996:132–133).

Physical Development

Gross and fine motor development problems are classified on the IEP as mild, moderate, or severe. A description of the child's functional abilities and limitations should be included on the IEP, such as

- activities of daily living (toileting, dressing, and feeding);

- ability to transfer; and
- mobility status (whether the child walks or uses a wheelchair, and under what conditions).

Specific lifting, handling, and positioning instructions should be addressed in this section as well.

Physical Therapy

A physical therapist designs and implements a program of therapeutic exercises and techniques to improve quality of movement, gross motor balance, strength and coordination, functional posture, and mobility within the school setting. The physical therapist assists the student with ways to safely manage the physical environment and provides

- activities that develop self-help, mobility, and transfer skills;
- instruction in the use of adaptive equipment, wheelchairs, and braces to permit management of personal needs in the classroom and school; and
- training for wheelchair mobility, gait training with walking devices, and ambulation to enable freedom of movement.

Adaptive positioning devices may be used in the classroom to improve overall comfort, prevent joint contractures, and provide a means for alternative weight bearing. The physical therapist can provide suggestions to the student and make recommendations to school personnel regarding adaptation of the school environment. The physical therapist may also provide consultation on physical

---

When looking for a school, go to the school before you decide. Make sure you can enter the front door in the wheelchair, and do not have to use the maintenance door. Take your wheelchair into the bathroom and the cafeteria. See if you can reach the locker shelves and the water fountain. Do not assume everything is accessible for you.

Daniel Cornejo, age 11

I explain to the other students that I am a nice person in a wheelchair, not an alien. I tell them, "Your bones are like carrots—thick and hard to break. My bones are like celery and snap easy."

Antonella Verderosa, age 11

modifications and low-level assistive technology accommodations.

Physical therapy may be provided in the classroom (called "push-in") or as a "pull-out" service outside the classroom. The specific therapy goals usually dictate whether the service can be performed during classroom instruction or outside the classroom.

Occupational Therapy

An occupational therapist plans and implements a program of purposeful activities to develop and maintain skills for daily living. School-based occupational therapy is designed to improve the physical, sensory, and cognitive functioning of students in all instructional activities.

An occupational therapist provides activities that

- develop independence in feeding, dressing, toileting, grooming, mobility, and object manipulation;
- assist with organization and attention skills in the classroom;
- develop eye-hand coordination;
- develop gross and fine motor functioning; and
- enhance thinking for better organization, problem solving, planning, memory, etc.

The occupational therapist may give an orientation to school personnel illustrating specific positioning, use of adaptive devices, and handling methods to facilitate the student's comfort and ability to learn. The occupational therapist can be consulted for specific assistive technology recommendations.

Therapeutic Evaluation and Assessments

Evaluative testing is often required to determine the need for therapy services in school programs. Selecting an assessment instrument to evaluate the student with OI can be challenging. The assessment tools may be inappropriate for children with fragile bones. If standardized testing is required, the evaluator should review the testing activities in advance and consult with parents regarding the child's specific medical history and physical restrictions before initiating the test. It is helpful to include a narrative statement describing the testing restrictions in the report, so an accurate description of the student's abilities is demonstrated.

Annual Goals and Objectives for Related Services

Goals for related services, such as physical and occupational therapy, must relate to improving the student's ability to benefit from instruction within the school. Other goals related to the child's health and function but unrelated to her school participation may be addressed in a private or medical setting. The school therapists will require written medical clearance to resume services following a fracture or surgery.

Parents should ensure that the stated goals on the IEP are appropriate regardless of a change in the child's functional status, and select goals that will allow the therapist to continue working with the child following a change in medical status. The school therapist is bound by the frequency and duration of services and the goals established on the IEP. For example, following a fracture or surgery, a physician may request a temporary increase in physical therapy services to allow the child to return to her previous functional status. The school physical therapist, however, cannot increase the services provided in school without an amendment to the IEP. Many school districts will say that the additional therapy is a non–school-related medical goal, and should be addressed in a different setting. Parents and school personnel should keep this in mind when stipulating goals and service frequency on the IEP. If a child has a history of multiple fractures each year, a high frequency of therapy services may be appropriate. Children with milder forms of OI may need less frequent services.

A sample of a school physical therapy goal and objective is as follows:

> **Goal:** Demonstrate an improvement in mobility skills to successfully participate in educational activities and negotiate the school's physical environment.

Objective: John will demonstrate the ability to walk the length of a classroom using a walker with increasing independence.

An annual review of the child's IEP is usually scheduled during the second semester of the school year. Each related service provider treating the child will report on the child's status and make recommendations for the following school year.

Physical Environment Considerations

Architectural Barriers

For students with limited mobility, whether they use a wheelchair or walk, with or without assistance, physical barriers may prevent their full participation in school activities. These barriers must be addressed if they interfere with the child's educational experience. The following must be taken into consideration.

Busing/Transportation:
- Can a four-point strap tie-down system be provided to secure the wheelchair during transit?
- Can the wheelchair and student be transported in a forward-facing position to minimize side-to-side jerking movements?
- Can lower-body restraints be positioned over the pelvis, not the abdomen, at an angle of 30 degrees or greater to the horizontal?
- Can upper-torso restraints be provided to limit movement of the head and chest?
- Does the bus have air conditioning?
- What is the amount of time that the student will be on the bus?
- Are seat belts provided for students who can sit in a regular seat?
- If the student can walk, does he/she need help getting on and off the bus?
- Is accessible transportation available for field trips?
- Will the child be at risk of a fracture on very bumpy bus rides (particularly if the wheelchair tie-down is located at the back of the bus where the ride is often roughest)?

Building:

- Can the child independently enter/exit the building?
- Are there curb cuts on the school grounds that would enable the student to propel his/her wheelchair onto/off the sidewalk?
- Is the student able to open/close the doors without difficulty?
- Where is the accessible door entrance?
- What is the length and width of the hallways?
- How does the traffic pattern flow?
- How will the student safely navigate the crowds in the hallways?
- Can the student travel between classes in a timely fashion? If not, can he/she leave class a few minutes early to allow for travel time?
- Is the student able to access his/her locker and reach the hooks and shelves; if not, what is the alternative plan for storage of personal items?
- Is there an elevator in the building?
- Can the child access the elevator buttons?
- What is an alternate plan in the event of a power outage?
- What is the evacuation plan for fire drills/emergencies? (See the section later in this chapter on fire and emergency plans.)

Bathroom:

- What adaptations are present in the bathroom?
- Has the student attempted to use the bathroom to determine its accessibility?
- What are the child's transfer skills?
- Will a grab bar make his/her toilet transfers safer?
- Does the child need assistance in the bathroom?
- Are soap and towel dispensers low enough for the child to reach?

Cafeteria:

- Where is the cafeteria located?
- What is the height of the tables?

In elementary school, I was not allowed to participate much in gym class. During class I would sit by myself and usually draw or color. Even though I did not mind doing so, I felt left out. When asked by my classmates why I couldn't participate, I did not know how to respond. As I progressed into middle school I began participating in gym class, but I never enjoyed going to gym class and I would not put forth too much effort in the activities. I was also uncomfortable with myself because people would make comments about my size because I was so skinny. Even though their comments were compliments, I did not seem to think so. I was very quiet in my academic classes because of my lack of confidence. I looked at this disorder as a punishment from God. When I entered high school, I changed completely, mostly because of cheerleading. I was convinced to try out as a freshman by one of my friends. I made the Junior Varsity squad for freshman and sophomore year. Ever since joining the squad I have gained confidence, and I am very comfortable with who I am as a person. The last season of cheerleading this year, our Junior Varsity squad competed and we placed first, third, and fifth. At one of the competitions, they were giving out an award for "Outstanding Cheerleader," which I won out of all the JV cheerleaders in Western Massachusetts. That meant a lot to me because I have always been told by doctors and others that I cannot do anything athletic.

Christie Allen, 16 years old

- Can the child access the cafeteria line?
- How will the student navigate through the cafeteria with a lunchroom tray?

Physical Environment Solutions

Assistive Technology

The IDEA defines assistive technology as "any piece of equipment, or product system...that is used to increase, maintain, or improve functional capabilities of a child with a disability." The reauthorization of IDEA 1997 requires that every IEP team consider assistive technology for students with an IEP. Assistive technology may include mobility devices, adaptive equipment, electronic devices, and devices for activities of daily living. Any assistive technology required for the student must be indicated on the IEP.

Mobility

Independent mobility within the school and home environment is essential for academic, social, and emotional development. School therapists, with parental input, assist in determining which mobility options are best suited to meet the student's needs within the school environment. Strength and balance are also assessed to determine if the student can independently move about in the classroom and hallways without fear of falling. If there is a safety or endurance concern, an assistive device or wheelchair may be the alternative.

Walking Devices. The student should use his own crutches or walker in school. Students who are progressing from a walker to crutches may want to use the crutches in therapy or in specific classroom settings and continue with a walker in busy hallways or the cafeteria for safety purposes, until their agility and confidence with the device improves.

Wheelchairs. Depending on the student's mobility status and endurance level, the use of a wheelchair in school may be a consideration. The student wants to keep up with his peers and fully participate in student activities. Even a child who uses crutches or a walker at home may want to consider using a wheelchair in the classroom or just in the hallways. A student with good arm strength may want to use an ultralight wheelchair that maneuvers easily in small spaces and can propel easily between classrooms. Students who have moderate to severe arm involvement may opt for a power wheelchair to provide further independence and eliminate the need to be transported to class by an aide or another student.

When evaluating wheelchairs for a child with OI, consider the following features for school use:

- Even if the child has good head and trunk strength, consider a removable headrest and harness for use on the school bus or when negotiating uneven terrain, such as grassy areas.
- Shock-absorbing footrests may help the student on bumpy bus rides.
- A seat extension attachment may allow the student to return to school with legs immobilized.

- The rental of a full recliner wheelchair may allow the student to return to school in a spica cast.

- Notify the transportation company in advance if the child gets a new wheelchair, to ensure proper tie-down on the school bus.

Adaptive Equipment

- **Height Adjustable Desk:** An individual height-adjustable desk will allow for adequate clearance of a wheelchair and/or casts, as well as adjust to shorter body and arm reach.

- **Classroom Chairs:** The student's posture must be evaluated in the chair to ensure his body is upright and the height is appropriate for writing at the table. The chair must be the proper height for standing and wheelchair transfers. A wheelchair does not need to be the student's desk chair if he can transfer safely into another chair. His ability to move about in the classroom must be considered. Using a classroom chair vs. a wheelchair will depend on the dynamics and the student's safety within the classroom.

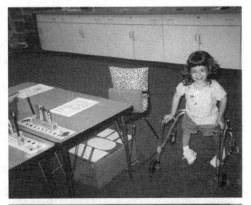

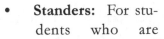
This student uses cushions and a footrest so she can sit comfortably at the classroom work tables.

- **Standers:** For students who are

I have OI and I have a son with OI. When I first put my son in kindergarten he got sick and had to stay in the hospital. I found out while he was there that he had more than five compression fractures in his back due to the rough bus ride to and from school. Several doctors said Austin needed to get off the bus and get other transportation. The city schools told me that if I put Austin in a special school and class, they would give him anything I wanted. To me that was not fair. I tried to get him a 504 plan so he could get what he needed. The school system told me he was too smart to get a 504 plan—they did not know that you could get a 504 plan for a physical disorder. Austin also required an aide on the playground with him, and they were not going to do that either. They even sent a note home saying he would be suspended if they caught him on the monkey bars. I had to get two of the local news channels in on the whole mess and it got the school board a little scared. It took the whole year just about, but he finally got the aide and the transportation.

Tonya Muncy, mother of Austin Bibb, age 7

nonambulatory or recovering from surgery, a standing device such as a prone or supine stander may be used in the classroom as a weightbearing activity. Following surgery, medical clearance from the student's physician is required for using a stander.

Low-Technology Classroom Adaptations

All low- and high-level adaptations must be specifically indicated on the IEP. Once they are documented on the IEP, the school district must purchase these items for the student's use in school. Children with milder OI may not require any classroom accommodations, except following a fracture or surgery. Physical and occupational therapists can be consulted to identify the specific needs of students with moderate to severe involvement.

There are state assistive technology programs, funded by the National Institute on Disability and Rehabilitation (NIDRR) under the Assistive Technology Act of 1998. Contact the RESNA Technical Assistance Project (listed in the Resources section of this chapter) for individual state listings.

The following items may assist students with their classroom work if fine motor difficulties and/or hand weakness has been identified:

- **Pencil Grip**: This protects joints and decreases muscle fatigue. Square pencil grips also keep the pencil from rolling off the desk if reaching down is a problem.

- **Adapted Scissors:** Lever scissors eliminate the repetitive squeeze motion required to open and close scissors. This reduces fatigue. Other adapted scissors include those that are lightweight and those with varied handle sizes and shapes.

- **Page Turner:** This is an electronic device that stabilizes a book and via a single switch activates an electronic arm that attaches to and turns individual pages.

- **Soft Lead Pencils and Felt Tip Pens:** Less downward pressure is required on the writing implement to produce darker markings.

- **Reading Easel:** This device holds large or heavy books on a stand and positions them at a vertical slant. It eliminates strain on the back and neck from unnecessary forward bending.

- **Slant Board:** A table surface that slants allows for easier view of written work and better support of the forearm while the child is writing.

High-Level Technology

Adaptations can be made for more efficient keyboarding. Examples of such adaptations include the following:

- **Comfort Type/Writing Easel:** This positions a keyboard or reading materials at a vertical slant. It prevents strain on the back and neck by eliminating the need to bend forward.

- **Mini-Thin Keyboard:** This keyboard is small and lightweight. It prevents excessive reaching to access all quadrants. It can be effortlessly repositioned on the desk surface.

- **Trackball Adapted Mouse:** This mouse has a stationary base and a moveable ball portion. It requires only a finger and/or thumb to move the ball and ultimately the cursor. Shoulder and wrist movements are not necessary; energy is conserved.

- **Glide Pad Adapted Mouse:** This also has a lightweight base with a touch-sensitive pad. It requires movement of one finger gliding on the pad to move the cursor.

- **On-Screen Keyboard** (e.g. Wivik, Soft-type): This keyboard is displayed visually on the monitor and accessed via a mouse vs. direct finger-to-keyboard contact. Some on-screen keyboards are also accessible using a switch and scanning.

- **Rate Enhancement Software:** This program incorporates word prediction and word abbreviation. It reduces the number of keystrokes required to complete words and sentences. It eliminates repetition, which reduces strain and decreases fatigue.

- **Voice Activation Computer Access** (e.g. Dragon Dictate and Naturally Speaking): Both programs decrease the need for direct access to a mouse or keyboard. The computer is trained to recognize the voice. Once the computer is trained, the user can dictate text, control mouse movements, and issue commands by voice.

- **Eye Gaze Computer Access:** This also decreases the need for direct access. A camera and infrared light follow movements of the eye. As the student's eyes scan the letters of an on-screen keyboard, the camera picks up the eye movements and selects the letter on which the eye pauses.

Fire and Emergency Evacuation

The mobility accommodations outlined in a student's IEP may be difficult to implement during a fire drill or emergency evacuation. Students must quickly exit the building, and it may be unsafe to use elevators. It is vital that school employees develop a fire and emergency evacuation plan for a student with OI *before* an emergency occurs, and that they practice this plan during routine fire drills.

In single-level school buildings, educators should make sure that a child with OI, who may move more slowly than other children and be at risk of a fall if students are moving quickly or jostling each other, gets out of the building safely. Schools may want to assign a particular staff person to accompany a child with OI during a fire drill or emergency. For children in multilevel school buildings, their parents, physician, personal care aide, and/or physical therapist can often provide advice about how to evacuate the child in an emergency. It is possible for two adults to carry a child in a wheelchair safely down a flight of stairs. Leaving a child with OI inside during a fire drill is unacceptable; this places the child at risk during a true emergency, when personnel will be unprepared to help the child evacuate.

Accommodations for Hearing Loss

Children with OI who have hearing loss may wear assistive devices all the time, or only as needed for certain situations, such as oral exams and lectures. Devices include hearing aids, an FM system, a personal listening device, or a combination of several devices. In some cases, the teacher needs to clip on a microphone that works with the child's assistive device.

Additional accommodations that help a child with hearing loss participate in classroom activities include the following:

- Have the child sit near to where the teacher usually lectures.

- Give the child permission to move around the room as needed to be near the teacher. The child can have a clipboard to carry from place to place.

- Assign a "buddy" who can repeat verbal instructions if needed.

- The teacher should speak clearly, in a normal voice, and in full view of the child with OI. It is important not to speak more loudly than usual, or overenunciate words. This interferes with lip reading.

Extracurricular Activities

Clubs

Clubs are an ideal way for a student with OI to participate in social situations. They provide an opportunity for others to get to know the student for herself and not for her disability. "A Brownie," "the yearbook editor," or "a cheerleader" are more positive descriptors than "the girl in the wheelchair." Parents can actively participate in the student activities program by joining a parent/teacher association to ensure that the school offers programs in which their child can be actively involved. Students should not limit themselves and can be involved in some way in virtually any activity, including drama, band, art clubs, chess, yearbook staff, student government, service clubs, or other interest groups.

Sports

Students with OI can participate in recreational and competitive sports provided precautions are carefully thought about. Regardless of the sport, proper body mechanics and stabilization techniques must be considered to minimize unnecessary stress and strain on the joints and the potential for fractures.

A child participating in wheelchair sports should be stabilized with straps at the pelvis, upper thighs, ankles, and abdomen. The type of wheelchair to use will depend on the sport. The national sports associations can be contacted for specific information and resources regarding adaptive sports regulations, wheelchairs, and equipment. They will also be able to suggest possible wheelchair sports suited to a particular child.

Many students with OI participate in school sports by being a cheerleader, managing a team, keeping or announcing scores, and otherwise contributing to their school's teams even if they cannot physically participate.

References

Adams, R. 1994. Physical Activity and Exercise Guidelines for Persons with OI. In Glauser, H.C. (ed.), *Living with Osteogenesis Imperfecta: A Guidebook for Families*. Gaithersburg, Md.: Osteogenesis Imperfecta Foundation.

Allbrink, K. 1999. *Ability in Self Care Related to Upper Limb Range*. Presentation at the Seventh International Conference on Osteogenesis Imperfecta. Montreal, Canada. 29 August to 1 September.

American Mensa. 1991. *A Resource Guide for Parents*. Arlington, Texas: Author.

Anderson, W., S. Chitwood, and D. Hayden. 1997. *Negotiating the Special Education Maze: A Guide for Parents and Teachers*. 3rd Edition. Bethesda, Md.: Woodbine House.

Binder, H., A. Conway, and L.H. Gerber. 1993. Rehabilitation Approaches to Children with Osteogenesis Imperfecta: A Ten-Year Experience. *Archives of Physical Medicine and Rehabilitation* 74:386–390.

Bleakney, D. and M. Donohoe. 1995. Osteogenesis Imperfecta. In Campbell (ed.), *Physical Therapy for Children*. Philadelphia: W.B. Saunders.

Church, G. and S. Glennen. 1992. *The Handbook of Assistive Technology*. San Diego: Singular Publishing Group.

Cole, D.E.C. 1993. Psychosocial Aspects of Osteogenesis Imperfecta: An Update. *American Journal of Medical Genetics* 45:207–211.

Crockett, J B., and J.M. Kauffman. 1999. *The Least Restrictive Environment: Its Origins and Interpretations for Special Education*. Mahwah, N.J.: Erlbaum Associates.

Engelbert, R. et al. 1999. *Osteogenesis Imperfecta in Childhood: Profiles of Motor Development*. Presentation at the Seventh International Conference on Osteogenesis Imperfecta. Montreal, Canada. 29 August to 1 September.

Gerber, L. 1999. *Rehabilitation of Children and Infants with Osteogenesis Imperfecta.* Presentation at the Seventh International Conference on Osteogenesis Imperfecta. Montreal, Canada. 29 August to 1 September.

Hammond, M. 2000. Tech Around the House. *Exceptional Parent* 30:48–50.

Kranowitz, C.S. 1998. *The Out-of-Sync Child.* New York: Berkley.

Marcus, S.J., H. Cintas, J. Marini, and L. Gerber. 1999. *Temperament in Relation to Gross Motor Function in Children with Osteogenesis Imperfecta.* Presentation at the Seventh International Conference on Osteogenesis Imperfecta. Montreal, Canada. 29 August to 1 September.

Murin, L. and P. Haviland. 1998. *The Early Intervention Training Project Manual: A Workbook for Service Providers of Families with Children Birth to Three.* Albertson, N.Y.: National Center for Disability Services.

New York Department of Education. 1997. *Adaptive Physical Education: Regulations, Recommendations and Resources.* Albany: University of the State of New York.

Office of Vocational and Educational Services for Individuals with Disabilities. 2000. *The Regulations of the Commissioner of Education: Parts 200 and 201 Relating to the Education of Students with Disabilities.* Albany: University of the State of New York.

Osteogenesis Imperfecta Foundation. 1998. *Going Places: A Day in the Life of a Teenager with OI* (video and discussion guide). Gaithersburg, Md.: Author.

Osteogenesis Imperfecta Foundation. 1998. *Plan for Success: An Educator's Guide to Students with OI* (video and brochure). Gaithersburg, Md.: Author.

Sillence, D. 1999. *Management of Osteogenesis Imperfecta in Adolescents and Adults.* Presentation at the Seventh International Conference on Osteogenesis Imperfecta. Montreal, Canada. 29 August to 1 September.

Silverman, L.K. 1992. *How Can Parents Support Gifted Children?* ERIC Digest #E515. Reston, Va.: The ERIC Clearinghouse on Disabilities and Gifted Education.

Solano, T., and S. Aller. 2000. Tech for Tots: Assistive Technology for Infants and Young Children. *Exceptional Parent* 30:44–47.

Vernick, D. 1996. Hearing Loss. In Wacaster, P. (ed.) *Managing Osteogenesis Imperfecta: A Medical Manual.* Gaithersburg, Md.: Osteogenesis Imperfecta Foundation.

Widmann, R., F.J. Laplaza et al. 1999. *Quality of Life in Osteogenesis Imperfecta: A Preliminary Report.* Presentation at the Seventh International Conference on Osteogenesis Imperfecta. Montreal, Canada. 29 August to 1 September.

Willard-Holt, C. 1999. *Dual Exceptionalities.* ERIC Digest #E574. Reston, Va.: The ERIC Clearinghouse on Disabilities and Gifted Education.

Resources

Accessibility:
>   **The Access Board**
>   1331 F St. NW
>   Suite 1000
>   Washington, DC 20004
>   Phone: (800) 872-2253 or (202) 272-5434
>   TTY: (800) 993-2822 or (202) 272-5449
>   E-mail: info@access-board.gov
>   Internet: www.access-board.gov

Assistive Technology:
>   **ABLEDATA**
>   8401 Colesville Rd.
>   Suite 200
>   Silver Spring, MD 20910

Phone: (800) 227-0216
Internet: www.abledata.com

National Office Technology Access Center
2175 E. Francisco Blvd.
Suite L
San Rafael, CA 94901
Phone: (415) 455-4575
E-mail: ATAinfo@ATAccess.org
Internet:: www.ATAccess.org

RESNA Technical Assistance Project
1700 N. Moore St.
Suite 1540
Arlington, VA 22209-1903
Phone: (703) 524-6686
TTY: (703) 524-6639
E-mail: resnaTA@resna.org
Internet: www.resna.org/taproject

Disabilities:
Americans with Disabilities Act/
National Council on Disability
1331 F St. NW
Suite 1050
Washington, DC 20004-1107
Phone: (202) 272-2004
TTY: (202) 272-2074
E-mail: mquigley@ncd.gov
Internet: www.ncd.gov

National Information Center for Children and Youth with
Disabilities
P.O. Box 1492
Washington, DC 20013-1494
Phone: (800) 695-0285
E-mail: nichcy@aed.org
Internet: www.nichcy.org

Early Intervention/Preschool Special Education:
National Early Childhood Technical Assistance Center (NECTAS)
Frank Porter Graham Child Development Center
University of North Carolina at Chapel Hill
137 E. Franklin St.
Suite 500
Chapel Hill, NC 27514-3628
Phone: (919) 962-2001
TDD: (877) 574-3195
E-mail: nectas@unc.edu
Internet: www.nectas.unc.edu

Education:
Council for Exceptional Children/
ERIC Clearinghouse on Disabilities and Gifted Children
1110 N. Glebe Rd.
Suite 300
Arlington, VA 22201-5704
Phone: (888) CEC-SPED or (703) 620-3660
TTY: (703) 264-9446
E-mail: service@cec.sped.org
Internet: www.cec.sped.org

Office of Special Education and Rehabilitation Services
U.S. Department of Education
330 C St. SW
Switzer Bldg, Room 3132
Washington, D.C. 20202-2524
Phone: (202) 205-8241
Internet: www.ed.gov/offices/osers

Osteogenesis Imperfecta Foundation
804 West Diamond Ave.
Suite 210
Gaithersburg, MD 20878
Phone: (800) 981-2663 or (301) 947-0083
Internet: www.oif.org

State Parent Training and Information Centers: Each state has a Parent Training and Information Center (PTI) for parents of infants, toddlers, children, and youths with disabilities, and professionals who work with them. To reach the PTI in your state, contact the Technical Assistance Alliance for Parent Centers (The Alliance) or one of four regional centers.

Alliance National Coordinating Office
PACER Center
8161 Normandale Blvd.
Minneapolis, MN 55437-1044
Phone: (888) 248-0822 or (952) 838-9000
TTY: (952) 838-0190
E-mail: alliance@taalliance.org
Internet: www.taalliance.org

Northeast Regional Center
Parent Information Center
P.O. Box 2405
Concord, NH 03302-2405.
Phone: (603) 224-7005
E-mail: picnh@aol.com
Serves CT, DE, DC, ME, MD, MA, NH, NJ, NY, PA, RI, VT, Puerto Rico, and the U.S. Virgin Islands.

Midwest Regional Center
Ohio Coalition for the Education of Children with Disabilities
Bank One Building
165 West Center St.
Suite 302
Marion, OH 43302-2741.
Phone and TDD: (740) 382-5452.
E-mail: ocecd@gte.net.
Serves IL, IA, IN, KS, KY, MI, MN, MO, NE, ND, OH, SD, WI.

South Regional Center
Partners Resource Network, Inc.

1090 Longfellow Dr.
Suite B
Beaumont, TX 77706-4819.
Phone: (409) 898-4684.
E-mail: path@partnerstx.org
Serves AL, AR, FL, GA, LA, MS, NC, OK, SC, TN, TX, VA, WV.

West Regional Center
Matrix Parent Network and Resource Center
94 Galli Dr.
Suite C
Novato, CA 94949
Phone: (415) 884-3535
E-mail: matrix@matrixparents.org
Serves AK, AZ, CA, HI, ID, MT, NV, NM, OR, UT, WA, WY, Department of Defense Dependent Schools, and the Pacific Jurisdiction.

Home Schooling:
Home Education Magazine
P.O. Box 1083
Tonasket, WA 98855-1083
Phone: (800) 236-3278
E-mail: HEM@home-ed-magazine.com
Internet: www.home-ed-magazine.com

Home School Legal Defense Association
P.O. Box 3000
Purcellville, VA 20134
Phone: (540) 338-5600
Internet: www.hslda.org

National Home Education Network
P.O. Box 41067
Long Beach, CA 90853
E-mail: info@nhen.org
Internet: www.nhen.org

Sports Organizations and Foundations:
Casa Colina Adaptive Sports and Outdoor Adventures
2850 N. Garey Ave.
P.O. Box 6001
Pomona, CA 91769-6001
Phone: (909) 596-7733
E-mail: rehab@casacolina.org
Internet: www.casacolina.org

Disabled Sports USA
451 Hungerford Dr.
Suite 100
Rockville, MD 20850
Phone: (301) 217-0960
TDD: (301) 217-0963
E-mail: information@dsusa.org
Internet: www.dsusa.org
National Wheelchair Basketball Association
Internet: www.nwba.org

United States Golf Association Resource Center for Individuals with Disabilities
Mark Frace, Project Director
1631 Mesa Ave.
Suite D
Colorado Springs, CO 80906
Phone: (719) 471-4810 ext. 18
E-mail: mfrace@usga.org

United States Tennis Association
70 W. Red Oak Lane
White Plains, NY 10604
Phone: (914) 696-7000
Internet: www.usta.com

Wheelchair Track and Field-USA
2351 Parkwood Rd.

Snelville, GA 30039
Phone: (770) 972-0763

Accessible Playgrounds:
Boundless Playgrounds Hasbro National Resource Center
968 Farmington Ave.
West Hartford, CT 06107
Phone: (877) 268-6353
Internet: www.boundlessplaygrounds.org

Acknowledgments

The authors wish to give special thanks to the professional staff of the Henry Viscardi School in Albertson, N.Y. This multidisciplinary team is truly expert in adaptation and modification of the learning environment for students with physical disabilities. The team includes Joan Adickman, Dawn Baratta, Ellen Bergman, Marcia Burwell, Mary Anne Cicchillo, Andrea Ebert, Lillian Gabriel, Janet Gambinsky, Susan Giles, Suzanne Huber, Joy Krebs, Patrice McCarthy-Kuntzler, Richard Kuntzler, Jeanette Marinese, Catherine McGrath, Gail Nolan, Jeanne Obergh, Maggie Pipia, Ann Sande, and Patricia Ziev. Special thanks also go to the students and parents who shared their personal experiences with us.

Sample School Information Form

Elizabeth (Beth) Simmonds
(Home Address Here)

Parents: Sid and Barbie Simmonds
H) xxx-xxx-xxxx
W) xxx-xxx-xxxx (Barbie)
W) xxx-xxx-xxxx (Sid)

Medical Condition: Osteogenesis imperfecta (OI), Type I, mild, scoliosis

Background: OI is a genetic disorder whose primary feature is brittle bones. It occurs due to poor or insufficient formation of collagen. Collagen provides elasticity in the skin and bones, so when it is deficient, the bones do not have the support they need to absorb normal shock or trauma. There is a wide variation in both the severity and symptoms of OI. Some of the features that affect Beth are brittle bones, blue sclera, loose joints, hearing loss (mild), bruises easily, weak ligaments.

Practical Matters: The main area of concern is that Beth's bones fracture easier than most others. She has had 12+ fractures, mostly in her right leg and feet. Her fractures tend to result from a twisting motion of the bone. Turned ankles have been a common cause (this is why she usually wears high tops). She also wears a shoe orthotic and lift to correct her leg alignment as a result of prior fractures.

Our goal is to prevent situations where there is an increased risk of a fracture occurring. We know that we cannot prevent every fracture and do not expect this from her teachers and caregivers either.

We cannot envision every situation that Beth may encounter and indicate whether it is OK or not for her to participate. We believe it is important for her to always try new things and *not to be limited because of the possibility of a fracture.* Some activities may have too great a risk for her, such as roller skating and contact sports. Please let us know if you have any questions about planned activities.

Hearing Loss: Beth has a mild to moderate hearing loss in her left ear. This can be compensated for by seating her in front of a group and close to the speaker. When trying to get her attention in a noisy situation (cafeteria, playground) she may need a tap on the shoulder or a louder call. She wears a hearing aid, which she may remove for PE and lunch, and store in her case.

Back Brace: Beth was diagnosed with scoliosis and has been fitted with a back brace (8/99). She needs to wear it 16–18 hours a day. The time off can be throughout the day at her discretion. It should be removed for PE, any other strenuous activities, or when it is very hot. It is at the discretion of the teacher as to the best timing for taking it off and on to minimize her absence during any instructional time.

11

The Parent's Question: How?

Helping Children with OI Reach Their Full Potential

Kay Harris Kriegsman, Ph.D.

Key Points in This Chapter

- In healthy families, everyone's needs are recognized and addressed. Although the needs of a child with OI can sometimes dominate the family, it is vital that parents' and siblings' emotional needs are also met.

- Many parents benefit from addressing unresolved emotional issues from their own childhoods, as well as their feelings about having a child with a disability. Some parents consult a counselor or clergyperson for help in sorting out their emotional "baggage."

- The middle school years are full of change and stress for all children, including those with OI.

- Throughout children's growing-up years, and especially in the middle school years, there are four key areas of development that help children to reach their full potential: responsibility, socialization, experience, and risk.

- Parents of children with OI may find it especially hard to allow their children to take risks, but risk taking is an important part of growing into a competent adult.

Author's note: *This chapter is dedicated to my parents who, in hindsight, I now understand had the foresight to provide the responsibilities, experiences, social opportunities, and risk taking that allowed for me (who had polio at age seven) and my brothers and sisters to develop our full potential. They set no specific goals for us, only those we set for ourselves, which they encouraged us to meet. This chapter is based on that experience, along with my roles as wife, mother, grandmother, graduate student, psychologist, author, and facilitator for groups of parents of children, from toddlers to young adults, with physical disabilities.*

I hope that this chapter gives parents some notion of what lies ahead, and allows for the insights necessary to help prepare their child's journey through the middle school years into young adulthood.

My daughter, mother of an adventurous two-year-old, read this text recently and reported feeling "overwhelmed" by the enormity of the task of parenting. And, she added, her child doesn't have a disability. Let's address this issue so that those reading this chapter do not feel that this is "mission impossible." Because this is a condensed, all-in-one chapter, it is jam-packed. Please read it in small bites; it will be better digested.

My personal goal in writing this chapter is to help parents rise above the nitty-gritty to see the broader picture by encouraging parents to control what they can, and realize that they can't do it all. In so doing, parents will feel less at the mercy of random events.

Raising a child is a challenge. Raising a child with osteogenesis imperfecta (OI) is an added challenge. Now add the wide range of physical, sexual, and mental maturation going on in the middle school years and parents have their hands full! "How," asks the parent, "can I deal with all of these challenges and dare to hope that my child will reach adulthood, independent and feeling good about who he is and what he can do to contribute to the world?"

This chapter will look at the issues parents need to grapple with, especially during the middle school years, to prepare themselves and their children, both with and without OI, for the future. We will discuss the needs of parents, children, and siblings, and how they can be met to nurture healthy families.

Step 1: Taking Care of Mom and Dad

Parents of all children need energy, enthusiasm, and creativity to help their children traverse the slippery slopes of growing up. With parental support and guidance, children can reach adulthood feeling optimistic, competent, and eager to meet the challenges of maturity.

Add the OI factor. The amount of energy, enthusiasm, and creativity required is quadrupled. For not only do parents have the usual concerns about normal physical, social, spiritual, and psychological development, they have the added issues arising out of how OI affects the life of their child and family. OI's role—both positive and negative—in the family's present and future life cannot be dismissed. It is a reality. But only part of the reality.

Parental preparation for the long haul—that is, the child's growing-up years—is essential. To allow a child to develop as a healthy, whole person, the OI factor will need to blend in as but one of a number of factors that contribute to who he is. So, if parents feel that OI is the dominant factor in their child's or family's life, and are overwhelmed, it is time to take a step back to deal with their feelings. These feelings may come from two sources: unresolved, pre-child concerns; or from the birth of a child with a disability.

Unresolved Issues

If parents have old issues dating back to their childhoods or to problems with their own parents, it's time to confront, deal with, and get rid of that old baggage. It drains them of vitality and the ability to deal with their present life. For instance, parents may find themselves holding internal dialogues with their folks over old issues, leading to tension and anger, or they may feel physical stress and tension when family events, such as birthdays, weddings, or anniversaries arise. Parents need to examine their feelings and the reasons behind them, so they can confront them. Parents can find a helping professional they feel comfortable with to sort through this old problem. It's time for resolution.

Parental Feelings About Having a Child with a Disability

Some parents have not had the chance to deal with the emotional baggage that may arise when they have a child with a disability— guilt, anger, depression, frustration, or anxiety. These feelings may be overwhelming, and may resurface when parents are dealing with a new fracture or surgery. Parents may ask, "Why did this have to happen to my child?" These feelings are quite normal...but they certainly don't feel "normal"!

What do parents do with these uncomfortable feelings? Some parents are able to deal with them through prayer, introspection, reading, or observing how others handle this experience.

But many parents need to talk, to "get it out," to vent feelings. Sometimes family members or friends are able to be sounding boards, to hear the parent's emotions. However, often these rela-

tives also have unresolved feelings about what has happened and cannot be unbiased in their hearing and responding. When this happens, parents might turn to other parents of children with OI, or perhaps a clergyperson. But often parents would like to work with someone who is far removed from their situation, such as a psychologist, rehabilitation counselor, or social worker. This allows parents freedom to express thoughts that are hard to acknowledge to people close to them.

The important thing for parents to remember is that they are not bad people for having these feelings. They are just feelings, not actions. And they will fade in time as parents begin to focus on all of the wonderful attributes and ordinary "orneriness" their child possesses.

Early in life, parents are the most important people in their child's world. As a child grows, parents will still be important but less central. That is as it should be for normal development. Yet even as a child matures, the parent's role is still pivotal and affects a child's self-concept. The middle school years are especially important as children balance one foot in the children's playroom and one in the adolescent rec room.

Sometimes parents' unresolved issues and attitudes limit or get in the way of this normal development and limit the child's potential. If, on the other hand, parents resolve the issues that clutter their view, they will be able to distinguish the normal kid issues, and those that disability adds.

Tip for parents: A quick test to determine how you see your child (and to take your emotional temperature) is to ask yourself, "When I meet someone new, how do I describe my child—as Billy, who has OI and uses a wheelchair, or as Billy, who is into the latest rock band music and an ardent Yankees fan?" If the answer is the first description, give serious consideration to getting some help to get a new perspective, to free yourself and your child from such a limited view.

As these issues are resolved, parents will feel a new level of energy, and an openness to explore creative ways to deal with all the issues of a family plus the added dimension of OI. They will experience HOPE, something with which parents want to infuse all their children. To use an old bromide, they will be able to see the forest, not just the trees. They have taken the first crucial step to become a "grown-up" parent, thus allowing their children to be children.

People often assume that a parent with OI will be able to better understand what a child with the same disability has to confront. In many cases, it is true that having had a disability, the parent will be able to guide the child with keen awareness and insight. This does not, however, hold true in every situation. Parents with disabilities come with their own pre-child parenting "baggage," and have the same hopes and aspirations for their children that other parents have. Thus, their feelings about having a child with a disability may be similar to the feelings of parents without disabilities, and they will have to deal with them accordingly.

What about families where more than one child has OI? One might assume that this family will be better able to parent the second child because of their previous experience. That, however, will depend on how parents have resolved their feelings about the birth of the first child with OI, and also on the family's resilience. The "bounce back" factor—the ability to creatively and optimistically solve problems—will ensure a healthy family.

The Middle School Child

According to Dr. Beverly Celotta, a psychologist in private practice in Darnestown, Md., there is a wide range of physical, emotional, and sexual maturation during the middle school years. Some boys and girls are well along in their physical development while others have not begun. Some are worldly wise while others are still innocent. Generally this age group is conflicted about how they wish to be treated, as dependent or independent, child or adult.

There is some confusion over how to understand the developing body and the mood swings that accompany it. We're not quite certain of all the factors that go into the drop off of self-esteem during this time. Boys may measure their imperfections against others' "perfections," comparing self to others and coming up short. About 70 percent of middle school girls have low self-esteem, arising out of society's expectations of "beauty" as seen in teen magazines. Just as boys do, girls also measure their imperfections against others and feel lacking.

Middle school students are continuing a trend beginning around the fifth grade to show interest in the opposite sex and relationships. There is some fumbling as they learn the right words to say and how to indicate interest in one another. Many times this is done via friends: "Ask Jamie if he likes me." Thus friends become facilitators for the establishment of relationships.

At the same time, rebellion against parents begins to foment while allegiance to the codes of the peer group becomes strong. There may be pressure to try out drinking, smoking, or drugs. Early sex exploration may also begin.

Add to this mix the fact that adolescents are thinking more abstractly and are less tolerant of hypocrisy. The switch to middle school complicates all of these changes at a time when kids really need contained, small communities to address their individual needs. They are thrown into a situation where they have different teachers, different classrooms, and different students for each subject.

Dr. Celotta indicates that there are added issues when the middle school student has a physical disability. While the child needs to be working on a separate identity, it may be difficult for the child to figure out the difference between herself and others because she has less opportunity for differentiation, less time to distinguish self from parents. This is the result of less opportunity to be away from home and parents, doing what middle school students like to do, such as cruising the mall or going to slumber parties. The normal developmental task for this age group is to become part of a peer group, learning its norms

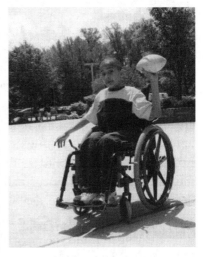

and receiving its support. If a child is not part of this process, he may feel isolated or ostracized, not doing what others his age are engaged in.

Challenging authority is another transitional hallmark for adolescence. Sometimes kids with disabilities have trouble challenging authority because they rely on authority figures for support and basic needs. Danny may feel reluctant to voice criticism of Mom's ideas and then ask her to help him reach the milk on the top shelf of the refrigerator.

The psychological concern here is that fusion with family, exclusion from peer groups, and inability to express true feelings, thus suppressing them, can lead to depression— a common part of the roller coaster emotional ride of adolescents. Another factor to consider is that normal development is like walking a stepping stone path, with each stone aligned so that we step one to the next. When we confuse the pattern, for instance, not learning the norms and expectations of our age group through peer groups, it will make future transitions more difficult. We may need to come back to repeat that step when we are older and others have long been through it. Thus we have little support as we make that attempt.

With this as background, what can we do to enable kids to develop the resilience, sense of competency, and belief in self they need to get through the present, and reach early adulthood ready for its challenges?

Preparing Kids to Figure Out "How?"

Over the past two decades, I have worked with many parents of kids with physical disabilities. I have been privileged to hear and to share the emotional pains and triumphs, the exhaustion and elation, the breaking free of conventional conceptions of disability, the creativity and innovations that have released children—and their parents!—from constricting expectations. These parents have what I call "vision"—the ability to find space and time to stand back, to see the big picture (Kriegsman 1999). They plan for the future, determining how best to deal with the present to reach their goals. They articulate problems and move toward solutions.

Bearing in mind the normal issues of preadolescence that Dr. Celotta elucidates, how can parents help their children along the way to adulthood? In my view, there are four areas of development that are crucial for all children to grow to be competent adults. Each requires parents to be creative and willing to adventure into new realms of "doing." (**Tip for parents**: As you consider what follows, RELAX! You probably have put much of this into practice already without verbalizing it.) In no order of importance, the four crucial areas of development are

1. responsibility,
2. experience,
3. socialization, and
4. risk evaluation.

Responsibility

For children born in centuries past, there was no question that they would bear a portion of the load necessary to maintain the family. They held steady the plow, or churned the butter, or helped preserve food for the winter. These children knew that their labor was necessary and contributed to their family's well-being. Their chores ingrained in them the idea that they were competent to contribute in some way to the family's good.

Learning to accept responsibility is one of the ways in which children grow. However, this lesson is often denied children with disabilities because caring, well-intentioned parents, grandparents, teachers, or youth leaders feel this child carries too much of a load already. For instance, it's so easy for an older brother to set the table; younger sister using the wheelchair needs more time, or has to have chairs moved back from the table so that she can maneuver close enough to set it. Thus, kids with a disability may be excused from activities or assignments given classmates and siblings.

There is a tricky caveat here for kids with OI. Independence and dependence are roles that come and go in their lives. For instance, normal responsibilities may take a hiatus when Joey has another break and is laid up for awhile. But the length of that respite needs continual evaluation so that when Joey is physically able, he resumes his old jobs. In fact, parents might think of some jobs for Joey while he is recuperating, such as doing some computer work for them or answering the phone and recording messages.

Jackie was the youngest of five children. She was pampered by the rest of her family, who catered to her smallest whim. At school she was treated as "special" by the teacher and her classmates' parents due to her "cuteness" as a girl with OI in a wheelchair. She was often exempted from classroom assignments and wasn't required to complete projects when she had medical appointments; other students were not exempt when they were sick. Her classmates resented Jackie's special status and didn't want to invite her to their parties. After Jackie was excluded from several celebrations, her mother called a couple of the other mothers to ask what the problem was. They were honest with her and told her of their childrens' perceptions. Working through the school counselor, Jackie's parents and her teacher began to work on more fully integrating Jackie into the fabric of the classroom, which included bearing the same responsibilities, adapted to her abilities, that the rest of the pupils had.

Tip for parents: Words are powerful. Jackie's designation as "special" elevated her to a level different from her classmates. It is essential that kids with OI be seen on a par with, not a notch above or below, their classmates. To illustrate, consider this: Do you tell jokes or the latest gossip to a saint (notch above) or a very young child (notch below)? My guess is the answer is no. The perception of Jackie as a notch above her peers prevented her from being just one of the kids. Within Jackie's family she also had a special status. Older siblings of children with physical disabilities sometimes resent the time they are required to help with the younger child, or the amount of time parents spend with the disabled sibling. They may also feel angry that the younger child is not asked to help out. These older siblings are often right about the abilities of their younger brother or sister. There are many ways in which a child can contribute to family life, such as loading the dishwasher, setting the table, answering the telephone and taking messages, or keeping a family calendar on the computer. So if you find yourself using the word "special" for all your children, go ahead. But if you apply it only to your child with OI, you need to do some redescribing.

There is one area for which no child can be responsible, yet it is sometimes assigned to the child with a disability. That role is the "cheerer up" of the family, the child designated to keep the sun shining for the rest of the family even when storm clouds hang overhead. This role is destined for failure; no person can be responsible for another's happiness or emotional stability. That is something each of us has to do for ourselves.

Experience

The way we come to know about life—and about ourselves and others—is through experience. We come to know what winter is all about by feeling the cold, tasting snowflakes, slipping on ice, sledding. We come to know about the forest by hiking its trails, stumbling over gnarled roots, feeling the coolness of a dense treed world, sighting a deer in a clearing. We come to know about wind by feeling it in our hair, standing against a vigorous gust, watching it carry dandelion seeds on its streams.

Most children have had these experiences; however, many children with OI have not. They often have to live life vicariously through books, TV, movies, and the tales of their siblings or parents. Yet, they can have similar experiences with some creative planning.

Madison's family had a Sunday afternoon ritual—an afternoon drive in the country. If they came to a roadside fruit stand, Madison's two brothers would pile out of the van with their folks to inspect the

Some of the best advice we were given for how to approach parenting a child with mild OI came from the geneticist who confirmed the diagnosis when Beth was a baby. He had consulted with many families dealing with OI over the years and told us, "There are worse things in life than a broken bone." Many of the families he encountered were protective of the child with OI to the extent that they never let the child participate because "you might break something." He felt that the regular exclusion of the child in this way created longer-lasting problems for the child than spending four weeks in a cast. We have tried to remember this over the years when making the tough decisions about when to say yes and when to say no.

Barbie Simmonds, mother of Beth, 12 years old

produce while Madison waited. Madison wanted to get out of the car with the family but she had overheard her folks complaining about the "hassle" of unloading her wheelchair, putting her in it, and then traversing the bumpy, stony parking lots. She felt she had no right get out if it were such a problem. One day she felt the tears burning behind her eyes when her family climbed back into the car with their berries and beans. Her father asked what the problem was; she broke into sobs, telling about how she felt left behind and excluded from the family. Beginning the following Sunday, everyone pitched in to make sure that Madison was part of the experience.

As much as possible, kids with OI need to do the things that other kids do routinely. For instance, most kids know the sensation of riding a bike. Seth did not; he had OI. One day his dad put Seth on the seat of his bike and walked with him to let him know the sensation of riding a bike. The other boys in the neighborhood were "into" their bikes and talked of them incessantly. Seth could better understand what the sensations were when riding a bike. If possible, parents might consider purchasing front-end bikes that attach to wheelchairs for their children. There are also three-wheeled bikes that can be powered by the operator's arms or legs.

Socialization

Recently I was talking with my friend, Ben, who is 11, of his worries about middle school. He said what he and his friends worried most about was fitting in, that they not be considered "dorky," or stand out. What did he recommend? He said wearing clothes like everyone else is the first step. Making sure that your eyeglasses are "cool" and that your haircut is "in" were also vital. Socialization, then, at the middle school level begins with the packaging. It seems to be the signal that "I'm safe to talk with."

Socializing is all about building bridges, breaking through the barriers, and establishing common bonds. So, if Ben's assessment carries over to other situations (and I think it does), then the first hurdle is the message that, "I'm okay on the exterior so I'll probably be okay within, too." Especially for kids with physical differences and appliances, the common threads of clothing, hairstyle, glasses, or lunchbag (or none) are vital. Extend that to their wheelchairs (e.g., neon colors, racing style) to make them even more inviting.

Parents can teach their child to begin building relationships by initiating conversations. Because parents are models for their child, they should share how they begin introductions. Parents can even share their own qualms and hesitancy with their child so that she realizes that many people share this anxiety. For shyer children especially, it helps to have some opening lines in the bag to pull out when necessary. Parents may want to rehearse some conversation openers, building on their child's interests. For instance, if a child is a baseball fan, he might say something like "What did you think about that game last night?" to establish a common bond.

When parents are working with children on social give-and-take in conversations, a good metaphor to use is that of the spotlight. Sometimes you are in the spotlight, when you are speaking and telling of your recent trip, and sometimes your friend is, when he is upset about losing his baseball game. It is about giving and receiving. Many children with disabilities do very well in the spotlight and some prefer the shadow. They all need the ability to work in either.

Remember Jackie? She was accustomed to the spotlight; she needed to learn the skill of standing back, listening, and supporting. Madison, on the other hand, probably needed help in accepting the limelight once in a while. While we can be designated extroverts or introverts in personality patterns, we can also learn to be outgoing or more quiet in different situations.

The most natural way for a child to become socialized is to be

All my life I have had to weigh almost everything I do against the risks involved. In many cases, the decision was easy, while in others it required a great deal of consideration. For example, I had to weigh risks a lot when deciding which school to go to and what activities to participate in. At first, I attended special schools designed for disabled children. In sixth to eighth grade, the school was 16 miles from home so I had to ride the bus. Riding the bus for more than one hour each way proved to be the most difficult part of those three years. Not only were the longer days difficult, but the buses rode very rough, and made me tired and caused back pain. It was only after those three years that we ever considered my going to a regular school. I was convinced that the risks of being hurt by being surrounded by "normal" children would be less painful than riding the bus. The neighborhood school was nearby and my friends went there, so I knew they would look out for me.

Participating in school activities during high school proved to be some of the best times I have ever had. These activities included starting a chess club, participating in the drama club, and working on the school yearbook. The most memorable activity by far was going on a senior trip to Washington, D.C. One of the teachers, Mr. Dilks, asked me if I would like to go with nine other classmates to learn how our federal government operates. My first response was, "Every picture of Washington, D.C., I have seen has monuments with steps. How will I get around?" Mr. Dilks said not to worry, he would take care of it. To my surprise, when I asked my parents if I could go, they said if I could find someone to take care of me, they would pay for it. I arranged with the school to provide my best friend, Terry, with a partial scholarship to go in return for taking care of me. I was very nervous when the day arrived, because it was the first time I had been on a trip without a family member along, and it was the first time I had flown on a commercial plane, except when our family moved from Texas to St. Louis when I was just a few months old. The only problem I had on the trip was being sick the first evening from all the excitement. I did not miss out on any of the activities, including being carried to the top of the Lincoln Memorial. I did not want to be carried up all the steps, but my buddies insisted they were not going to let me miss out on anything. At the time, I wondered if they were friends or daredevils.

Peter Dohm, adult with OI

After attending special schools for eight years, Pete came to me and said, "I want to go to regular school." I quickly said, "Are you aware of the teasing, stares, and questions other children will come to you with?" He said, "It won't bother me." I said, "Okay, but you must be prepared to talk to the principal." That he did. From then on, he was mainstreamed into regular school. I have always let Pete make decisions for himself. When he wanted to go away to college, that was the hardest thing I ever did. That was the first time I had to leave him in someone else's care. Since then, he has lived away from home. Now he has his own car and home.

Clara Dohm, mother of Peter Dohm

exposed to situations that require give-and-take, and require socially accepted behavior. There is no better way to learn this behavior, and also peer norms, than by joining youth groups, an opportunity many kids with disabilities don't experience. Parents need to ensure that all of their children have these learning and group fun experiences. Groups like 4-H, the Scouts, and youth religious groups welcome all kids. These socializing experiences with peers are particularly useful for children with disabilities who have spent lots of time in medical settings, where they develop a pseudo-adult manner of communication. They need to develop the social skills appropriate to their age level before moving on to a higher level of communication.

Middle schools typically have dances. Kids using wheelchairs need to be encouraged to attend; after all, most of the action is the chatting and cutting up around the edges of the dance floor at this age. And, who knows, a child might become the hit of the dance by dancing in his chair. Parents might find a "cool" young adult who is a good wheelchair dancer to teach their child some good moves!

As the mother of two children with OI Type I, I become somewhat overprotective at times. Because I also have OI, I had to think about how I was brought up. My son, who is now 17, is a typical teenaged adventurous boy. A few years ago, he was having a hard time because I would always tell him to please be careful. He is a skateboarder, bike jumper, and snowboarder. He had gotten hurt one day and turned around and told me it was my fault that he got the bone disease. I felt absolutely terrible about what he said. I told him he could do whatever he thought was safe to do, and life is a challenge. I try now to let him make his own decisions about what he can do. He still is adventurous and daring.

Maria Semprini-DeMartino, mother of Christopher, 17 years old, and Nicole, 13 years old

Attending day or sleep-away camps provides wonderful opportunities for learning how to interact with peers in a more natural environment. Children learn how to be independent, interdependent, and dependent when it is necessary. Whether a child attends a camp with other kids with physical disabilities, or a "regular" camp not based on disability depends on the child's and parents' wishes and abilities.

Tip for parents: Humor is a pathway to friendships. The ability to see the ironic or funny side of a situation is a wonderful gift that draws people in. If your child has that ability, help him to appreciate and develop it in his own characteristic way. Warning lights should flash, however, when you hear him use humor to ridicule and deprecate others.

Risk

The most problematic area for parents of children with OI to deal with is that of risk taking. I have been presenting workshops for parents for many years. When I have asked parents to choose which of these four areas we have been discussing to work on, they have shunned risk. I do understand where these parents are coming from, because for many, the very word "risk" conjures up visions of broken bones, ERs, and recuperating time.

So, let's defuse the term "risk," stepping back to realize that risk comes in many forms. For some, it's bungee jumping or participating in the Iditarod. For others, it's striking up a conversation with the kid at the next desk or trying out sponge painting.

For most people, disabled or not, risk taking has helped us to recognize our limits and also to learn that some things we thought ourselves incapable of, we can do! Risk is a motivator. It helps hone our definition of who we really are. It can also be a boon to our ego when we succeed at a task that we thought we couldn't accomplish. And if we fail, we come to know what our limits are.

Henry was an A student in grade school. When he entered middle school, he was urged to enroll in several honors classes. They sounded interesting but also difficult. Would he be able to maintain his straight A record? He had always been the top student in his class and wanted to continue at that level. His counselor was realistic, saying that Henry might be able to maintain his perfect record, but noting that these were difficult courses and they would require much more work. But, the counselor wondered, was the possibility of a less than perfect record a reason to deprive himself of the chance to try out new courses?

Henry's parents talked with him. They said that as he entered middle school he would be making more decisions, with some input from them. They talked about the risk of failing to continue his perfect grades. But they also talked about the risk of not being able to discover what his abilities were and the fun of the challenging coursework. In the end, Henry decided that he would take two honors classes. He would balance some "safe" courses with some riskier ones.

Henry was dealing with a mental risk. Parents are usually more fearful of the physical risks their children take.

In her final year of middle school, Claudia had finally made it into the "in" crowd of girls. She had worked hard at school, been active in many school activities, and become a leader. She liked this feeling of being one of the crowd. Claudia, although a bit shorter of stature and using crutches, always worked on finding ways to be like the other girls through her hairstyles and clothes.

One Friday night the crowd wanted to go to an amusement park. Claudia's parents were a bit apprehensive and asked her to discriminate between safe rides and those that presented a real possibility of breaking a bone. She assured them that she would be very careful in her choices, if they would just let her go. The evening at the amusement park was going well until someone suggested that the gang go on the bumper car ride. Claudia said she would watch from the sidelines; her friends were very upset that she would not go on the ride with them. They begged her to go, assuring her that it was a safe ride and nothing could happen; after all, no one else had gotten a broken bone that evening. Claudia relented, with some qualms. Halfway through, two boys rammed their car into Claudia's. Her arm, resting against the side of the car, was slammed into the door. She knew at once that she had a new break.

The down side of this experience was the pain and time the arm took to heal. But Claudia also learned from this experience. She learned that she had to listen to her own inner voice and not to the encouragement of others who didn't know the fragility of her bones. She couldn't buckle under to peer pressure. Although a painful lesson, she did learn about her own limits and her own need to evaluate what was safe for her. She had learned the consequences of one type of risk.

These four elements—responsibility, experience, socialization, and risk evaluation—are the bedrock for the development of middle school-age students. Ideally, these are planted in a strong family philosophical or spiritual core. This belief system will provide internal guidance and sustenance to each member of the family, paving the way through good and difficult times.

And What About the Sibs?

Recently, recognition has at long last been given to the needs of brothers and sisters of children with disabilities. For years, the emphasis was on the child with the disability, with some small attention given to the parents and almost none to brothers and sisters. If this were reflected in a photo, it would place the child with the disability up front and center, with parents in back, and beyond, the siblings in a somewhat fuzzy background. We know that this arrangement makes for an unbalanced, out-of-kilter family. A family is composed of the parents and ALL of the children. All of their needs are equally important.

Several years ago, while working with a group of families, each having children of various ages with disabilities, I met a father who was very angry with his college-age son who had no disability. This son had accused the father of babying and pampering his 25-year-old sister, who used a wheelchair, by driving her to and from work every day. The brother insisted that his sister had indeed, on occa-

sion, used mass transit and had reached her destinations successfully. The father said, "What if it rains?"

"Well, Dad, Molly will get wet, just like I do."

"But I have the time so why don't I just do it? It's so much easier
for her to go in the car than on the subway," said Dad, newly retired.

The argument continued, Dad stressing how he could make
life easier for his daughter, while brother was disgusted that his
sister wasn't being given the opportunity to take some risks and
take responsibility for herself. As I listened, it was clear that the
brother was advocating for his sister's growth toward independence,
while Dad wanted to shelter and protect his daughter.

Equality of opportunity and responsibility among brothers
and sisters, whether disability is involved or not, has always been a
contentious issue. But I do find that when disability is involved,
brothers and sisters make pretty accurate assessments of what their
siblings with a disability can really do.

Parents' time and emotional involvement is another issue that
often burbles up in a discussion by nondisabled siblings. They recall times when physical therapy and routine doctor's appointments
kept parents from attending their Little League games or the dress
revue at the county fair. Parents need to balance the needs of all
their children, not overemphasizing the needs of the child with
OI. Overemphasis breeds bitterness and resentment toward the
parents and the child with the disability. How do parents balance?
Perhaps physical therapy and doctor's appointments can be resched-
uled or even scaled back a bit so that everyone's needs can be met.
A good barometer for parents is listening to their "gut reaction."
If they feel uneasy, it usually means some element is out of order.

To balance this equation, one has to note that sometimes the
situation is reversed, and the child with the disability is in the fuzzy,

I think having OI is fine just as long as you have a little freedom. I think when you have
OI you need to have a little independence. I'm very independent. I love going shopping
and doing things with my friends.

Monique Pierson, 13 years old

gray background. Again, one needs to balance her needs along with the rest of the family's members.

The Challenge

Yes, indeed, raising a child is a challenge. Disability adds another dimension. And a dollop of middle school children's developmental needs makes this time in a child's life a wallapalooza!

But this is not an impossible task, this raising of an interdependent, competent, optimistic child who just happens to have OI. First of all, Mom and Dad need to take care of their own unresolved personal issues and feelings about disability so that they are fully free to invest themselves as parents. They will feel free to invest in hope, so that the question will not be "Why?" but instead, "How?". The next task will be to discern between "normal" adolescent issues and those that arise out of disability. Then the building and planning can begin. Parents will have moved from a responding, reacting stance to one of initiating and creating. They will be parents with vision.

Suggestions for When You Discover Your Child Has a Disability

1. Be gentle with yourself. Know that grief and loss reactions are normal; allow yourself time to work through them. These reactions don't mean that you love your child any less or that you are a bad parent. You simply need time to readjust and reorient your expectations. Grant your spouse, family, and close friends the space to reorient as well. And remember that you and those around you will not be experiencing the same reactions at the same time; listen, share, and care.

2. Talk out your feelings with someone you trust—a person who can listen and not dictate how to deal with your emotions. This person might be a relative, friend, minister, priest, or rabbi.

3. If you feel "stuck," find professional help. You might choose to work with a psychologist, social worker, counselor, psychiatrist, or pastoral counselor. Advocacy organizations can sometimes recommend experienced therapists. Friends may also be able to recommend someone. Remember: You are not "sick" if you get such help. You are a problem solver.

4. Get in touch with other parents of kids with disabilities. If possible, contact parents of children who are your child's age for your own understanding and "co-trail blazing." Parents of children older than yours may also be helpful in charting difficult turns of the trail. Caution: Keep a balance in maintaining friends who have children with and without disabilities. Most of the issues kids with disabilities have are shared to varying degrees by all children. It is important to have that perspective to eliminate feelings of "apartness" or "specialness."

5. To chart your progress, keep a log of your reflections and feelings. Review them to note how the passage of time and the intervention of people or events have helped you on your journey. Logs also help by allowing us to pour out our feelings without being judged.

6. Gather information about your child's disability, and about technological and legal advances, so that you become a true partner in medical/educational decisions concerning your child. Remember that no other person has the broad perspective and knowledge of your child that you do.

7. Watch your own sense of balance. Have you been tickled by the absurd recently? Did you see the brilliance of last night's

sunset? When did you last feel your body completely relaxed? Heard a symphony lately?

8. If you find yourself overly concentrated on your child with the disability, it is time to reconsider your parenting. This over-emphasis is not healthy for you, your spouse, your child with OI, or your other children. It is time to step back, to allow all of you some space.

9. Remember that perfection is not required, or even possible, in parenting. "Good enough" will get us through, erase guilt about meeting impossible standards, and will surely free your children to be complete human beings.

10. An added nugget to think about: The usual thrust is to prepare the child with the disability for the nondisabled world. It would be nice once in a while for your child's nondisabled friends to come into his world—to see what a hospital or physical therapy is like, for example—to gain appreciation and understanding.

How Can You Judge When You Have Reoriented Your Thoughts and Feelings About Disability?

Here are some key signals:

*   You see the boy in the suit, not his crutches or wheelchair.

*   The little girl is misbehaving and you feel free to discipline her just as you do her nondisabled brothers and sisters.

*   You call to reschedule the orthopedist's appointment because it conflicts with his piano recital or his sister's Little League game.

*   You go out for the evening with your spouse or accept a date, leaving your child with a babysitter, and do not think of your child for the entire evening.

- You no longer ask "can?" or "should?" but instead ask only "HOW?".

Resources

Kriegsman, Kay Harris. 1999. Families with Vision. *Breakthrough: The Newsletter of the Osteogenesis Imperfecta Foundation* 24:4. July/August.

Kriegsman, Kay Harris, Elinor Zaslow, and Jennifer D'Zmura-Rechsteiner. 1992. *Taking Charge: Teenagers Talk About Life and Physical Disability.* Bethesda, Md.: Woodbine House.

Osteogenesis Imperfecta Foundation
The OI Foundation provides many opportunities for families to give and receive mutual support, including online chat rooms, a mentoring program for preteens and teens with OI, local support groups, peer support sessions at national conferences, and more.
804 West Diamond Ave.
Suite 210
Gaithersburg, MD 20878
Phone: (800) 981-2663 or (301) 947-0083
Internet: www.oif.org

12
Caring for Unaffected Siblings

Rose-Marie Chiasson

Key Points in This Chapter

- Siblings of children with OI have special needs and concerns.

- Siblings may sometimes feel jealous, left out, guilty, angry, sad, or afraid.

- Common concerns include the time that parents must devote to caring for the child with OI, the sibling's guilt over not having OI or over causing a fracture, separation from parents and the child with OI due to hospitalization, and resentment that the child with OI is treated differently than siblings.

- Open communication allows siblings to express their feelings, and parents to respond to their needs. Parents can initiate conversation by asking questions about how the sibling feels about the child with OI.

- Parents can help siblings feel secure by involving them in planning for how the family will deal with fractures, and making special arrangements for siblings' care when parents accompany the child with OI to the hospital.

Families are composed of individuals who are unique in many ways. Each member contributes to the family's complexity and establishes his or her place and role within this unit. Each family member has his or her own level of maturity, set of coping skills, and ways of expressing needs and concerns. Ideally, families establish a compatible lifestyle and become a secure family unit. The extended family must also be included as contributors to the family's functioning.

When a couple has a new baby, their lifestyle changes and they are faced with many new challenges. They must adapt to a very different home situation and at the same time, continue to promote the health, well-being, and development of all family members. The birth of a child with a disability further compounds the challenges faced by parents. Needs and concerns change suddenly; they become amplified and appear to dominate the family. Likewise, the siblings of children born with a disability have special needs and concerns. As the parents tend to the numerous pressing demands of the child with osteogenesis imperfecta (OI), siblings often feel left out and/or rejected. Parents must find creative strategies to deal with the inevitable new challenges and possible negative feelings of siblings. The goal of this chapter is to recognize issues that families face and then suggest solutions that may be adapted to each individual.

Textbooks describe common stages of grieving, and sibling reactions to a new sibling with OI may mirror those stages, such as denial, anger, bargaining, depression, and acceptance. Other difficult issues for siblings are periods of separation from parents or the sibling with OI, jealousy of the attention given to the child with OI, anxiety over the affected sibling's health, guilt over causing a fracture or over not having OI, and feelings of a double standard related to discipline or performing household chores.

When the health of children with OI significantly improves because of specific interdisciplinary treatments, including the experimental approach of bisphosphonate medications, rodding surgery, or physical therapy, or simply by growing older, their profile changes. They become more mobile and have more energy. These changes bring on new issues for families to deal with as the child is still fragile but may have new abilities.

Communication

Siblings, whether older or younger than the affected child, must be included in the process of learning to live with a child with OI. The family environment can be a safe network in which to learn to communicate positive and negative feelings. The initiative for interaction must come from the parents, who must recognize the need for and promote healthy communication. Parents must also educate the siblings on the complexity of OI. These interventions will help normalize sibling reactions to what is happening and help them understand the physical limitations of OI. With communication and disclosure, the sibling is no longer isolated with her thoughts and feelings. She is reassured that it's okay to be angry and/or feel sad. The sibling as a bystander feels alone, afraid, or rejected. These feelings may dissipate, only to reappear at different stages in her life. Coping skills acquired as a young child will be useful when new challenges occur. Parents can promote problem-solving skills and basic communication skills, such as the "I" statement, in which family members are encouraged to talk about their feelings using the "I" pronoun, rather than talking about someone else. For example, a child is encouraged to say, "I feel angry when my brother gets all the attention," instead of saying, "He gets all the attention," or "You never pay attention to me." Parents can help develop

and enhance existing coping skills and reassure all family members that their feelings may be expressed freely and that these expressions will be understood.

Parents can ask the following questions to promote open communication and interaction with siblings. They can adjust the interaction according to the child's age.

- Do you sometimes wonder if you will get OI?
- Would you like to have OI so you could go to the hospital with your parents?
- Do you sometimes wonder if your sibling with OI will grow?
- Do you sometimes wonder if/when your sibling will walk?
- Do you sometimes wonder if your sibling will die?
- Can you tell someone (your teacher, minister, friends, parents) when you feel sad or worried?
- Do your friends have questions or tease you, and do you know how to answer?

Parents can role play to help children come up with answers to common questions or responses to teasing. (See Chapters 14 and 15 for ideas on how to respond to teasing and questions.) Parents can also encourage siblings to tell children who tease them that it hurts their feelings to hear comments about their brother or sister. It is also helpful for siblings to talk to their friends about their brother or sister with OI before those friends come to visit. Parents should expect that the siblings may want to enjoy their friends without the child with OI around; this situation occurs in most families, regardless of disability.

Feelings of compassion, jealousy, bitterness, guilt, embarrassment, and/or shame are common to siblings of a child with a disability. Siblings will benefit from dispelling common myths about people with disabilities, or about how parents deal with difficult times. These discussions must include all members of the family.

Examples of myths to discuss with family members are:

I am 41 years old and the oldest of eight children. The five girls all have OI Type I, and our three brothers are not affected. My sisters and I have a different relationship than our brothers, even though we are a close family. We girls are always in and out of the hospital, casts, surgeries, etc. It is a normal way of life for us. We have been to hell and back many times. Our brothers can't really understand what we have gone through. We are our own support system.

Maria Semprini-DeMartino, adult with OI

- Children in wheelchairs are "dumb."
- Children with a disability can't have a normal life.
- What they have is catching.
- People with OI will never have a boyfriend/girlfriend, never get married, and/or never be parents.
- Real men do not express their feelings or cry.
- Parents must always be strong.

Issues to Consider

The issues identified concerning siblings give rise to many negative feelings. These feelings are then translated into behaviors that affect the family's functioning. Feelings that siblings may harbor include anger, jealousy, confusion, rejection, sadness, fear of the unknown, moodiness, and hostility. These behaviors may be reflected by poor performance at school, lashing out and temper outbursts, bullying, and/or using bad language. It is important for parents to address these feelings and help siblings find appropriate ways of expressing what upsets them. (For examples of interventions, see Meyer, Vadasy, and Fewell 1996.)

The following general suggestions may prove to be helpful to parents:

Our daughter Carmen was born with OI Type III and was one small (4 lb., 8 oz.), broken baby. Carmen's brother Brian was three-and-a-half years old at the time and was thrilled to have a baby sister. We talked to Brian before Carmen was born and let him know that Mommy and baby would stay in the hospital for two days and then we could bring the baby home. After Carmen's birth, Brian asked why we weren't coming home like he expected. It was a hard time for everyone. We explained to Brian that Carmen was very fragile, and she needed to stay in the hospital a little longer.

We tried to have Brian be involved as much as possible with Carmen. He did hold his baby sister a couple of times with a lot of assistance. He loved that, and when he didn't hold her, he would still sit and touch Carmen, sing to her, and give her lots of gentle kisses to her head. We were very thankful many, many times for Brian being a gentle kind of kid.

We don't remember a lot of jealous behavior at the time, but about six months later, Brian's calm, cooperative behavior disappeared for almost a year. Brian became quite defiant and was miserable to his parents most of the time. We are still not sure if his behavior was just a stage, or if that was his way of getting our attention.

Brian always talked and sang to and played with Carmen. He always said he loved Carmen, but a few times he said things like, "I wish Carmen had strong bones so I could wrestle with her," or "I wish Carmen could walk so we could play in the snow and have snowball fights."

We thought and talked lots about whether to have another baby. We were pretty busy dealing with our two children. Could we handle three? What was the chance of having another baby with OI? (We were told it was a 3 to 5 percent chance.) We did decide to have another child, and Ashley was born two-and-a-half years after Carmen. Brian's first question was, "Does the baby have strong bones?" We were all relieved to know Ashley did not have OI.

Carmen always loved babies, and when she saw her baby sister, she was all smiles. She would lie beside Ashley on the bed and just watch her. Brian could hold Ashley whenever he wanted and was a proud big brother.

Brian enjoyed playing differently with Ashley than he did with Carmen. Carmen enjoyed playing with Ashley too, until Ashley was old enough to grab Carmen or take a toy from her. Not only did Carmen have a new fear of her baby sister hurting her, but the stress we felt as parents was high. We had to watch Carmen and Ashley constantly. Some fractures did happen as a result of Ashley pulling a toy away or bumping Carmen. Those were sad times, but we tried not to blame Ashley. We taught Ashley to be extra gentle with Carmen, just as we had taught Brian. When Carmen would fracture because of what a sibling did, it was most important to be understanding and use the incident as a teaching opportunity. We didn't want Brian and Ashley to be afraid to play with Carmen.

Carmen learned so much watching her baby sister, and would try to copy her movements. Ashley has been a great motivator for Carmen. Although we didn't see much jealousy between Carmen and Brian, Carmen and Ashley were a different story. When Ashley was two and Carmen was four, some sibling rivalry began. If we were holding Ashley, Carmen wanted to be held. If we were holding Carmen, Ashley wanted "up"! We spent a lot of time figuring out how to split our attention among all three children.

Carmen is now five, and is very much involved in playing with her siblings, with each of them knowing her limits. Carmen has a power chair, and thus will play hide and seek, or just chase around the house with them. She will laugh with them and encourage them to play if she has a fracture that limits her participation. Carmen always feels included, even though she's not always physically involved. Carmen goes everywhere we go, with friends or family. If she can't participate in an activity, she will watch, visit with us, and laugh with us.

Not all times are so wonderful. We have a noisy home most of the time. Carmen and Ashley fight over toys, and Brian, now nine, enjoys getting his sisters to scream. Most of these behaviors are just typical, we think. The one thing that's different with our kids is that they know they must be gentle physically. Ashley, who can be a "hitter," gets mad at Carmen, winds up to hit her, then stops short. She knows she can't hit Carmen.

We are really glad to have three children in our family. We will always be aware of the attention each of our children need and deserve—families do that whether or not they have a child with a disability. It might be magnified a little more for us because Carmen does need more hands-on attention. Our children are also so accepting of people with disabilities. We think that Brian and Ashley will be better people because of their experiences with their sister Carmen.

Ed and Mary-Lou Sims, parents of Brian, 9 years old, Carmen, 5 years old, and Ashley, 3 years old

- Seek the help and guidance of specialized professionals (social workers, psychologists, child life specialists, nurses, etc.). Some siblings may benefit from seeing a therapist or counselor.

- Explore whether your local hospital or other organization offers special support groups for siblings of children with disabilities. (The OI Foundation provides these groups at national conferences. See the Resources section at the end of this chapter for other organizations.)

- Recognize the frustration that siblings may have concerning financial and social limitations (e.g., holidays, costly special outings, barriers to accessibility, etc.) and that spontaneous outings may not always be possible.

- Explore with older siblings the genetic ramifications of OI through genetic counseling. Although there is usually little genetic risk for unaffected siblings (see Chapter 1), they may need reassurance or help in determining if the family has an unusual genetic profile.

- Discuss with and reassure older siblings of the long-term financial and continuing care plan for the affected child.

- Discuss ways of coping with other parents at an OI support group meeting or while the child is hospitalized.

- Maintain a good sense of humor.

Chores and responsibilities, as well as privileges and discipline, can be decided according to the age and abilities of all family members, including the child with OI. This will help to avoid feelings of jealousy and unfairness, and will prevent the creation of a double standard. Parents may also determine responsibilities for siblings at the time of a fracture, which is a very stressful time. Siblings will feel powerless, out of control, or guilty at this time, and having some responsibilities will help. Perhaps the sibling can get the splinting kit, or prepare toys and a snack for the trip to the hospital, while the parents tend to the child in pain. Families can rehearse a fracture incident just as they would any other crisis (e.g., a fire drill).

Parents can help siblings understand OI treatment by installing a cast or a symbolic IV on a doll. They can also engage in medical play with siblings if appropriate. For example, if a sibling seeks attention by saying he can't walk because his leg hurts, the parent can "treat" him. The sibling can try riding in a wheelchair, or put a cast on a doll or stuffed animal. Medical play toys are very useful as well.

It is also important for parents to create and supervise a safe environment for siblings to play with each other, and to outline a set of rules to prevent injury as much as possible. If a fracture occurs when siblings are playing, it is very important to acknowledge the sibling's feelings and reassure him that everything will be okay. Let the sibling draw on the cast or prepare a surprise for the return home (a drawing, homemade cookies, etc.).

Siblings who have been encouraged to interact with the child with OI will understand the affected child's needs, understand his pain, and be able to help. These responsibilities may be redefined as the siblings get older.

Leaving Siblings at Home

When parents accompany the child with OI to the hospital and leave the siblings at home, the following suggestions may help to diminish stress for the siblings:

- Spend special time with the siblings before leaving and upon returning.

- Prepare a family album, video, or tape to be left with the children at home.

- Obtain a picture of the hospital, hotel, etc. so that the children will know where the parents have gone.

- Leave "love notes" with the caregivers to be given at appropriate times.

- Find something precious (a keepsake) to leave with siblings for comfort.

Having a disabled child does not only affect the child and parents but also the immediate family members, and also grandparents, aunts, uncles, and cousins. My brother Peter was the only disabled child in a family of six, which is not to say the other five were perfect children. We all had the markings of normal, active, growing children, with all the emotional upsets and physical growing pains that accompany growing up. I don't think there is any "normal" child for we each are so unique and different.

Peter was the "baby" and so got a lot of attention, and even more so because of his severe disability. In Pete's defense, I must say the attention was given very willingly. We all had heartfelt gladness each time Pete accomplished a new task as simple as the ability to sit up solo without hurting himself. In our family, we were raised to look at a difficulty and try to resolve it. Necessity was the mother of all inventions that were made around our home for Pete. We never excluded Pete from any outings; it simply was not even a consideration. We just picked up each side of the wheelchair and up the stairs to the baseball stadium Pete went.

We siblings were raised to appreciate our good physical abilities and use them to help others, but never to look down or stare at a disabled person. As we grew, married, and had children of our own, we passed this positive attitude onto our children. Our children all look at Uncle Pete as being just "normally different," just like anyone else.

Marilyn Rapplean, sister of Peter Dohm

I was the oldest sister and my brother, Peter John, born with OI, is the youngest of six children in our family. I remember vividly going to the hospital within hours of his birth and seeing this small fragile baby that wasn't supposed to live. Helping care for him when he came home was not always pleasant, because of the pain we unintentionally inflicted on him. Sometimes we caused breaks just by handling him. I have always felt that I'm truly sorry for what he has had to suffer, but so grateful for the better, more caring people he has made everyone in our family. There were many times when the extra effort was made or the decision easy—"If Pete can't go or can't do it, it is not that important to the rest of us."

Juanita Gruenloh, sister of Peter Dohm

- Siblings may exchange a toy with the child with OI.

- Plan a special time for phone calls.

- Establish a support system (grandparents, relatives, neighbors, etc.) for when siblings are left at home.

- Clarify the rules and parameters with the sitter and the support system to ensure continuity of the everyday routine while parents are away.

- Prepare letters in advance to advise teachers and/or daycare providers that parents will be absent for a period of time due to hospitalization.

It's okay to enroll a sibling as a "partner" and for her to offer suggestions and find solutions. Value the children's ideas and utilize them to enhance their self-worth. Parents tend to protect their children by hiding their own feelings, which only tends to increase  children's fear that something is wrong. In any family unit, siblings react constantly to their surroundings. These reactions are not age-related or dependent on the physical abilities of other siblings. Talking to members of families who do not have an affected child may help families understand normal sibling rivalry. Recognizing how other families function may help parents avoid feelings of guilt, discouragement, or anxiety.

Resources

Association Française de Recherche Génétique. 1998. *L'Impact Familial et Social des Maladies Génétiques Orphelines*. Paris: Les Presses D'Expressions.

Darnell Good, Julia, and Joyce Good Reis. 1985. *A Special Kind of Parenting*. Franklin Park, Ill.: La Leche International.

Glauser, Heidi C. (ed.) 1994. *Living with Osteogenesis Imperfecta: A Guidebook for Families*. Gaithersburg, Md.: Osteogenesis Imperfecta Foundation.

Klein, Stanley D., and Maxwell J. Schleifer (eds.). 1993. *It Isn't Fair!: Siblings of Children with Disabilities*. Westport, Conn.: Bergin and Garvey.

Kriegsman, Kay H., Elinor L. Zaslow, and Jennifer D'Zmura-Rechsteiner. 1992. *Taking Charge: Teenagers Talk About Life and Physical Disabilities*. Bethesda, Md.: Woodbine House.

Meyer, Donald J., Patricia F. Vadasy, and Rebecca R. Fewell. 1996. *Living with a Brother or Sister with Special Needs: A Book for Sibs*. Seattle: University of Washington.

Miller, Nancy B. 1997. *Nobody's Perfect*. Baltimore: Paul H. Brookes.

Osteogenesis Imperfecta Foundation. 1999. *Breakthrough: The Newsletter of the Osteognenesis Imperfecta Foundation* 24(4). (Issue devoted to family and sibling issues.)

Osteogenesis Imperfecta Foundation. 1999. *Psychosocial Needs of the Family*. Gaithersburg, Md.: Author.

Simons, Robin. 1985. *After the Tears*. Denver: Children's Museum of Denver.

Vanzant, Iyanla. 1999. *Don't Give It Away!* New York: Fireside.

Verhaeghe, Pierre. 1999. *L'Ostéogénèse Imparfaite, Maladie des Os de Verre*. France: Edition Frison-Roche.

Sibling Support Project
Phone: (206) 368-4911
Internet: www.chmc.org/departmt/sibsupp
   The Sibling Support Project is a national program based at

the Children's Hospital and Regional Medical Center in Seattle. The project is dedicated to the interests of brothers and sisters of people with disabilities. The project has publications available, including curricula for sibling workshops, children's books, newsletters, and a web site. They conduct workshops for siblings (called Sibshops) in the Seattle area, and will provide technical assistance to those who wish to start a Sibshop in their own area. Two computer listservs—one for young siblings, and one for adult siblings—provide a forum for brothers and sisters to communicate with each other about growing up as the sibling of a person with a disability.

13
Landing in Holland

Healthy Relationships When OI is Part of the Family

Kathy Shine

Key Points in This Chapter

- Some parents grieve the loss of a dream when their child is diagnosed with OI. Bitterness, fatigue, and sadness can sabotage parents' mental health and their family relationships.

- It is vital for parents to nurture their connection with each other by talking regularly, going out on dates, and appreciating what their spouse does to support the family.

- Siblings of children with OI may become resentful of all the attention given to their sibling, or of the rules instituted to protect the sibling from fractures. Siblings need one-on-one time with their parents and reassurance that they are as important as their brother or sister with OI.

- Many parents find it hard to ask for help and become worn out by trying to do it all. Extended family and friends can help lighten the load.

I am often asked to describe the experience of raising a child with a disability—to try to help people who have not shared that unique experience to understand it, to imagine how it would feel. It's like this...

When you're going to have a baby, it's like planning a fabulous vacation trip—to Italy. You buy a bunch of guide books and make your wonderful plans. The Coliseum. The Michelangelo David. The gondolas in Venice. You may learn some handy phrases in Italian. It's all very exciting.

After months of eager anticipation, the day finally arrives. You pack your bags and off you go. Several hours later, the plane lands. The stewardess comes in and says, "Welcome to Holland."

"Holland?!?" you say. "What do you mean Holland?? I signed up for Italy! I'm supposed to be in Italy. All my life I've dreamed of going to Italy."

But there's been a change in the flight plan. They've landed in Holland and there you must stay.

The important thing is that they haven't taken you to a horrible, disgusting, filthy place, full of pestilence, famine, and disease. It's just a different place.

So you must go out and buy new guide books. And you must learn a whole new language. And you will meet a whole new group of people you would never have met.

It's just a different place. It's slower-paced than Italy, less flashy than Italy. But after you've been there for a while and you catch your breath, you look around...and you begin to notice that Holland has windmills...Holland has tulips. And Holland even has Rembrandts.

But everyone you know is busy coming and going from Italy...and they're all bragging about what a wonderful time they had there. And for the rest of your life, you will say, "Yes, that's where I was supposed to go. That's what I had planned."

And the pain of that will never, ever, ever, ever go away...because the loss of that dream is a very, very significant loss.

But...if you spend your life mourning the fact that you didn't get to Italy, you may never be free to enjoy the very special, the very lovely things...about Holland.[1]

This story was written by Emily Perl Kingsley to describe the experience of raising a child with a disability, and every time I read it, it touches me deep within my heart. Of course Italy and Holland are purely metaphors for our own life experiences. The experience of the unknown, the challenges of "I don't know what to do," and most important, the unique styles of communication that bombard us every day, take us on a journey that we did not plan on.

The underlying message of the story is loud and clear. First, we need to acknowledge that, yes, "Italy" was where we were supposed to go. The next step (and it's a big one) is to move on. If we spend the next year or two mourning the fact that we didn't get to Italy, we will not be free to enjoy the very special, very lovely things that Holland has to offer.

So what does this story have to do with family relationships? Everything! In my own experiences, my emotions, attitude, inner strength, style of communication, resistance, and direction of my affection have all been challenged. My feelings and reactions to situations have affected my relationships with my husband, my sons, my sisters, my parents, and in-laws. This journey has certainly become one of a lifetime.

My "Italy" was a simple dream. I would grow up to marry a loving man with values similar to my own. I'd take my kids to the

---

[1] ©1987 by Emily Perl Kingsley. All rights reserved. Reprinted by permission of the author.

park, pushing them as high as they could go on the swings. We would ride like the wind on our bikes, rush to get the kids to basketball and soccer practice, and teach them Chinese jump rope. I'd be a playground monitor and "cupcake mom" at school. I wished for this dream ever since I was a little girl.

My journey to Holland began about six years ago, when my husband, Dan, and I were accused of child abuse. Our youngest son, Joey, was only 18 months old. We couldn't explain the multiple femur, rib, and tibia fractures that showed up on x-rays when we took Joey to the hospital after an accident that occurred at a park. Needless to say, my emotions got the better of me. Animosity and bitterness toward Child Protective Services (CPS) and some members of the nursing staff began to affect my interaction with my family.

The good news was the immediate outcome: Joey was not removed from our custody, and the charges against us were dismissed. But most important, the physician in charge of CPS who headed the accusation against us learned through his experience with our family that even if the x-rays suggest abuse, it is entirely possible that the child may have OI. I have been told that since his encounter with us, that physician has become an advocate for the OI Foundation.

Without getting into a deep explanation of the six months following the accident at the park, let me simply say that the time was difficult. Learning about OI can be overwhelming. The feelings of helplessness and bewilderment when I was told that my child has a rare disorder were a major heartache for me.

Never in my dream did I ever imagine having an unhealthy child. I never considered how caring for someone with special needs would change my life, or how much strain it could put on a family. And I never thought that a child so dear, with such a sweet and loving smile, could challenge my inner strength to such a degree that it would threaten a dream I had since I was so very young.

My heart was set on my dream. But instead of going to the park, we went to the hospital. Instead of riding like the wind, we had to watch for every bump in the sidewalk. And instead of rushing to basketball and soccer practice, my son and I bounced among physical, occupational, and hydrotherapy.

Recognizing the loss of my dream was very hard; I denied it for a long time. I was angry. Resentful. Moody. Sad. Unpredictable. But I also remember the specific moment when I heard my flight attendants announce that I had landed in Holland.

I had been active in the moms' group at my parish for nearly a year. We met on Wednesday mornings in the church basement just to mingle and hang out with other moms, while the kids played together in another room.

The names of my flight attendants were Terri and Rosemary. I vividly recall watching their sons run out of the nursery room and jumping up into their arms at the end of a session. My son followed, wheeling himself in his new little Etac wheelchair. He had trouble getting through the doorway, and too many chairs blocked where I was sitting. So I made my way to him for the "hug exchange," only too late because now the children were playing "ring around the mommies." Terri's son was fast, zipping in and out between the chairs. Rosemary's son was hiding under the tables, and Joey was doing his best to keep up with both of them.

I know that Joey was fortunate to be active in a group, with-out any care that he couldn't do what the other boys did. But on this particular day, I finally got in touch with my emotions, my own dream that I had for so long.

At the moment that I missed my hug, I sat down and cried like I had never cried before. It was the first time that I recognized the pain of my lost dream, and understood for the first time how truly important my dream had been to me. I remember thinking to myself, "My son is never going to run into a room and jump into my arms like that."

As I sat there crying, Terri and Rosemary came and sat next to me. They each put their arms around me and said, "Kathy, he's no different than any other kid. He just has wheels instead of feet." As they spoke and comforted me, they told me in their own words that I had landed in Holland. They encouraged me to move on so I could enjoy all the wonderful and lovely things that Holland has to offer. And they were right.

From the time they told me where I had landed, things got better. I did take the time to catch my breath. I realized that my Holland not only had windmills and tulips, but it also had a kid with the widest, brightest smile, unending bedtime hugs, morning kisses, and a heart as precious as gold.

Therapy became a place of resources and friends who continually offered me support. Therapists taught me safe ways to entertain, play, and interact safely with both of my children.

I've met new colleagues to help me balance caring for my family with my other ambitions. I've discovered new opportunities to channel my energies into affirming actions, and have gained knowledge that I would never have if I had gone to Italy.

Think of me as a tour guide to make those first few years in Holland a bit easier. Think of the next part of this chapter as a road map to help you enjoy your new life in Holland. Based on my own family's experiences, I can point out events you don't want to miss and help guide you away from potential disasters. Please take the time to catch your breath, and I guarantee that you'll discover wonderful, beautiful things.

Rediscovering Tulips: Nurturing a Marriage

One of the beautiful and natural things about Holland is their tulips. They're cheery, wistful, lovely, and no matter where you are in Holland, you'll find them in unexpected places.

I encourage you to rediscover tulips, but not necessarily the ones growing in the fields. The tulips I want you to discover are right above your spouse's chin. Those lovely lips that can kiss away a bad day, the lips that say, "I love you," the lips that whisper the truth when you may be too afraid to say it yourself.

A challenge that Dan and I face on a regular basis is communicating our feelings with one another. I tend to be more emotional, and Dan more matter-of-fact. I notice that our relationship is stronger when we take brief moments and share a kiss, or whisper a kind word to one another. Sound too simple? Believe me, it's not.

After a week, or sometimes even a day of balancing therapy, homebound school instruction, homework, laundry, and the constant entertaining of a six-year-old, I get pooped out! Enter the older son, Anthony. He needs help with his homework and wants lots of attention too, just like his little brother. So I make the extra effort and have a tickle fight, then get off the floor to make dinner. Then Dan walks in the door. Do I have any desire to give him a hug or say, "Hi, honey. How was your day?" Nope. Nothing is left in my energy tank. I'm dry to the bone.

If this process continues, I question whether our marriage would last. It's so important to make time for each other, to go out on a date, or perhaps just out for a walk…even if my energy level is zero. The time together will be well worth it. And when we make the time for each other, the relationship is better, stronger, happier.

So what's my first bit of advice to make the relationship with your spouse strong? Go on a date at least once a month (more often if you can). Visit a comedy café on a regular basis so you remember how to laugh together. Hold hands walking into church, through a parking lot, or even in the car on the way to the gas station. Rekindle the passion as often as you can, because without it, your marriage will be terribly stressed.

Another situation that brought Dan and me together was his commitment to "fix something." I've heard several men whose children have OI comment that if they can't "fix it," they don't feel like there is anything they can do to help.

Dan brought his expert problem-solving abilities into the picture. When we couldn't safely take Joey to the park and swing, Dan custom built a swing for Joey, and added on a few fun features for Anthony. I think Dan worked on the swing chair for Joey for nearly a week, and my, did it make him feel important. He not only did a great job, but I recognized that he found a way to "fix" a part of Joey's OI, by allowing Joey to play safely and have fun outside with his brother.

Dan also put his know-how to work by constructing a mini drafting table for Joey to write on while in a hip spica cast. With some lightweight PVC piping and a sturdy board, Dan made homework, coloring, and painting a joy for Joey and a simpler task for me.

The success of Dan's projects directly affected my relationship with him. By taking tasks that were difficult for me to do with Joey, and implementing some custom-made design, he made my daily obligations to Joey less stressful, and my energy level high enough to welcome Dan home.

Another relationship-building strategy that we use is pretty basic—we talk to one another. Now I admit, it's not as frequent as I would like, and sometimes it's not on the emotional level that I prefer, but when we take the time to talk, we grow closer. When he shares his work with me, I see the passion that drives him. I can take a moment to admire his dedication, take pleasure in knowing how valued he is, and in turn, understand why he works so many hours.

When Dan listens to me, I get the support of knowing that all my efforts with our children will pay off in the long run, and that my time is as valuable as his, even though I don't work outside of the home. I often second-guess myself, and Dan lets me know that I'm a capable, talented woman. (Now, if he would just bring me flowers on occasion…)

The key to a strong relationship with your spouse is to balance constant daily demands with pleasure, moments of solitude with the needs of caretaking, work with play, and activity with rest. Nap with your spouse. Go out on dates. Have friends over. And nurture one another. Give kisses and hugs, and say the words, "I love you." Even if the words are written in frosting on a cookie, they'll go a long way in building your relationship.

Rembrandt: Portrait of a Sibling

I did mention that I have an older son, Anthony, didn't I? He is three years older than Joey, and he is someone that I forgot for a while. It's not that he wasn't around, or that I didn't feed him or send him off to school, but I got so wrapped up in the day-to-day responsibilities of caring for Joey that I didn't give enough attention to Anthony.

Anthony was five years old when Joey was diagnosed with OI. When that happened, lots of new rules entered our lives. Safety first. No wrestling with your brother. Slow down. No running in the house. No jumping on the couch. It's okay to talk to strangers if we're in a hospital. And the biggie: Be careful of your brother!

Do I really need to write that Anthony became resentful? For a five-year-old who had the run of the house, the ceiling came crashing down when Joey's health became the top priority.

While I recall sitting down and talking with Anthony many times about Joey's condition, I believe it took Anthony many years before he realized he too has landed in Holland. When Anthony was in child care, he was a "good kid." He didn't bully anyone, and the teachers always liked him. He was fun and happy.

Dan and I noticed that once Anthony started kindergarten, he changed. It probably wasn't a coincidence that this new behavior began when Joey was diagnosed with OI. Anthony seemed to constantly get into trouble. He didn't respect the teacher, and often fought with other children. I didn't understand what was happening to Anthony, and I was already overwhelmed with the responsibilities of Joey's care.

I discussed this frustrating situation with a friend from my moms' group, and she suggested I join a parent support group for families with special needs. After a month of consideration and with some resistance, I packed up my boys and went.

It took nearly four months of sharing what was happening with me and our family before one of the counselors recommended that we take Anthony to see a therapist. She suggested that he needed equal opportunity to share his thoughts on what was happening in his life with an "expert."

Dan and I were surprised to learn how angry Anthony was at us. We were equally surprised at how angry he was at Joey for breaking all the time. What we learned from having Anthony in therapy was that he needed as much attention as Joey did. Again, another seemingly obvious concept, but when you're living the reality of life, simple concepts like this can be easily overlooked.

We learned how important it was to dedicate quality one-on-one time with Anthony. We learned that Anthony needed a safe way to vent his frustrations without Joey getting hurt. We learned that Anthony needed time to roughhouse with his friends, and that he needed to be told how important he was, even if he wasn't the one getting all the attention.

Another vital lesson we learned was to encourage quality, safe play between Anthony and Joey. Now remember, we had set up lots of rules, and Joey had broken a bone from simply popping the popper on the game "Trouble." What could the boys do together that would work?

Pokemon to the rescue! I know that some parents think this card collecting game is over the top, but it brought our sons together. They collect, trade, and share, and they read together about each Pokemon's powers and Ash's adventures. Pokemon led to GameBoy and Nintendo 64, and after nearly two years, the boys are still playing together. Of course, other families will find their own "Pokemon"—a shared interest that brings siblings together despite differences in physical abilities.

My advice to other parents is to set aside specific times for you and your spouse to play with your other children. While it is important to spend time together as a family, it is sometimes more important to dedicate one-on-one time with each child. Take him to a movie or the park. Play a board game with him while your spouse cares for the child with OI. Have marshmallow fights when your child is upset with you or her sibling. Give your children the chance to have friends over to play hard and roughhouse. No matter how hectic your schedule is with therapy and doctor appointments, set aside some time to take your other children to swimming class, soccer practice, or Sunday school.

Most of all, tell your children that you love them, no matter what. Share stories of how you felt when they were born. Show them their baby pictures. Make them feel as special as your child with OI. And be sure to hang up their artwork, because you never know who the next Rembrandt may be.

Windmills: Getting the Support You Need

I've always enjoyed watching windmills spin. Whether they're in a movie or in a neighbor's garden, there is such a simple tranquility about them.

The beauty of windmills in our lives is that each vane represents people who are willing to help you and your family. There can be windmills that energize you, windmills that help you relax, and windmills that give you a hand. Your vanes may be therapists and doctors, business associates, clergy, and friends and family members near or far away.

My family members became the vanes that empowered me when my life became overwhelmed with the responsibilities of taking care of Joey. They have been an incredible source of personal strength when I have felt low or depressed. They've been my inspiration and motivation to do things for myself. They've encouraged me to be active in groups outside of OI, like Toastmasters and the American Business Women's Association, and have let me know that it's okay to get a massage or pamper myself with a new outfit or two. Their simple suggestions, the time they spend babysitting for my boys, and their plain words of encouragement have all meant so much to me.

Both Dan's and my family have come to the rescue so I could get away from the house. Whether it was by allowing me to go shopping, take a walk, attend a concert, or even to go on a date with Dan, family has played an important role in helping me stay energized.

Another windmill in my life was the people who simply listened to me when I felt most depressed. When I was in doubt, I phoned my brother and sister-in-law who lived several hundred miles away, because I knew they could offer me a fresh perspective on the situation. They always helped me feel better and get ready to tackle another day.

Over the years I've come to depend on my windmills. My sister stepped in to be with Anthony while Dan and I were in the hospital with Joey. My parents and in-laws spent time at the hospital with Joey so I could be with Anthony when he came home from school. My sisters regularly take Anthony someplace special, simply because he is so special. A dear neighbor friend who signed her daughter up for swimming lessons offered to have Anthony join them. It was a wonderful experience for him, and he got his first swimming certificate.

But I didn't always look to my windmills for peace of mind or help.

Look at me. I am "supermom." I can take care of it all. I don't need your help. I don't need sleep. I can bathe the kids, make break-

fast, schedule the doctor appointments, wash the dishes, and feed the dog with my hands tied behind my back. I am invincible!

Oops. Wait. Reality check. That's my advice. Well, actually, it was my sister's advice—advice I should have listened to long before I got tired, long before I felt like I could use a hand. That reality check is more of the common sense advice that many of us don't want to take.

Take a long, hard look at your reality. Are you trying too hard to do everything yourself by being a supermom (or superdad)? I have to admit that in the beginning, this high-level supermom commitment was a way to deal with my grief, and at times with my anger. I know that burying myself in work often helped me get through the crisis of another fracture. But just as Dan would leave because he couldn't fix things, I worked harder when I most needed help or when I was so very tired. Getting Joey to therapy and making certain that he completed his homework was a way to help me get through my day. In retrospect, my energy wasn't always spent loving what I did, but rather coping with the tough times.

There are people willing to help you. Haven't you had a neighbor, friend, or family member say, "If you need anything, just call"? And how many times have we failed to pick up the phone and say "I need your help!"

As any mom can tell you, grocery shopping with a child can be quite an adventure. When you add a child in a hip spica cast, shopping becomes more of a challenge. The wheelchair takes up the trunk, and the child takes up the back seat. By the time you're ready to load the groceries, there's no room. This is the perfect opportunity to ask for help. Whether someone will meet you at the store when you're done shopping, or watch your children while you're gone, don't hesitate to tell friends or family members your dilemma. They'll understand, and more than likely, will be glad you called to take them up on their offer of help.

It doesn't matter what you need—support, a friendly ear to listen to you, a babysitter, or a Sunday morning alone at church—the power and energy generated by the vanes on your windmills should not be ignored. You can't just walk by a windmill without realizing what it has to offer. Each vane will contribute something different, so admire the beauty, but be sure to utilize its strength. The windmills are certain to make your time in Holland easier.

Life is a journey. Most of the time, you expect to go to specific places, but sometimes the flight pattern changes and you wind up in a completely different destination. It's not necessarily better or worse than your desired destination, it's just different. Take the time to learn the new culture, and enjoy what the new place has to offer.

Take a moment and catch your breath. You'll begin to notice the windmills, the tulips, and even Rembrandt.

Welcome to Holland!

Tips for Healthy Family Relationships

- Nurture your marriage.

- Recognize and rely on each other's strengths.

- Recognize your personal limitations.

- Provide time for siblings of a child with OI.

- Help siblings develop a healthy relationship with their brother or sister who has OI.

- Involve your extended family as much as possible.

- Seek help from caring professionals when needed.

- Take friends and neighbors up on their offers to help.

Resources

American Business Women's Association
9100 Ward Parkway
PO Box 8728
Kansas City, MO 64114-0728
Phone: (800) 228-0007
Internet: www.abwa.org

MUMS Parent-to-Parent Network
150 Cusler Court
Green Bay, WI 54301-1243
Phone: (877) 336-5333 or (920) 336-5333
Internet: www.netnet.net/mums

National Fathers Network
16120 NE 8th St.
Bellevue, WA 98008-3937
Phone: (425) 747-4004, ext. 218
Internet: www.fathersnetwork.org

Osteogenesis Imperfecta Foundation
The OI Foundation provides many opportunities for families to give and receive mutual support, including online chat rooms, a mentoring program for preteens and teens with OI, local support groups, peer support sessions at national conferences, and more.
804 West Diamond Ave.
Suite 210
Gaithersburg, MD 20878
Phone: (800) 981-2663 or (301) 947-0083
Internet: www.oif.org

Sibling Support Project
Phone: (206) 368-4911
Internet: ww.chmc.org/departmt/sibsupp

Toastmasters International
PO Box 9052
Mission Viejo, CA 92690
Phone: (949) 858-8255
Internet: www.toastmasters.org

Ban Breathnach, Sarah. 1995. *Simple Abundance: A Daybook of Comfort and Joy.* New York: Warner Books.

PAIRS Foundation. 1992. *Daily Temperature Reading.* HB-2-49. PAIRS Foundation, Ltd.

PAIRS Foundation. 1992. *Shared Meaning and Empathic Listening.* HB-3-79. PAIRS Foundation.

14
Relationships with Peers

Heidi and Trey Glauser

Key Points in This Chapter

- Children with OI are as capable as other children of having close friendships and loving relationships. OI severity seems to have little to do with social success.

- Some children with OI experience social isolation at different times in their lives. Many children with OI have developed successful coping skills to overcome this isolation.

- Issues such as transportation and accessibility can be addressed to help children participate in play dates and social events.

- Dating is delayed for some teens with OI, but many teens and adults with OI report that they have satisfying dating relationships.

Authors' note: *During the spring and summer of 2000, we contacted dozens of teens and young adults living with OI. Through a survey and interviews, we gathered data about their experiences. Their stories, along with our own family's experience, provide the information in this chapter. We are grateful to the young people who shared their stories with us and have given us their permission to be quoted in this chapter.*

"Life with OI can be great or miserable. It is whatever you make of it. I wouldn't have the courage and determination that I have today without all that I have faced due to my bone disorder. If someone doesn't like you because of your OI, then don't be discouraged."

Mary Alice Birdwhistell, 13 years old

Like all people, children with OI benefit from close friendships and loving relationships. Some children may experience difficulty initiating play dates and nurturing friendships. Parents can help their child maintain a healthy attitude when social interactions are strained due to the child's OI. Natalie Cinman, age 17, summed it up best when she said, "There are a lot of obstacles in life, but with every obstacle you and the people around you become stronger—physically and emotionally."

Coping with Isolation

The severity of a child's OI seems to have little to do with determining social success. A child with very severe OI can feel completely accepted, while one with a milder form can feel excluded. When asked if she had ever been excluded from an activity, a very severely affected teen with OI stated, "No, my friends don't do that. I invite them and they invite me." Another, age 14, stated, "My classmates and friends include me in everything they do. They like me because I am normal except for the physical part."

Conversely, a child with milder OI stated, "Almost every day I feel isolated from my peers. Many kids are jealous of the special attention I receive. They say that I break my bones on purpose. Also, many students are jealous of my grades. Therefore I'm not in 'the group.' Many times I feel like boys won't go out with me because of my condition. I feel especially isolated at recess and PE when I can't do what they do."

A crucial factor concerning peer relationships is the child's conception of him- or herself. When parents encourage strong self-esteem, and help their child to develop a healthy attitude about being different, children with OI generally find themselves surrounded by wholesome and cherished friendships. A 13-year-old with OI suggested that kids keep in touch with several friends with OI. She stated, "You will be amazed at the situations you can help each other through."

Another way to help a child with OI feel accepted is to help him or her discover and develop a skill, hobby, or interest in which he or she can excel, and find strong peer relationships. Kristen Antolini, age 17, stated, "I have felt isolated from my peers in school. This isolation usually occurred during physical education or lunchtime, since the cafeteria was downstairs. It also happened when I was hurt and in my wheelchair. My classmates could never get used to me being hurt and of-ten were shy about including me in activities because of their fear of hurting me or thinking that I was not as capable because of my injury. It is important to talk to your peers because they usually do not realize they are leaving you out. I also feel isolated when my friends are involved in organized sports. My best friend is an amazing athlete, but I cannot connect with her favorite activity, softball. When I was five years old, I began piano as a result of my frustration of not being able to join the teeball team with everyone else. I have always used music as an outlet to vent my frustration about things that I cannot do. I am truly thankful that I was led to music because it is my greatest joy and talent."

Some children will carry a sense of isolation even though their friends try often to include them. Julie Hocker, age 17, stated, "I always feel isolated from my peers. I feel so much different from

them, in almost every way possible. They always try to invite me and make me feel included, but it's just a feeling I have and something I need to work at. I think this is mainly because I view things differently sometimes. I've had different experiences than them and I've had to deal with different issues than they have."

Angela Rowe, age 21, expressed it well when she said, "I think everyone with OI has been excluded at some time or another. It is just fact that we cannot play Red Rover or go on a slip-and-slide. But there are lots of things we can do, and my parents were very good about enrolling me in music and art classes. I also took dance classes. I think that even people that are 'normal' get excluded from things too. It is part of life and everyone learns to deal with it in their own way."

And Elizabeth Simmonds, age 12, focuses on one positive aspect of having OI. She said, "I think it's kind of cool to have OI, because I'm different, and I like being different. My friends treat me regularly. They don't care about OI. They look for what's inside."

Often, children with OI gravitate toward adults and older playmates. Michelle Bunker, age 17, believes that children with OI have to be able to communicate with adults in order to speak up for themselves. Angela Rowe believes that she relates to adults more because they are less willing to do dangerous activities. She has always been close to her mother, and so it was natural that she went places with her and her friends and got comfortable with that. She believes that having OI has made her grow up fast and deal with very grown-up issues. These relationships help her to be more mature and to relate to adults better.

"I definitely relate to adults better," says Julie Hocker. "I guess it's because I spend more time with them than most kids my age. I'm just used to being around doctors and other adults, and not being afraid to tell them what's going on. I have friends who are older than me too. It just seems like they understand me better and I feel like I can relate to them well. It seems like adults look at things with a different perspective, which definitely helps, and they are less likely to jump to give you advice. Adults are more likely to talk something over instead." Parents of children with OI should encourage them to foster and develop relationships with people of all ages.

Educating Others About OI

Often it is necessary to educate peers and their parents about OI, and to dispel any fears that may exist. Also, when a child meets a person outside the family, school, or neighborhood who doesn't know about OI, someone must often explain it. Helping the child learn to be comfortable in teaching new acquaintances about OI is important. Sometimes strangers can be abrupt or offensive, and it is important to help a child learn to courteously handle difficult or potentially embarrassing situations.

Mary Alice Birdwhistell, age 13, states, "When people are kind and considerate and ask questions about my disorder, I am happy to explain my condition. I tell them that I have a brittle bone disorder and I break my bones easily. However, when people ask me what is wrong with me, I just say that nothing is wrong with me, and I walk away." Ryan J. Donnelly, age 14, uses a technique unique to him. He states, "When I don't feel like telling people about OI, I just say, 'It's hard to explain.' "

Kristen Antolini states, "I was always willing to answer people's questions to the best of my ability. I even did a huge oral report about OI and brought pictures of my OI friends. By the end of my three years at that school, the teachers and kids hardly noticed my disability. It became part of their routine to help me. They nicknamed my walker 'Bob' and my leg braces 'Harry and Larry.' I was very fortunate that one of my teachers learned everything about OI and she was a great physical help to me. Because I was in a Christian school, it helped me and my classmates to look at it from a Catholic viewpoint through prayer. I think that it is very important to be open when talking about your disability and to make a presentation about OI and the equipment that you use."

Sometimes, especially when a new injury is evident and visible, repeatedly explaining what happened becomes tiresome. Angela Rowe says, "I think the hardest part is telling people over and over why your arm is in a cast. Or having people say things about my parents and how they treated me. It seemed like people, even kids, thought my parents beat me."

"I feel very comfortable talking about OI," states Julie Hocker. "OI is just one part of me and I'm okay talking about it. I do not like it when strangers approach me with questions, and I do not feel it is my obligation to entertain their questions. I do not go up to someone in public and ask them why they might have chosen to wear a certain color shirt, so I don't think they should ask me about my disability. They usually ask 'What is wrong?' and I say 'Nothing.' There is nothing wrong with me; I have a disability and that is not right or wrong. If someone familiar to me asks 'What is wrong?' I very politely reply, 'Do you mean, what is my disability?,' and then I talk to them about it. I do go and speak publicly upon request, and I am comfortable with that. When I am becoming friends with new people I try to make them comfortable without overdoing it. I might just bring up a time I fractured or something such as that. Sometimes that brings up more questions and I always try to make the person feel comfortable asking questions. I think people need to be comfortable with OI and know what to do if ever there is a problem. I don't want people to panic if I was to break a bone in front of them so I try to let them know it's a possibility."

Transportation and Accessibility Challenges

Sometimes a social event may present an accessibility challenge for a child. Perhaps a friend may invite the child to visit her home or other location that is not accessible. Or the occasion may require someone to lift the child. Parents will need to decide if it is safe to allow their child to ride in another family's car, or to travel with an older friend who can drive. In the teenage years, youths with OI want to socialize with their peers without a parent being constantly present.

Mary Alice Birdwhistell says, "Most of the time, I invite people over to my house. It really frustrates me when I am not invited somewhere, most likely because my friends are not sure if I can go up steps or be comfortable in their houses or other places. However, it also makes me sad when I do go to someone's house and can't take part in activities because I am physically unable or they are too wild. Sometimes people exclude me because they are afraid I will get hurt in the situation. Sometimes friends' mothers don't want me to come over because it is such a hassle to help me."

Becky Sisco, age 14, regrets the times she is unable to travel with friends. She says, "I don't go in my friends' cars because they are inaccessible. I feel isolated because I miss some great times to chat while riding." Yuri Ellis, age 14, needs to consider whether there will be someone at the location who is strong enough to carry him if needed.

Open communication is the key to enjoying successful social interactions. If parents and children can discuss any potential obstacles and simple methods to overcome them, the problems usually resolve themselves. Kristen Antolini said it best when she stated, "I usually talk with my friends about what is different about transporting me than their other friends. All of my friends have been with my parents and me, so they usually have seen what help I needed. I question my friend about what type of vehicle they have since some vehicles that are high off the ground are very difficult to get into. I also ask if there is room for my wheelchair or walker in their car. I always bring my handicapped sticker with me or ask that I be dropped off at the door. I need extra help if it is raining or snowing because I am not strong enough to keep myself steady on slick surfaces."

Sometimes it may be a little embarrassing for a child to explain transportation needs to others, but like many other aspects of living with OI, it's better to communicate than to miss the opportunity because it may be difficult to get there. If the child's class will be going on a school field trip, and the transportation needs of the child with OI are different than the needs of the rest of the class, one suggestion is to invite other students to ride in the accessible van that follows the school bus, or in the parents' car if they are driving.

"When I used a wheelchair, transportation was a really big

The social pressures of life are a challenge for everyone. But when you are different, an entire new set of hurdles are set up to be overcome. Having OI in our society seems to cross the line of where it's cool to stand out from the crowd. I didn't choose my wheelchair in the same way I did my belly button ring!

Throughout my childhood and high school years I was surrounded by a supportive and loving group of friends. My first of many sleepovers came later and with more plans than most, but I enjoyed the experience in my own time. At a young age, my friends developed skills to safely push me or maneuver up and down curbs. Before long, they were showing their parents how to put my chair in the car or how best to get me in the house. In high school, I went to parties, stayed extremely active in school, and enjoyed friendships with a variety of groups and "cliques." Dating was challenging as so much focus is on physical appearance at this age. I did experience sadness of not being asked to some dances. Looking back, I realize it wasn't just related to OI. I didn't have the self-confidence to form close friendships with boys, and that is the start of any relationship. As I gained self-esteem and realized how strong I can be as an independent woman, I easily formed friendships and never missed another dance.

My mom's advice on dating had been that it would get better as I got older. The boys would change. Of course, I always thought, "Yeah, right. She has to say that. She's my mom!" But she was right! When I went to college, I was a little caught off guard by the change in attitude some guys showed toward me. I began dating and trying out all the levels of relationships I had missed over the years. At first it was strange because I didn't have years of "practice" that other girls had. I didn't know how to react when a guy flirted with me, what to say when he said I was beautiful, what to do when some of them broke my heart. But I learned fast!

Many guys I feel compatible with or attracted to would never consider dating me because of my wheelchair. For this reason, I can honestly say I am thankful for the gift of OI. It has become the best filter I could have to screen out people who only see and feel skin-deep. I am assured that the guys who approach me are automatically a few rungs up the ladder of character and strength as a person.

My advice to others is, as you build relationships, be careful not to lose yourself. After years of waiting for attention, it is hard not to settle for anyone who looks your way. I'm still waiting for my Prince Charming, but I know that enjoying the rewards of a normal relationship is definitely possible no matter what your disability. We have so much to offer the world. OI is for me a small but important part of my personality, and I have learned to incorporate it into the confusing world of guys and friends, and make the most of it!

Kara Sheridan, 20 years old

deal," says Michelle Bun-
ker. "I worried about the
chair not fitting in the car
and getting in and out on
my own. In order to avoid
this, my parents usually
ended up driving me and
since I didn't want them
driving me certain places
I missed out on a lot.

However, now I have my own car and my social life has changed
dramatically! It was the extra push I needed in order to start using
a walker so that I could go out on my own without having someone with me to take the wheelchair in and out of the trunk for me.
Whenever I feel unsafe, I voice my opinion...loudly!"

For children with OI, going away on an overnight trip unac-
companied by parents provides a welcome short spurt of independent living. While invaluable to a child with OI, these times away
from Mom and Dad seem to occur very rarely. One parent found
that enrolling her older child in an overnight camp not too far
from home provided excellent practice for her son to learn to live
on his own.

One teen with OI stated, "When we have one hotel room, I
get concerned about my friend finding out that I wear diapers and
then telling everyone or laughing at me." Another stated, "I have
never been on a weekend or longer trip with my friends. My friends
have come with my parents and me on trips instead."

Dating

For many teens with OI, dating is delayed. Peers in the teen years
are generally very self-absorbed. Often it isn't until later that
meaningful relationships develop. Julie Hocker recognizes that
"there are a lot of people that look at others and see past physical
beings." But rarely is that "special someone" mature enough to
devalue physical appearance in the teen years.

Julie continued, "I know that when guys first meet me they

have a lot of thoughts that run through their head. I don't want to tell them they are wrong, I just like to show them they are. Most guys are eventually able to see past the wheelchair I sit in."

Kristen Antolini said, "My biggest concern is that maybe a guy wouldn't ask me out because of the way I look as a result of my OI. It does hurt my feelings though when a guy is not interested when they find out I have OI."

Angela Rowe echoed Kristen when she stated, "My biggest concern when I started dating was that they wouldn't want to date me because of OI. I got real scared that I would never get married because my children could have OI. I have learned that there are alternate ways to have a family, and I have educated my dates on OI. I think they get a class in OI 101 when they date me! I am so short, I had to first find a guy that was not too tall, then find a dress that was not too long and find shoes that I wouldn't kill myself in. From having sprained and broken feet the shoe thing was the hardest!"

Teens with OI have enjoyed attending dances. Mary Alice Birdwhistell states, "I have learned that while in a wheelchair or while using a walker you can dance just as well as everyone else. When I slow dance, I am able to stand and dance like everyone else. I can do wheelies in the wheelchair in fast dances, and everyone loves it. I'm also not nervous at all to ask a boy to dance." Some teens with OI who use wheelchairs report that their dance partners (either male or female) get on their knees to dance with them. One girl said that her dance partner lifted her: "I guess we just worked it out."

Conclusion

Where peer relationships are concerned, living with OI can often present challenges for a child. Parents should make every effort to keep the lines of communication open wide and to teach their child with OI techniques for overcoming the challenges that are bound to surface. Christine Nelson, age 16, summed it up when she said, "Growing up with OI is hard, but with the support from friends and family you learn how to cope and deal with it."

Tips for Healthy Peer Relationships

- The severity of a child's OI is not the determining factor for his or her social success.

- Self-concept is a crucial factor for successful peer relationships.

- Developing skills, hobbies, and other interests facilitates healthy peer relationships.

- Focus on the positive as much as possible.

- Keep the lines of communication between parent and child open.

- Identify the causes for feelings of isolation and address them.

- Be prepared to educate others about OI.

- Children and teens with OI will benefit from learning to advocate for themselves.

- Use creative problem-solving skills to address transportation and accessibility problems.

- Participate in school and community activities.

- Remember the old saying: "To have a friend, be a friend."

Resources

Osteogenesis Imperfecta Foundation
The OI Foundation provides opportunities for teens and young adults to give and receive mutual support. Opportunities include biannual national conferences, a mentoring program, and KeyPals—a peer support network.

> 804 West Diamond Ave.
> Suite 210
> Gaithersburg, MD 20878
> Phone: (800) 981-2663 or (301) 947-0083
> Internet: www.oif.org

15
Coping with Being Different

Suzanne Marie Richard

Key Points in This Chapter

- Every human being is unique and therefore "different."

- Because OI causes some obvious outward differences, people with OI sometimes confront misunderstanding, ignorance, teasing, exclusion, or other challenges.

- A certain amount of denial about OI can be healthy. It helps children see themselves as capable people without limitations.

- Children with OI benefit from learning to speak up for themselves.

- Families can develop strategies for responding to questions, teasing, or staring with information, humor, and understanding.

- Though explaining OI to others is often helpful, people with OI are not obligated to answer every question or respond to every look or comment.

- Children with OI may sometimes feel sad about being different. These feelings are understandable, and parents can help children work through them in healthy ways.

- Resilient people possess certain qualities that allow them to bounce back from difficult experiences and become healthy, happy adults. Families will benefit by identifying and nurturing these qualities.

N o matter how loving and accepting an environment parents create for their child, there will always be times when he or she feels different. In this chapter, we will discuss issues of difference and useful coping skills.

Growing up with Type IV OI, I have faced these issues head on. By becoming a professional actress, I have chosen to take a very public approach to understanding difference. Besides playing a large variety of roles as a person with a disability, I also speak publicly on disability issues. Difference should not be ignored, nor should it become become all-consuming. I hope that by reading this chapter, families can develop strategies that work for them.

Step 1: Everyone is Different

When I speak to groups about what it is like to be different, I always start with a chuckle. Everyone has differences that make them feel alienated at times from their peers. Maybe they have glasses, a big nose, an allergy, or their skin is a different color than most of the people they see. By encouraging children to recognize the differences that every person feels, parents can help them take the focus off of their difference.

All children feel different sometimes, and this feeling increases as they enter the teen years. When a child happens to have a disability, that becomes the focus of their feeling of difference. It is important that both parents and children keep in mind that everyone goes through this feeling of not fitting in as they grow up.

I tell my son that everyone is different in their own little way. With some people you can see their difference, and with others you can't. He asked me if we show that we are different. I told him yes, we show it with our brittle bones and our blue sclera. He knows he is different and in what ways, and he also knows that he is loved a lot.

Wendy Shiflett, mother of
Zachary, 6 years old

This can be a great opportunity for parents to share some of their own childhood experiences. Whether or not they grew up with an identified disability, parents can share with their child what made them feel awkward and different from their peers. Knowing that their parents went through some of the same things can help alleviate children's feelings of isolation that difference can foster.

Encourage children to talk to their peers, disabled or not, about what they are feeling. They will probably be surprised how similar others' experiences can be. An insightful friend can relate his or her own feelings to those experienced by the child with OI. Many kids with OI tend to express their feelings of "being different" from their peer group by claiming that they relate better to adults than to their peers. Parents can encourage children to talk to the other adults or mentors in their lives about difference.

Denial Ain't Just a River in Egypt

For years I told people that my parents had raised me in denial, and I thanked them for it. I define denial as the ability to ignore differences whenever possible, and downplay them whenever necessary. Once parents and children have an understanding of differences and similarities, denial allows them to take the focus off the child's disability. A parent's example is probably the best way to do that; mention OI and limitations only when necessary, stress similarities rather than differences between the child and her peers or siblings, and avoid overpraise for accomplishments if the peers and siblings are not getting the same treatment.

It is important for parents to remember that their child's state of being is to have OI. To her, broken bones and the rest are normal. This is perfectly healthy to foster in a child. Try to make disability-related activities as routine as possible. For example, after a child with OI puts her socks on, then her long-leg braces, she puts her pants on one leg at a time just like everyone else. Families can set up a regular routine to deal with a broken bone. The more the child knows what to do in a stressful situation, the easier it will be to accept it as a normal part of her life.

Denial also allows parents to take a firmer stand with their

People often ask me if it bothers me when people, especially children, stare at me or deliberately avoid me because I look different. I tell them that the reaction of some adults, especially the parents of a child who asks questions, bothers me the most. It bothers me when parents scold their children for asking questions or staring. I have on many occasions, much to the parents' amazement, made a deliberate effort to approach the child to answer his questions. When a small child asks me, or his parents, why I am so small or use a wheelchair, it means he is wanting to learn. I try to take the time to respond to the child in a way that I think he will understand.

If I feel the child is too young for a detailed explanation, I may simply say, "My legs are not strong enough to walk," or joke, "I did not eat my vegetables." When I feel the child or an adult will understand, I will explain what OI is. I hope to educate the child and the parent about OI and make them feel more comfortable being around someone who is disabled. Even when I'm in a hurry or am tired and would rather not be bothered with questions, I feel a responsibility to help educate people about OI and what being disabled is like. A friend of mine told me that because of my interaction with her son when he was young, he is not afraid of being around disabled people.

Peter Dohm, adult with OI

When asked in public, "What's wrong with your child?" we always look down to our daughter to allow her to answer, showing she is human and should not be left out of the conversation as "different." It seems to put everyone at ease.

Michelle Hofhine, mother of Nicole, 6 years old

child when he is trying to get out of something because of his disability. If the family environment is such that the child has no *meaningful* difference from siblings and peers, then periods of self-pity or tantrums can be easily defused. Pointing out that his siblings and friends have to do their homework or do chores to get an allowance can turn these times into affirming experiences.

Tell It Like It Is: What is OI?

As a child enters school, she enters a larger peer group whose questions and sometimes misconceptions about disabilities will need to be addressed. What children don't understand can turn into fear. Sometimes the best defense is a good offense. Getting factual information to a child's peer group can help ensure that the classroom culture is accepting and nurturing. A team approach to addressing peer concerns is highly effective.

First, enlist the help of the child's teacher. The more he or she knows about OI, the more he or she can help the child and others by incorporating OI into the classroom culture. Suggest he or she make time for the child to present a report on OI so that the other children can have the opportunity to understand and ask questions.

Next, parents can work with their child to create an effective report on OI. Make sure the child understands OI and can explain it at his or her grade level. Again, the teacher can help determine grade-appropriate concepts and wording. (Chapter 1 lists some science experiments that can help children understand OI.) Encourage the child to share personal experiences and describe any equipment he uses. Younger children are fascinated by the hardware of disability.

Finally, make sure the child is comfortable with this approach. Find out if there are things that would make speaking in front of the class easier. Perhaps a parent can accompany him, assist with some of the presentation, or steer clear, depending on the child's preference.

I can still remember the report I gave in first grade with my proud parents looking on. My classmates were fascinated that traces of OI had been found in Egyptian mummies. I was a hit!

With milder forms of OI that are to some extent "invisible," families may question the need to share with the peer group. This is, of course, an individual decision, but it may help to stem any misconception of unwarranted special treatment if any activities need to be restricted or adapted.

Speak for Yourself: Encouraging Self-Advocacy

Once a child understands what OI is and can explain it, she has a valuable tool to begin advocating for herself. Children will be entering a world with a lot of opportunities for, and many obstacles to success. Always keep in mind that, as with any child, one of a parent's jobs is to help create a self-sufficient adult.

The more control a child feels over her environment, the more confident she will become. Parents can use the need for special assistance in school to foster self-advocacy. Bring the child to administrative meetings aimed at drawing up Individual Education Programs (IEPs) whenever possible so that she can help define her special needs. Then encourage her to take responsibility for daily implementation of these plans, secure in her own rights and the knowledge that she has the support of her parents and the school administration to deal with any problems.

Parents can also take advantage of what is known as a "teaching moment" with their child. Helping a child learn to talk to her own doctors can help her gain confidence. When strangers or acquaintances ask about the child's disability, parents can direct them to the child for the answer. The more parents let their child know that they respect her ability to speak for herself, the more she will feel comfortable discussing her differences.

Do You See the Word "Information" Written on My Forehead?: It's Okay to Say No

Once a child feels more confident talking about his disability, let him know it is okay if he doesn't feel like doing it all the time. It may be that he is having a bad day and just doesn't want to have to answer. Or perhaps he is having a great day and the question catches him off guard. These are perfectly reasonable reactions that he has every right to feel.

Discuss ways that he can firmly yet politely refuse to answer a question. Together, families might strategize quick answers to the most common questions. Perhaps the child can move the conversation in another direction. Asking the other person about him- or herself can also be a way of redirecting. Funny answers can put others and the child at ease. Friends of mine with OI have used a variety of witty comebacks to divert the curious. When asked "Why do you look so different?", one man sometimes answers, "I'm waiting for the Mother Ship to return." Another friend responds to

As I'm getting older I'm realizing that having OI is not so bad—there are things I like about it. For example, many other kids don't like to carry their backpacks but I don't have to carry my backpack, I just put it on my wheelchair. But there are times when I wish I could walk and be like everybody else. My friends always say "I wish I was in a wheelchair." They think it's cool. What they don't know is that it's hard being in a wheelchair. People tease you. It makes you feel small. Some people tease me because I'm short, but I just don't pay attention. It was hard growing up. I had to learn that I am no different than the rest of the kids. Just because I'm in a wheelchair doesn't mean I'm different.

Monique Pierson, 13 years old

"Why are you so short?" with "I didn't drink enough milk."

A person unfamiliar with differences or just curious can sometimes phrase a question in such a way that it disturbs or offends the child. Getting angry with the person usually only perpetuates this lack of knowledge. Parents can help their child understand that these comments are usually made out of innocent ignorance.

Sometimes people may stare at a child with OI, and she may express anger or frustration with this behavior in others. Parents may also feel annoyed. It's natural to feel this way. Keep in mind that often people who are staring aren't really aware they are doing it. Often catching their eye and and/or a quick smile will make people aware of what they are doing and end the behavior.

Tears of a Clown: It's Okay to Feel Bad

A number of years ago, a list of symptoms of OI was compiled to be put on medical alert bracelets and given to medical professionals who were not familiar with this disorder. Among the symptoms listed was "a cheerful disposition." In recent years, this description has been removed from most literature describing OI, at the request of many adults with OI.

Although it may appear flattering to be thought of as cheerful, and parents may observe this about their children with OI, that expectation can become a burden. Everyone gets overwhelmed sometimes, and allowing a child to express those feelings is important. Encourage him to draw or write at those times and ask him to identify what is making him sad. This is a tool that will help him move on.

It is important to urge children to move on after sadness. There is a tendency in our society to pity people and especially children with disabilities. Self-pity can be more debilitating than OI. Give children time to grieve a perceived inequity, but as soon as possible, start looking for solutions to that challenge.

One way for parents to help their children develop coping skills is to supply them with books they can relate to. There are hundreds of books, both fiction and non-fiction, written by and about children with disabilities and their families. Many of them deal head-on with teasing, hospitalization, and emotional ups and downs. Other books may provide spiritual or emotional inspiration, such as poetry collections or prayer books.

Teasing: Sticks and Stones

Kids will be kids and they can be cruel. It is not inevitable that a child with OI will be teased, but it is something to be prepared for. Just as everyone can experience feeling different, let the child know that everyone can get teased about something. Of course, sometimes that knowledge doesn't make it right or hurt less.

When a child is teased, it can shake her confidence in herself. It can make her feel powerless, and it is the parents' job to help her regain her power. Start by explaining that the child doing the teasing is probably feeling threatened or afraid and needs to find some way to feel better than the child with OI. Sometimes understanding the reason for seemingly unfair actions can make the sting fade a little. Maybe the child with OI does better in school, has more friends, or gets more attention than the teaser. Talk to the child about the good qualities she has that might be making the other child jealous. This also helps the child get out of any cycle of negative thinking that that the teasing may have caused.

A child's first and natural reaction to teasing may be to strike back. Remember, sticks and stones can break your bones (and in the case of OI that ain't just whistling Dixie!), but names can never hurt you. Develop strategies to deal with teasing when it occurs. There are many approaches to teasing; I will list a few suggestions that have worked for me. First, the child can try agreeing with the teaser. For instance, the child could respond to, "You short weirdo!" by saying, "Yes, I am short, but I'll keep trying to grow if you like." This is very disconcerting to the teaser because it is the opposite reaction he was expecting. The teaser wants the child to get upset. Other children and the teaser will realize that he hasn't succeeded. Make sure the child realizes that she does not have to really believe what the teaser says, but the important thing is for her to retain the power that the teaser is trying to take away.

Another strategy is to compliment the teaser. Again, this is not the reaction that the teaser expects or desires. Using this come-back makes the child with OI seem more mature to any other kids watching the exchange. The child could also try changing the subject. This can change the direction of the conversation and keep it from getting any more negative. Finally, humor is another way to lighten the mood. If the child can make the teaser laugh, he'll probably forget what was going on.

I remember in fifth grade, I was disagreeing with a boy in my class and he got very angry and shouted, "Shut up, you stupid…girl on crutches!" in the middle of class. The whole class and my teacher took a collective gasp and waited. I was a fairly popular kid and never really had been teased about being disabled. I remember blinking at him and then laughing and repeating "stupid girl on crutches!" Everyone found this hysterical and rather lame and the whole incident was smoothed over. The boy was still angry (not without cause) about our original argument, but we worked it out in a more appropriate manner.

If teasing becomes a continuing problem, teaming up with a teacher or other adult in the situation can be helpful. Class discussions and role playing can be useful, and the child with OI does not have to be singled out in the process. As a last resort, a conference with the teaser may be necessary. This is a double-edged sword, however, because the child with OI may end up feeling less power-ful. Try working with the child to find a solution using some of the above suggestions or other strategies.

Bouncing Back: Exploring Resiliencies

Out in the world, a child with OI may face some difficulties because he is different. In my years working with children, I have worked with children whom educators label as "at risk." These children are struggling to overcome hardships such as racism, poverty, and broken homes. It became apparent to me that having a disability can sometimes cause the same stumbling blocks to a child's development as these other hardships can cause.

Sybil Wolin, Ph.D., and Steven Wolin, Ph.D., have done a lot of work trying to discover how certain resilient individuals are able to overcome a difficult childhood and thrive as adults. (For more information on their work, go to their web site at

Figure 1

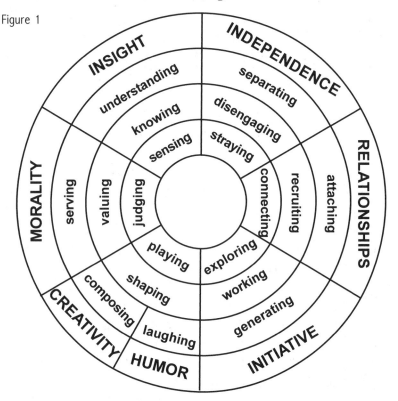

www.projectresilience.com or find their many publications in your local library. Their work is cited here by permission.) The results of their research are described in Figure 1.

The inner circle is the infant, reflecting a self-focused view of the world. As you move outward, each circle represents childhood, adolescence, then the attainment of a healthy adult understanding of the environment. The outer circle contains the common factors that the Wolins found among people who have successfully come through trying childhoods. They define insight as asking hard questions and giving honest answers, independence as establishing emotional and physical distance from sources of trouble, and relationships as making meaningful connections with other people. Initiative is the ability to take charge of problems, creativity is expressing oneself in artistic forms, humor is finding the lighter side of tragic things, and morality is acting on an informed conscience.

Parents can encourage children to develop in these areas. For instance, with children with OI it seems that watching their every move is the only way to keep them from getting hurt. But exploring is necessary in childhood to begin the journey to initiative as an adult. Find safe ways for children to explore and then let them go. If these terms don't seem to apply to a particular family, families can make their own diagram, listing qualities that help them get through tough times and recalling how they learned these behaviors. Soon the family will be able to bounce back from anything.

Bet You Wish You Were Me: Celebrating Difference

At the end of the day, we live on an incredibly diverse planet. Human beings are just one of a million species on our planet, and we ourselves come in all shapes and sizes, colors and abilities. If everyone were the same, there would be no Michael Jordans, or Michel Petruccianis, or Marilyn Monroes, and this would be a very boring world.

Diversity ensures that everyone has the chance to make unique contributions to the world. The differences that we all have give us the opportunity to focus on our own strengths and find things that we are good at doing.

Resources

Osteogenesis Imperfecta Foundation

The OI Foundation has a 15-minute video for preteens and teens, titled *Going Places,* that profiles a high school girl with OI. The video focuses on how this teenager is both similar to and different from her peers. A discussion guide is included with the video to foster conversation in classrooms or youth groups. The OI Foundation also provides opportunities for teens and young adults to give and receive mutual support. Opportunities include biannual national conferences, a mentoring program, and KeyPals—a peer support network.

804 West Diamond Ave.

Suite 210

Gaithersburg, MD 20878

Phone: (800) 981-2663 or (301) 947-0083

Internet: www.oif.org

Project Resilience

www.projectresilience.com

About the Authors

Caroline Anderson, Ph.D., received her undergraduate degree in psychology from Cornell University and her graduate degree in psychology from the University of Chicago. For the past 13 years, she has held the position of clinical psychologist at Shriners Hospital for Children in Chicago. In addition to assessing and treating children with physical or cognitive disabilities, she also works with parents and conducts long-term outcome research. She is part of the multidisciplinary team that works with children with osteogenesis imperfecta and their families.

Melanie Bland, CCLS, CTRS, is a certified child life specialist and recreation therapist. She graduated from Indiana University in 1997 with a degree in recreation, with emphasis in therapeutic recreation. Since then, Ms. Bland has worked for the Shriners Hospitals in Lexington, Ky., and currently, in Chicago. In the last three years, she has supported and educated children and their families while they are hospitalized for surgeries and difficult procedures. She enjoys her role in helping children with osteogenesis imperfecta learn about community resources and enhance their growth and development.

Rose-Marie Chiasson is a social worker at the Montreal Shriners Hospital for Children, where she works with a team of professionals providing treatment and services for children with OI and their families. She helped organize the 1999 International Family Conference on OI in Montreal, and has participated in several OI Foundation national conferences.

Holly Lea Cintas, Ph.D., graduated from the University of Colorado in 1965 with a B.S. in physical therapy and received a Ph.D. in developmental psychology from the University of Pennsylvania in 1990. She is the physical therapy research coordinator, Rehabilitation Medicine Department, National Institutes of Health. Past president of the Section on Pediatrics, American Physical Therapy Association (APTA), she received the Lindback Award for Excellence in Teaching, and the APTA Section on Pediatrics Dissertation Award for Outstanding Research Pertaining to Pediatric Physical Therapy. Dr. Cintas is board certified in pediatric physical therapy. Her current research interests are nonkinetic variables influencing motor performance for children with osteogenesis imperfecta. She collaborates with Dr. Lynn Gerber to focus on children's capabilities, rather than their limitations.

Ellen Painter Dollar is a writer and editor with 10 years of experience managing publications and communications for nonprofit organizations. She served for two years as the OI Foundation's director of public relations and events. She now works on a freelance basis from her home in Connecticut, where she lives with her husband and one-year-old daughter. Ms. Dollar and her daughter both have Type I OI.

Lynn Hurwitz Gerber, M.D., graduated from Smith College magna cum laude in 1965, and from Tufts University Medical School in 1971. She is board certified in internal medicine, rheumatology, and physical medicine and rehabilitation. She is currently chief, Rehabilitation Medicine Department, Clinical Center at the National Institutes of Health, where she has served since 1976. Dr. Gerber is adjunct associate professor of internal medicine at George Washington University, and clinical professor of internal medicine at Georgetown University. Dr. Gerber has developed evaluations and treatments for infants and children with osteogenesis imperfecta to achieve upright posture and ambulation.

Heidi and Trey Glauser, mother and son, have been active members of the OI Foundation since 1982, when Trey was born with Type III OI. Mr. Glauser is a student at Brigham Young University, where he is studying computer science. Ms. Glauser served as the OI Foundation president from 1989 to 1991, and edited the 1994 book *Living with Osteogenesis Imperfecta: A Guidebook for Families.* The Glauser family has attended most of the OI Foundation national conferences and innumerable support group meetings. They believe that the most worthwhile information about OI is gained from valuable and rewarding associations with others with OI.

Marilyn Marnie King, OTR/L is the clinical advisor for occupational therapy (OT) and therapeutic services at A.I. duPont Hospital for Children in Wilmington, Del. She has been employed at the duPont Hospital 17 years, having served as the rehabilitation coordinator for occupational therapy, and the director of occupational therapy before assuming her current position. Ms. King develops and provides specialty treatment in pediatrics, and coordinates OT clinical support for children with several disorders, including osteogenesis imperfecta. In 1995–1996, she collected data for a research project on hand and upper extremity function in children with OI.

Kay Harris Kriegsman, Ph.D., is a licensed psychologist and certified professional counselor in Bethesda, Md. She holds a Ph.D. in counseling and a master's degree in rehabilitation counseling, both from the University of Maryland. Currently in private practice, Dr. Kriegsman has extensive experience counseling individuals, couples, and families, and facilitating groups of children with disabilities and their families through hospitals, schools, and nonprofit organizations. She is a frequent speaker at OI Foundation national conferences, the author of numerous book chapters and articles, and a coauthor of *Taking Charge: Teenagers Talk About Life and Physical Disability.*

Bonnie Landrum, M.D., obtained her undergraduate degree from the University of Texas, and graduated from medical school at the University of Texas Health Science Center in San Antonio. She completed her pediatric residency and neonatal fellowship at the University of Minnesota Hospitals and Clinics. She has worked in the Newborn Intensive Care Unit at Childrens Hospital and Clinics, Minneapolis, for the last 16 years. She resides in Minneapolis with her husband, Mike, and three children, the youngest of whom has osteogenesis imperfecta.

Maureen McCabe, P.T., graduated from Sargent College at Boston University's physical therapy program in 1984. She received her NDT certification in pediatrics in 1990. She has been the rehabilitation advisor for A.H.U.C.E. (the OI Association in Spain) since 1996. For the past 16 years, Ms. McCabe has been working with children and adults with OI in a variety of treatment settings, including the Hospital for Special Surgery, early intervention programs, and private practice. She currently works as a physical therapist at the Henry Viscardi School in Albertson, N.Y., and has a private practice.

Mark A. Peck is an investment advisor with Michigan Financial Group in East Lansing, Mich., where he has worked for 18 years. Mr. Peck has OI, as does his daughter Elizabeth. His mother Midge Peck was one of the founding members of the OI Foundation, and Mr. Peck has served on the organization's board as well. He frequently lectures on financial topics, especially estate planning for families touched by disability. He also enjoys motivational speaking, an avocation that has taken him to three continents as well as numerous states. For fun, he flies a specially equipped sailplane in mid-Michigan, where he lives with his wife of 19 years, Kim.

C. Michael Reing, M.D., received his medical degree from Georgetown University, and has been in practice in Northern Virginia since 1979. Dr. Reing is board-certified in orthopedic surgery and pediatrics. He performed two residencies, one in pediatrics at Duke University, and one in orthopedics at Georgetown University. He also completed a fellowship in pediatric orthopedics and spinal surgery at Vanderbilt University. He serves as a consultant to the National Institutes of Health on pediatric orthopedics and osteogenesis imperfecta, and has published several articles on OI.

Suzanne Marie Richard is a professional actress in the Washington, D.C., area. She also works at the National Endowment for the Arts as an accessibility specialist in the Office for AccessAbility. She has a bachelor's degree in theater from the University of North Carolina at Chapel Hill.

Nina Rosalie, M.S., is a special educator at the Henry Viscardi School in Albertson, N.Y. She has taught and advocated for students with physical disabilities and other health impairments for more than 20 years. In 1982, Ms. Rosalie earned a master's degree in special education from Adelphi University, and has recently completed postgraduate course work in educational leadership at Long Island University at C.W. Post. Along with her work as a special education teacher, Ms. Rosalie has taught a graduate course, *Teaching Children with Physical and Multiple Disabilities*, for the education department at Dowling College.

Kathy Shine is a volunteer for the Wisconsin OI support group, and cochaired the OI Foundation's 2000 national conference committee. She has been married to her husband, Dan, for 14 years and they have two children. Her youngest son, Joey, has been diagnosed with Type VI OI by the Shriners Hospital in Montreal. Ms. Shine is an active volunteer in her church and her children's Christian formation program, is editor for Southwest Toastmasters, and was awarded "Year 2000 Woman of the Year" by the Milwaukee Chapter of the American Business Women's Association. Without her son's diagnosis, she believes she would have missed out on strong friendships and caring relationships she has developed over the past six years with her family, medical professionals, and other families living with OI.

Sue Simmonds, an attorney and freelance writer from Arlington, Va., is currently earning her keep as a home-based legal editor with the Lexis-Nexis Group. She has a sister-in-law and niece with Type I OI, who, together and individually, serve as ongoing sources of education and inspiration.

Peter A. Smith, M.D., received his medical degree from New York University and completed residency training in orthopedic surgery at the University of Chicago. He has been a full-time pediatric orthopedic surgeon at Shriners Hospital in Chicago for 10 years. He is director of the hospital's osteogenesis imperfecta clinic, which is one of the oldest and largest in the world, having been founded by Dr. Harold Sofield and then led by Dr. Edward Millar. Dr. Smith has special interests in osteogenesis imperfecta, gait analysis, and orthopedic care in underdeveloped countries, and has written books and articles on these subjects.

Priscilla Wacaster, M.D., graduated from the University of Arkansas for Medical Sciences in Little Rock, Ark., then completed an internship in family medicine at Riverside Regional Medical Center in Newport News, Va. She and her two children, ages nine and three, have Type I OI, and the family has experienced more than 35 fractures in the past eight years. The Wacasters are traveling the United States in a 40-foot fifth-wheel camper and Freightliner truck, but call Texas and Arkansas home. Dr. Wacaster serves on the Medical Advisory Council for the OI Foundation and edited the 1996 book *Managing Osteogenesis Imperfecta: A Medical Manual*. She has spoken at OI Foundation support group meetings and at the national OI Foundation conference in Milwaukee. She is a strong advocate for early intervention and full participation in all aspects of life for children with disabilities.

About the Osteogenesis Imperfecta Foundation

The Osteogenesis Imperfecta Foundation was founded in 1970 when a group of parents of children with OI joined together to provide mutual support, enhance public and professional awareness of OI, and promote research. The Foundation's dual purpose continues to shape our vision: funding research to find a cure, and providing support to help people with OI and their families cope with daily life. The mission of the Osteogenesis Imperfecta Foundation, Inc., is to improve the quality of life for people with osteogenesis imperfecta through education, increasing awareness, encouraging mutual support, and promoting research to find treatments and a cure.

How the Osteogenesis Imperfecta Foundation Helps

People with OI can and do live satisfying and successful lives. Like other children, those with OI attend school, make friends, go on family vacations, and even participate in sports. Like other adults, those with OI earn advanced degrees, socialize with friends, build careers, marry, and have families. Those living with OI also face daily challenges due to their bone disorder. The OI Foundation helps people with OI face those challenges and improve their lives through information, support, research, education, and awareness.

Information

The OI Foundation provides information resources to educate people about this bone disorder. The OI Foundation has answers for parents just learning about their child's OI diagnosis, adults grappling with the lifelong medical problems associated with OI, and medical professionals seeking information to improve treatment for their patients. Information resources include *Breakthrough*, a free bimonthly newsletter, as well as an informative web site, webcasts, fact sheets, brochures, videos, audiocassettes, and books. The Foundation also provides individualized responses to every inquiry.

Support

Through a network of volunteer-run support groups and support volunteers, the Foundation connects people in need with people who can share similar experiences, coping techniques, and resources. An online chat room is available through the Foundation's web site at www.oif.org.

Research

The OI Foundation has doubled funding for research every five years since 1970. The OI Foundation provides grants for research into the causes and treatments of OI, as well as postdoctoral fellowships to attract promising new scientists to OI research. The Foundation also coordinates scientific workshops that focus attention on solving research problems and developing new areas of study.

Education and Awareness

Because OI is rare, many people are unfamiliar with the disorder. Even many medical, education, and social services professionals—those on whom people with OI rely for assistance—look for opportunities to expand their knowledge of OI. The Foundation enhances public and professional awareness of OI through professional conferences, medical education resources, and media relations. A biannual national conference draws hundreds of people affected by OI together for several days of learning and support.

Contact the OI Foundation

The Osteogenesis Foundation welcomes all inquiries, and provides opportunities for volunteers with an interest in helping the Foundation fulfill its mission. Learn more about the Foundation by visiting our web site at www.oif.org, calling the Foundation at (800) 981-2663, or writing to us at the address below.

Osteogenesis Imperfecta Foundation
804 West Diamond Ave.
Suite 210
Gaithersburg, MD 20878
(800) 981-2663 or (301) 947-0083
www.oif.org

About the Million Dollar Round Table Foundation

T his book and its companion book for children were funded with the generous support of the Million Dollar Round Table (MDRT) Foundation. The MDRT Foundation is the philanthropic arm of the Million Dollar Round Table, an international, independent association of more than 23,000 of the world's best life insurance and financial services professionals from approximately 65 nations and territories. MDRT members demonstrate exceptional product knowledge, strict ethical conduct, and outstanding client service. Membership is recognized internationally as the standard of excellence in the life insurance and financial services business.

The MDRT Foundation was created in 1959 to provide Round Table members with a means to give back to their communities. Since its inception, the Foundation has donated nearly $8 million to more than 930 worthy charities around the world. The majority of these funds were raised by MDRT members from MDRT members.